Marx, Engels, and Marxisms

Series Editors
Marcello Musto, York University, Toronto, ON, Canada
Terrell Carver, University of Bristol, Bristol, UK

The Marx renaissance is underway on a global scale. Wherever the critique of capitalism re-emerges, there is an intellectual and political demand for new, critical engagements with Marxism. The peer-reviewed series Marx, Engels and Marxisms (edited by Marcello Musto & Terrell Carver, with Babak Amini, Francesca Antonini, Paula Rauhala & Kohei Saito as Assistant Editors) publishes monographs, edited volumes, critical editions, reprints of old texts, as well as translations of books already published in other languages. Our volumes come from a wide range of political perspectives, subject matters, academic disciplines and geographical areas, producing an eclectic and informative collection that appeals to a diverse and international audience. Our main areas of focus include: the oeuvre of Marx and Engels, Marxist authors and traditions of the 19th and 20th centuries, labour and social movements, Marxist analyses of contemporary issues, and reception of Marxism in the world.

More information about this series at
https://link.springer.com/bookseries/14812

Marcelo Badaró Mattos

The Working Class from Marx to Our Times

Translated by Rebecca Freitas (revised by Semaj Moore)

palgrave
macmillan

Marcelo Badaró Mattos
Brazilian History
Fluminense Federal University
Niterói-RJ, Brazil

Translated by
Rebecca Freitas
Fluminense Federal University
Niterói, Brazil

ISSN 2524-7123 ISSN 2524-7131 (electronic)
Marx, Engels, and Marxisms
ISBN 978-3-030-97354-4 ISBN 978-3-030-97355-1 (eBook)
https://doi.org/10.1007/978-3-030-97355-1

Cover illustration: Frank Rothe Photography/GettyImages

This Palgrave Macmillan imprint is published by the registered company Springer Nature Switzerland AG
The registered company address is: Gewerbestrasse 11, 6330 Cham, Switzerland

To Renata

Titles Published

1. Terrell Carver & Daniel Blank, *A Political History of the Editions of Marx and Engels's "German Ideology" Manuscripts*, 2014.
2. Terrell Carver & Daniel Blank, *Marx and Engels's "German Ideology" Manuscripts: Presentation and Analysis of the "Feuerbach Chapter"*, 2014.
3. Alfonso Maurizio Iacono, *The History and Theory of Fetishism*, 2015.
4. Paresh Chattopadhyay, *Marx's Associated Mode of Production: A Critique of Marxism*, 2016.
5. Domenico Losurdo, *Class Struggle: A Political and Philosophical History*, 2016.
6. Frederick Harry Pitts, *Critiquing Capitalism Today: New Ways to Read Marx*, 2017.
7. Ranabir Samaddar, *Karl Marx and the Postcolonial Age*, 2017.
8. George Comninel, *Alienation and Emancipation in the Work of Karl Marx*, 2018.
9. Jean-Numa Ducange & Razmig Keucheyan (Eds.), *The End of the Democratic State: Nicos Poulantzas, a Marxism for the 21st Century*, 2018.
10. Robert X. Ware, *Marx on Emancipation and Socialist Goals: Retrieving Marx for the Future*, 2018.
11. Xavier LaFrance & Charles Post (Eds.), *Case Studies in the Origins of Capitalism*, 2018.

12. John Gregson, *Marxism, Ethics, and Politics: The Work of Alasdair MacIntyre*, 2018.
13. Vladimir Puzone & Luis Felipe Miguel (Eds.), *The Brazilian Left in the 21st Century: Conflict and Conciliation in Peripheral Capitalism*, 2019.
14. James Muldoon & Gaard Kets (Eds.), *The German Revolution and Political Theory*, 2019.
15. Michael Brie, *Rediscovering Lenin: Dialectics of Revolution and Metaphysics of Domination*, 2019.
16. August H. Nimtz, *Marxism Versus Liberalism: Comparative Real-Time Political Analysis*, 2019.
17. Gustavo Moura de Cavalcanti Mello and Mauricio de Souza Sabadini (Eds.), *Financial Speculation and Fictitious Profits: A Marxist Analysis*, 2019.
18. Shaibal Gupta, Marcello Musto & Babak Amini (Eds.), *Karl Marx's Life, Ideas, and Influences: A Critical Examination on the Bicentenary*, 2019.
19. Igor Shoikhedbrod, *Revisiting Marx's Critique of Liberalism: Rethinking Justice, Legality, and Rights*, 2019.
20. Juan Pablo Rodríguez, *Resisting Neoliberal Capitalism in Chile: The Possibility of Social Critique*, 2019.
21. Kaan Kangal, *Friedrich Engels and the Dialectics of Nature*, 2020.
22. Victor Wallis, *Socialist Practice: Histories and Theories*, 2020.
23. Alfonso Maurizio Iacono, *The Bourgeois and the Savage: A Marxian Critique of the Image of the Isolated Individual in Defoe, Turgot and Smith*, 2020.
24. Terrell Carver, *Engels Before Marx*, 2020.
25. Jean-Numa Ducange, *Jules Guesde: The Birth of Socialism and Marxism in France*, 2020.
26. Antonio Oliva, Ivan Novara & Angel Oliva (Eds.), *Marx and Contemporary Critical Theory: The Philosophy of Real Abstraction*, 2020.
27. Francesco Biagi, *Henri Lefebvre's Critical Theory of Space*, 2020.
28. Stefano Petrucciani, *The Ideas of Karl Marx: A Critical Introduction*, 2020.
29. Terrell Carver, *The Life and Thought of Friedrich Engels, 30th Anniversary Edition*, 2020.
30. Giuseppe Vacca, *Alternative Modernities: Antonio Gramsci's Twentieth Century*, 2020.

31. Kevin B. Anderson, Kieran Durkin & Heather Brown (Eds.), *Raya Dunayevskaya's Intersectional Marxism: Race, Gender, and the Dialectics of Liberation*, 2020.
32. Marco Di Maggio, *The Rise and Fall of Communist Parties in France and Italy*, 2020.
33. Farhang Rajaee, *Presence and the Political*, 2021.
34. Ryuji Sasaki, *A New Introduction to Karl Marx: New Materialism, Critique of Political Economy, and the Concept of Metabolism*, 2021.
35. Kohei Saito (Ed.), *Reexamining Engels's Legacy in the 21st Century*, 2021.
36. Paresh Chattopadhyay, *Socialism in Marx's Capital: Towards a Dealienated World*, 2021.
37. Marcello Musto, *Karl Marx's Writings on Alienation*, 2021.
38. Michael Brie & Jörn Schütrumpf, *Rosa Luxemburg: A Revolutionary Marxist at the Limits of Marxism*, 2021.
39. Stefano Petrucciani, *Theodor W. Adorno's Philosophy, Society, and Aesthetics*, 2021.
40. Miguel Vedda, *Siegfried Kracauer, or, The Allegories of Improvisation: Critical Studies*, 2021.
41. Ronaldo Munck, *Rethinking Development: Marxist Perspectives*, 2021.
42. Jean-Numa Ducange & Elisa Marcobelli (Eds.), *Selected Writings of Jean Jaurès: On Socialism, Pacifism and Marxism*, 2021.
43. Elisa Marcobelli, *Internationalism Toward Diplomatic Crisis: The Second International and French, German and Italian Socialists*, 2021.
44. James Steinhoff, *Automation and Autonomy: Labour, Capital and Machines in the Artificial Intelligence Industry*, 2021.
45. Juan Dal Maso, *Hegemony and Class Struggle: Trotsky, Gramsci and Marxism*, 2021.
46. Gianfranco Ragona & Monica Quirico, *Frontier Socialism: Self-organisation and Anti-capitalism*, 2021.
47. Tsuyoshi Yuki, *Socialism, Markets and the Critique of Money: The Theory of "Labour Notes"*, 2021.
48. Gustavo Moura de Cavalcanti Mello & Henrique Pereira Braga (Eds.), *Wealth and Poverty in Contemporary Brazilian Capitalism*, 2021.
49. Paolo Favilli, *Historiography and Marxism: Innovations in Mid-century Italy*, 2021.

50. Levy del Aguila Marchena, *Communism, Political Power and Personal Freedom in Marx*, 2021.
51. V. Geetha, *Bhimrao Ramji Ambedkar and the Question of Socialism in India*, 2021.
52. Satoshi Matsui, *Normative Theories of Liberalism and Socialism: Marxist Analysis of Values*, 2022.
53. Kei Ehara (Ed.), *Japanese Discourse on the Marxian Theory of Finance*, 2022.
54. Achim Szepanski, *Financial Capital in the 21st Century*, 2022.

Titles Forthcoming

Vesa Oittinen, *Marx's Russian Moment*
Kolja Lindner, *Marx, Marxism and the Question of Eurocentrism*
Adriana Petra, *Intellectuals and Communist Culture: Itineraries, Problems and Debates in Post-war Argentina*
George C. Comninel, *The Feudal Foundations of Modern Europe*
Spencer A. Leonard, *Marx, the India Question, and the Crisis of Cosmopolitanism*
Joe Collins, *Applying Marx's Capital to the 21st century*
Jeong Seongjin, *Korean Capitalism in the 21st Century: Marxist Analysis and Alternatives*
Marcello Mustè, *Marxism and Philosophy of Praxis: An Italian Perspective from Labriola to Gramsci*
Shannon Brincat, *Dialectical Dialogues in Contemporary World Politics: A Meeting of Traditions in Global Comparative Philosophy*
Francesca Antonini, *Reassessing Marx's Eighteenth Brumaire: Dictatorship, State, and Revolution*
Thomas Kemple, *Capital After Classical Sociology: The Faustian Lives of Social Theory*
Xavier Vigna, *A Political History of Factories in France: The Workers' Insubordination of 1968*
Attila Melegh, *Anti-migrant Populism in Eastern Europe and Hungary: A Marxist Analysis*

Marie-Cecile Bouju, *A Political History of the Publishing Houses of the French Communist Party*

Peter McMylor, Graeme Kirkpatrick & Simin Fadaee (Eds.), *Marxism, Religion, and Emancipatory Politics*

Mauro Buccheri, *Radical Humanism for the Left: The Quest for Meaning in Late Capitalism*

Rémy Herrera, *Confronting Mainstream Economics to Overcome Capitalism*

Tamás Krausz, Eszter Bartha (Eds.), *Socialist Experiences in Eastern Europe: A Hungarian Perspective*

Martin Cortés, *Marxism, Time and Politics: On the Autonomy of the Political*

João Antonio de Paula, Huga da Gama Cerqueira, Eduardo da Motta e Albuquer & Leonardo de Deus, *Marxian Economics for the 21st Century: Revaluating Marx's Critique of Political Economy*

Zhi Li, *The Concept of the Individual in the Thought of Karl Marx*

Lelio Demichelis, *Marx, Alienation and Techno-capitalism*

Dong-Min Rieu, *A Mathematical Approach to Marxian Value Theory: Time, Money, and Labor Productivity*

Salvatore Prinzi, *Representation, Expression, and Institution: The Philosophy of Merleau-Ponty and Castoriadis*

Agon Hamza, *Slavoj Žižek and the Reconstruction of Marxism*

Éric Aunoble, *French Views on the Russian Revolution*

Terrell Carver, Smail Rapic (Eds.), *Friedrich Engels for the 21st Century: Perspectives and Problems*

Patrizia Dogliani, *A Political History of the International Union of Socialist Youth*

Alexandros Chrysis, *The Marx of Communism: Setting Limits in the Realm of Communism*

Stephen Maher, *Corporate Capitalism and the Integral State: General Electric and a Century of American Power*

Paul Raekstad, *Karl Marx's Realist Critique of Capitalism: Freedom, Alienation, and Socialism*

Alexis Cukier, *Democratic Work: Radical Democracy and the Future of Labour*

Christoph Henning, *Theories of Alienation: From Rousseau to the Present*

Daniel Egan, *Capitalism, War, and Revolution: A Marxist Analysis*

Genevieve Ritchie, Sara Carpenter & Shahrzad Mojab (Eds.), *Marxism and Migration*

Emanuela Conversano, *Capital from Afar: Anthropology and Critique of Political Economy in the Late Marx*
Marcello Musto, *Rethinking Alternatives with Marx*
Vincenzo Mele, *City and Modernity in George Simmel and Walter Benjamin: Fragments of Metropolis*
David Norman Smith, *Self-emancipation: Marx's Unfinished Theory of the Working Class*
José Ricardo Villanueva Lira, *Marxism and the Origins of International Relations*
Bertel Nygaard, *Marxism, Labor Movements, and Historiography*
Fabio Perocco (Ed.), *Racism in and for the Welfare State*
Marcos Del Roio, *Gramsci and the Emancipation of the Subaltern Classes*
Tomonaga Tairako, *A New Perspective on Marx's Philosophy and Political Economy*
Matthias Bohlender, Anna-Sophie Schönfelder, & Matthias Spekker, *Truth and Revolution in Marx's Critique of Society*
Mauricio Vieira Martins, *Marx, Spinoza and Darwin on Philosophy: Against Religious Perspectives of Transcendence*
Jean Vigreux, Roger Martelli, & Serge Wolikow, *One Hundred Years of History of the French Communist Party*
Aditya Nigam, *Border-Marxisms and Historical Materialism*
Fred Moseley, *Marx's Theory of Value in* Chapter 1 *of* Capital*: A Critique of Heinrich's Value-Form Interpretation*
Armando Boito, *The State, Politics, and Social Classes: Theory and History*
Anjan Chakrabarti & Anup Dhar, *World of the Third and Hegemonic Capital: Between Marx and Freud*
Hira Singh, *Annihilation of Caste in India: Ambedkar, Ghandi, and Marx*
Salvatore Engel-Di Mauro, *An Introduction to Ecosocialism*

Preface to the English Edition

The first edition of this book was published in Brazil in mid-2019, just over a year after it was written. In preparing this translation for an English readership, about two years after the book was released in Portuguese, we believe that not many changes to the original text were necessary. After all, as the most substantive part of the book corresponds to a synthetic approach of texts by Marx (and Engels) about the working class, written in the nineteenth century (although some of their study notebooks and manuscripts are only coming to the public now in the twenty-first century), there is not much to be ***updated***. Even so, as we discuss contemporary debates on Marx's texts, we have made some additions and revisions, particularly in the "New Subjects?" section. We have also updated some of the statistical information about the working class today, both worldwide and in Brazil. It is worth noting that we chose to keep the section on Brazil in the book, as, although originally written with the country's audience in mind, the Brazilian case may be of broader interest regarding the conditions of exploitation of the working class in the Global South.

However, we cannot say that "only" two years have passed since the first edition in Portuguese. Because historical time, in certain circumstances, seems to accelerate, sharpening social contradictions that are already explosive. In this particularly dramatic situation, the objective of the book appears to gain even greater relevance. Since the beginning of 2020 until now, nearly five million people have lost their lives to the COVID-19 pandemic, approximately two million of them concentrated in three countries—the United States, Brazil, and India. Without going into further discussions about the reasons for this concentration, one cannot ignore the weight of social and political factors in explaining the uneven impact of the pandemic in each region and country of the world, as well as social consequences that are also unevenly distributed. Regarding the working class, the subject of this book, the sanitary, economic, and social crisis situations intensified/heighten by the pandemic experienced a degree of precariousness of labour relations, social inequality, and vulnerability of the living conditions in which billions of workers around the world are subjected.

In the first half of 2020, when the confinement of a large part of the planet's population was adopted to contain the virus's circulation, the centrality of social care/reproduction occupations and the essential nature of the work carried out by new occupations, such as delivery workers—subjected to labour relations with a lot of information technologies and little labour rights—was clear to any observer. In contrast, one could also see the selectivity with which governments declared certain activities "essential", forcing workers to unnecessary exposure to the virus, under pressure from the interests of capital.

As early as April 2020, the *International Labour Organization* (ILO) had already reported that the approximately 1.6 billion informal workers on the planet were at serious risk of losing their jobs and income as a result of the paralysis of many economic activities, living under a severe threat of extreme poverty and hunger.[1] Months later, in its annual report on labour market trends, the ILO estimated an 8.8% reduction in hours worked during 2020 worldwide, which helps explain the loss of 114 million jobs during that year, adding to existing liabilities to calculate a deficit of 144 million jobs globally, resulting in about 220 million unemployed people.[2] As a result, labour income has suffered a sharp drop for such a short period of time. According to the same report:

> Global labour income, which does not include government transfers and benefits, was US$3.7 trillion (8.3 percent) lower in 2020 than it would have been in the absence of the pandemic. (...) Relative to 2019, an estimated additional 108 million workers are now extremely or moderately poor, meaning that they and their family members are having to live on less than US$3.20 per day in purchasing power parity terms.[3]

Thus, the total number of people living in poverty, according to World Bank parameters, had an estimated increase from 1.2 to 1.4%, with a global poverty rate estimated at something between 9.1 and 9.4%.[4] On the other side of the global social pyramid, the planet's billionaires saw their wealth grow a few trillion more in the year of the pandemic. According to Oxfam,

> Worldwide, billionaires wealth' increased by a staggering $3.9tn (trillion) between 18 March and 31 December 2020. Their total wealth now stands at $11.95tn, which is equivalent to what G20 governments have spent in response to the pandemic. The world's 10 richest billionaires have collectively seen their wealth increase by $540bn over this period.[5]

The association between the pandemic, precarious labour relations, and extreme inequality reveals only the surface of social contradictions of the moment in which we live. After all, if moments of crisis exacerbate and make these contradictions more visible, their existence is inherent to capitalist social relations in their long-term historical dynamics. In order to understand the dimensions of the abyss, to whose margins we are increasingly being pushed by the destructiveness of these social relations, Marx becomes even more *current* and the recovery of some aspects of his analysis of the working class, at this precise moment, seems now more justifiable than ever.

Before moving on to the book itself, I would like to leave some important records. For this edition aimed at the English-speaking public to come into existence, I owe warm thanks to Marcello Musto, who was interested in the work which at the time was still in production and who, with his peculiar enthusiasm and affection, invited me to publish it in the *Marx, Engels and Marxisms* collection. Mariana Rezende did a competent and essential work of bibliographic research for the preparation of the English manuscript. The English edition would not have been possible without the work of Rebecca Freitas, who combines refined translator skills with an in-depth knowledge of Marx's work and the Marxist debate. Nor can I fail to mention, in a book about workers, the careful editorial work of the Palgrave publishing team.

Niterói-RJ, Brazil Marcelo Badaró Mattos
October 2021

Notes

1. ILO, *ILO Monitor: COVID-19 and the world of work*, 29/04/2021, p. 1. Available at: https://www.ilo.org/wcmsp5/groups/public/---dgreports/---dcomm/documents/briefingnote/wcms_743146.pdf. Accessed in September 2021.
2. ILO, *World Employment and Social Outlook*, Geneva, ILO, 2021, pp. 11–13.
3. Ibid., p. 12.
4. World Bank, *Poverty and Shared Prosperity 2020: Overview—Reversals of Fortune*, Washington D.C., World Bank, 2020, p. 5. The World Bank uses daily individual income of up to US$1.90 to define a poverty situation.
5. Oxfam, *The Inequality Virus. Bringing together a world torn apart by coronavirus through a fair, just and sustainable economy*, Oxford, Oxfam, 2021, p. 12.

Contents

CHAPTER 1

Introduction

The term class, referring to a classification or social stratification, is part of our society's everyday vocabulary. A few years ago, for example, the public sphere in Brazil was dominated by a debate in which the improved living conditions of the poorest strata of the population, interpreted as social upward mobility, were seen in terms of a change in the class of these strata.

In 2011, the then Brazilian president, Dilma Rousseff, stated that among the most important legacies of her predecessor, Luiz Inácio Lula da Silva was the social upward mobility of almost 30 million Brazilians who had gone from "class D" to "class C", constituting a "new middle class": "This new middle class is one of the great achievements and the biggest and best legacies I have from Luiz Inácio Lula da Silva's government".[1]

The association between "classes" and letters (A, B, C, D, E) wasn't invented by politicians. It has been used for a long time by research institutes, advertisers and companies in general to establish a stratification of social groups based on their consumption capacity. Such use of "class" as a category of analysis, however, is also shared by social scientists. The Brazilian situation mentioned above was described by the sociologist Rudá Ricci as "the greatest sociological phenomenon in Brazil", when commenting on a 2008 survey by Marcelo Neri from the Getúlio Vargas

M. B. Mattos, *The Working Class from Marx to Our Times*, Marx, Engels, and Marxisms,
https://doi.org/10.1007/978-3-030-97355-1_1

Foundation, which found that the so-called new middle class accounted for almost half of the Brazilian population. According to the survey:

> The class C is currently made up of 91.8 million Brazilians. For FGV, a family is considered middle class (class C) when it has a monthly income between R$1,064 and R$4,591. The economic elite (classes A and B) earn more than R$4,591, while class D (classified as low-income) earns between R$768 and R$1,064. Class E (poor), in turn, brings together families with incomes below R$768.[2]

New consumption patterns, lower education levels and a political susceptibility to fall for "neo-populisms" are some of the elements that, in Ricci's assessment, distinguish this "new middle class" from the "traditional" middle class.

The expression "new middle class" has older sociological roots. The term became well known from Wright Mills' classic book, published in 1951, on the rise of the "white collars" as the "new middle class" in the United States.[3] Mills compared an "old" middle class, made up of small businessmen and typical self-employed workers (from the so-called liberal professionals to small capitalist "entrepreneurs", such as small business owners, small farmers and owners of craft workshops) to the "new" middle class, composed of managers, medium waged workers and non-manual workers, especially in the service sectors.

In Mills' terms, however, the contrast between the "old" and the "new" middle classes involved their position in relation to property, their degree of subordination in labour relations and reverberated on collective mentalities, with no decisive weight to the income parameter. After all, his white-collar typology ranged from the "top", made up of managers of large companies and bureaucrats in suits, to "lower positions", where there were "office workers": "secretaries and typists, entry clerks, billing clerks, corresponding clerks—a thousand kinds of clerks; the operators of light machinery, comptometers, dictaphones, addressographs; and the receptionists".[4] So, according to his comparison:

> The nineteenth-century farmer and businessman were generally thought to be stalwart individuals—their own men, men who could quickly grow to be almost as big as anyone else. The twentieth century white-collar man has never been independent as the farmer used to be, nor as hopeful of the main chance as the businessman. He is always somebody's man, the corporation's, the government's, the army's; and he is seen as the man

> who does not rise. The decline of the free entrepreneur and the rise of the dependent employee on the American scene has paralleled the decline of the independent individual and the rise of the little man in the American mind.[5]

However, even among the classics of sociology, the category of analysis "social classes" can be found associated with a position in a specific social classification stratified according to income levels, properties, and more generally, positions in the market. According to Max Weber, the situation of a social class is defined by some components of this relative position, and one can speak of a class:

> when (I) a number of people have in common a specific causal component of their life chances, insofar as (2) this component is represented exclusively by economic interests in the possession of goods and opportunities for income, and (3) is represented under the conditions of the commodity or labour markets. This is "class situation."[6]

Competition in the market, "aiming at exchange", creates specific life opportunities, marked by the distinction between owners and non-owners, in which the former are certainly more favoured in accessing "much desired goods". "Property" and "lack of property" are, therefore, the basic categories of all class situations", according to Weber. Therefore, according to the same author, "Class situation is, in this sense, ultimately market situation".[7]

It is interesting to note, however, that, insofar as references to class as a criterion of social stratification measured by income and defined by differentiated access to consumption in the market are abundant today, there is little mention of the term class associated with a position in the production process, in labour relations, or even in certain forms of collective action driven by a sense of class.

Therefore, we hear and read a lot about "class A, B, C", etc., or about new and old "middle classes" (and a little less about "rich" and "poor"), while the use of expressions such as "working class" or "proletariat" is increasingly rare in the media (as expressions such as "bourgeoisie" and "ruling class"), in political discourses and even in the academic elaborations of social sciences.

It is not just the categories of analysis that are absent, but the consequent perception that such social classes have objectively opposed worldviews, interests, and political projects, which confront each other in different moments of social life. In other words, what is omitted is the class logic of the fundamental social conflicts in which we are immersed.

The author of this work is among those who see these current uses of the term class, as well as efforts to conceptualize class exclusively from phenomena associated with consumption, income, and market, as reductionist, for they limit the class situation to a strictly economic dimension (and circumscribe economic phenomena to the competition of individuals and groups of individuals for income and consumption in the market). Such reductionism prevents the comprehension of social classes in their articulation to the totality of social dynamics.

For this reason, this book privileges another perspective, which identifies classes based on the relationships that men and women, living in society, establish with each other to produce and reproduce themselves socially. These relationships establish limits and pressure the collective behaviour of the class, which raises the need to understand other dimensions of these fundamental social groups, such as their collective conscience and political action. In this way, one can perceive classes, and the conflicts among them, as historically situated processes and relationships, which are decisive for understanding the broader dynamics of social transformation. The theoretical starting point for such a perspective is historical materialism.

Naming historical materialism as a reference may not be enough since the term itself is an object of controversy.[8] Thus, the book you are now starting to read is intended to be an introduction to the debate on the working class based on the work of Marx. The central thesis defended here is that the general lines of the critical analysis of capitalism developed by Marx and Engels and especially the categories of analysis of social classes, class struggle, and working class remain relevant as a way of understanding the world in which we live.[9]

Defending the validity of the critique and categories outlined by Marx does not mean to see them as a finished and closed set. Nothing is farther from the dialectical complexity of Marx's proposed apprehension of society than a rigid doctrine. The best proof of this is that over more than 130 years that have followed Marx's death so far, his contribution has continued to be the object of study, reinterpretation, and controversy, even among those who explicitly claim it.

For this reason, this book will focus on an analysis of Marx's contributions to the debate on the working class but will draw on several contributions within Marxism(s), seeking to elucidate polysemic and/or controversial aspects of Marx's analysis and even highlight the different interpretations his work generated.

As for the formal division of the book, the first part seeks to synthesize some of Marx and Engels' main contributions (and, in a complementary way, of twentieth-century Marxist authors) to the understanding of social classes, class struggle, and the working class in particular. This first part—which is the most extensive in the book—was divided into different moments, initially addressing the encounter between Marx, Engels, and the working-class movement at the time of the making of this class in the European continent.

Next, I discuss the difficulties and peculiarities of the vocabulary through which we seek to approach the working class. The two discussions are inseparable; after all, vocabulary is incomprehensible outside the social relations within which it emerges and is transformed. Therefore, it is defended here that the period in which the working class emerges as a social subject corresponds to its self-definition as a class. Marx and Engels are contemporaries of this first moment of the formation of the working class and they "were introduced" to it in real social processes.

Amidst this meeting, they identified with this collective subject and sought to build a set of analytical and political references about social classes and class struggle, whose ultimate objective was to overcome class society in the existing world. The centre of this part of the text and of the book, therefore, is the effort to present such a contribution. We resorted to a didactic cut between the objective and subjective dimensions of the concept of the working class which Marx and Engels employed in different moments of their production. Such a distinction between the two dimensions, evidently, does not exist in the "real life" of the class. Moreover, to operate it even in the presentation of Marx's reflections, it is necessary to proceed much more by juxtaposing the layers of analysis than by separating aspects of the class.

The remaining parts are different exercises dialoguing between Marx's discussions of the working class presented in the first part and empirical elements of the reality of class today, as well as social science and historiographic debates about this same class. Thus, in the second part, a very synthetic picture of the data of the composition of the working class in Brazil and in the world in the first years of the twenty-first century is presented. Then, we suggest some analytical possibilities, coming from these elements of the current profile of the working class and considering the conceptual references presented from Marx's work. Thus, I intend to think historically and theoretically, from a historical materialism perspective, about the current situation of the working class.

The next part addresses some controversies around the characterization of the profile and social protagonism of those who live off their own labour today, paying special attention to some propositions by authors from the Northern Hemisphere, which have gained wide dissemination in recent decades and have in common a relativization or even denial of a central aspect of Marx's analysis of the working class, namely: its potential as a historical subject of an emancipatory transformation. This moment leads to another defence of the analytical validity and the topicality of the concept of working class, whose general lines were traced by Marx and Engels, this time from a critical dialogue with the contemporary production of the social sciences.

Thinking about the topicality of the concept is not restricted to defending its relevance in understanding the world we live in today, but also realizing its explanatory efficacy for analysing the history of capitalist societies. Therefore, the last part of this work is dedicated to the debate about the working class among historians, maintaining the analogies of the discussion about contemporaneity made in the previous part.

Given that the purpose of this text is to introduce and synthesize, the main concern was not to present an original contribution, but to gather information and introduce analytical references that could be useful to readers in the university environment, but also outside it. The author's desire is to reach a readership involved in the broader effort of working-class transformative intervention in current social relations.

This book is not my first exploration of the subject. To avoid self-remitting footnotes in each chapter, at the bibliography I list the most recent past work on the debate about class, class struggle, the working class, and the specific historical studies that I have developed. All of them nurtured this book, directly or indirectly. Many passages originally presented in them have been recovered, revised, and reorganized, although most of the material gathered here has been written specifically for this book.

The time and conditions necessary to carry out this undertaking were guaranteed to me by a leave for a research internship that the Department of History of the Fluminense Federal University, to which I am professionally linked, granted me in the period from August 2016 to July 2017.

Likewise, I must acknowledge that I was very welcomed by the Institute of Contemporary History of Nova University Lisbon, where I developed the internship, under the supervision of Professor Fernando Rosas, participating in the activities of the Research Group on the Global History of Work and Social Conflicts.

I thank them and the whole group for their welcome and fruitful exchanges. I am also grateful to Marcel van der Linden, who warmly welcomed me back to my brief return to the International Institute of Social History in Amsterdam and with whom I kept a dialogue at other times during the internship period in Portugal.

In the debates on Marx and Marxism in general, I owe a lot to the collective learning provided to me by the whole of the *Núcleo Interdisciplinar de Estudos e Pesquisas sobre Marx e o Marxismo* [Interdisciplinary Centre for Studies and Research on Marx and Marxism] (NIEP-Marx), at the Fluminense Federal University. In the same way, the theme of the working class has been the object of so many discussions in the last decade and a half in the research group *Observatório da História da Classe Trabalhadora* [Observatory of the History of the Working Class], which I have so far coordinated, that it would be impossible to thank the friends in the group enough for everything I learned from them. Among them, I leave special thanks to Amanda Cezar, Dani Jardim, Lívia Berdu, Marcelo Ramos, and Wesley Carvalho, who read the first part of the manuscript and contributed with key comments and suggestions.

Notes

1. Leandro Nossa & Tânia Monteiro, "Nova classe média é uma das grandes conquistas do País, afirma Dilma", *O Estado de São Paulo*, 26 April 2011, available at http://politica.estadao.com.br/noticias/geral,nova-classe-media-e-uma-das-grandes-conquistas-do-pais-afirma-dilma,710974, accessed in January 2017.
2. Rudá Ricci, "O Maior Fenômeno Sociológico do Brasil: a nova classe média", available at http://www.escoladegoverno.org.br/artigos/209-nova-classe-media?tmpl=component&print=1&page=, accessed: December 2016. In December 2016, US$1.00 was equivalent to R$3.30, approximately. For a critique of this idea of a "new middle class" see, for example, Marcio Pochmann, *Nova classe média? – O trabalho na base da pirâmide social brasileira*, São Paulo, Boitempo, 2012.

3. C. Wright Mills, *White Collar. The American Middle Classes*, London, Oxford University Press, 1956.
4. Ibid., p. X.
5. Ibid., pp. XI–XII.
6. Max Weber, *Economy and Society. An Outline of Interpretative Sociology*, Berkeley, University of California Press, 1978, p. 927.
7. Ibid., pp. 927–28.
8. Here, we share the definition of historical materialism outlined by the historian E. P. Thompson. In his debate with Marxist structuralism in the 1970s, he resumed the struggle he had been fighting since 1956 against Stalinism, proposing that there was a gap between two traditions that claimed Marx's thought. He claimed historical materialism as a tradition of active reason, open inquiry and criticism: "For the gulf that has opened has not been between different accentuations to the vocabulary of concept, between this analogy and that category, but between idealist and materialist modes of though, between Marxism as closure and a tradition, derivative from Marx, of open investigation and critique. The first is a tradition of theology. The second is a tradition of active reason. Both can derive some license from Marx, although the second has immeasurably better credentials as to its lineage." E. P. Thompson, *The Poverty of Theory and Other Essays*, London, Merlin, 1978, p. 380.
9. The importance of Engels for the themes that will be discussed here is not only measured by the texts they co-signed. As most of the texts cited are by Marx and as Engels himself acknowledged, on more than one occasion, considering the prevalence of Marx's reflection in the proposition of the great framework of historical materialism, I refer only to Marx in most of this book. I would like to stress, however, that both participated in the elaboration of most of the categories of analysis and theses summarized here.

CHAPTER 2

Marx, Marxism, and the Working Class

Marx, Engels, and the Working-Class Movements

This is a book about categories of analysis—social class, working class, class struggle, etc.—and the first impression we get when we discuss categories is that, as abstractions, they constitute pure theory, arising from the elaboration of brilliant minds. Categorical abstractions, however, are attempts to apprehend living realities, which are always complex and contradictory.

Thus, at times, a category of analysis is constructed to account for a reality experienced by men and women based on parameters external to their everyday life references, but in other situations, the abstractions used to analyse reality come from categories already shared by people from a certain time and space, by giving them a more general meaning. The category "social class" and its correlates can be used in these two senses when we study the history of human societies. After all, most societies in the past did not see themselves as divided into social classes, but the dynamics of their social conflicts can be apprehended by resorting to the category of social class (as well as class division, especially class struggle). Since the nineteenth century, however, it has been possible to say that significant portions of the men and women who lived and live off their own labour began to define themselves as belonging to the same class, distinct from others. Class was added to a repertoire of shared

M. B. Mattos, *The Working Class from Marx to Our Times*, Marx, Engels, and Marxisms,
https://doi.org/10.1007/978-3-030-97355-1_2

collective identification parameters (compatriots, citizens, members of the same sex or gender, ethnic, and racial self-identifications, etc.) to express a fundamental inequality. It referred to new identifications that previous designations for different social positions—such as castes, orders, estates—no longer seemed to account for.

The English historian Edward Palmer Thompson presented the question by distinguishing two dimensions of the employment of the category social class, differentiated as follows: "a) with reference to real, empirically observable corresponding historical content; b) as a heuristic or analytic category to organize historical evidence which has a very much less direct correspondence".[1]

As an analytical category, historians and other social scientists use the term social class to refer to different conflicting society conformations over time, in which those who worked and those who lived mainly on the surplus produced by the former did not see themselves as classes and did not employ this definition.

The first dimension corresponds to the historical process experienced by workers since the first decades of the consolidation of industrial capitalism, initially in England and then in other regions of Western Europe. In his best-known work on the making of the English working class, Thompson investigated the period between the beginning of the French Revolution and the 1830s, when a collective, class-minded movement, self-identified as a working-class movement, gained national proportions around union struggles and the struggle for the expansion of political participation.[2]

In the 1830s, Marx and Engels spent their youth in the social space that later became the German State. Both were interested in philosophical studies, which were conducted by Marx in a more academic sense, resulting in a doctoral thesis in philosophy and an unsuccessful career plan as a university professor. Engels, on the other hand, had more dilettante contacts with university life while he served as an officer in the armed forces and, due to family (class?) "fate", he was unable to plan an academic career.[3]

In the early 1840s, however, the encounter with social and political movements of the working class changed both their life trajectories, especially after Engels' trip to England to work at a family weaving factory and Marx's trip to France, seeking an environment with enough political freedom to carry out the journalistic, intellectual, and political work he had tried to develop in his own land.

In a sense, from different starting points, these two German thinkers, engulfed by the social and political conflicts of their time, converged on a common positioning and started to intervene in these conflicts from a clear class perspective. The early 1840s is the decisive moment for this taking of a position.

Engels was the son of a religious and conservative family of industry owners in the city of Barmen, and from a young age, he was pushed to take on tasks in the family businesses, which led him to study commerce in Bremen. While serving in the military in Berlin in 1841, he attended courses in philosophy at the local university and approached the ideas of the group known as "young Hegelians".

His interest in philosophy and the social concern that led him to denounce the living conditions of workers in his homeland grew continuously in the following years, but he was sent by his father, at age 22, to work in a factory co-owned by the family in Manchester, the industrial heartland of England. Arriving in Manchester in December 1842, he soon got in touch with the Chartist movement, which months earlier had been responsible for a great general strike in North England.[4] He also established contact with the radical movement of German exiles, united in the *League of the Just*. While still in Manchester, he started a relationship with Irish worker Mary Burns, who he stayed with until her death. Mary and her sister Lizzie introduced Engels to Manchester's impoverished working-class communities and played a central role in his political activity in the following decades.

Before leaving for England, Engels had already collaborated with the *Rheinische Zeitung*, a newspaper edited by Marx and had met him in the newspaper's editorial office in 1842, in a meeting that had left no special impression on either of them. About two years later, however, he wrote an article on political economy for the *Deutsch-Französische Jahrbücher*, a magazine whose first (and last) edition was directed by Marx in Paris.

The article made an excellent impression on Marx, who ended up inviting Engels to a meeting in Paris, resulting in the beginning of the collaboration and great friendship between the two that would last until the end of his life. At that time, Engels was already writing about English workers, and in 1845, he published *The Condition of the working-class in England*. The book contains a thorough analysis of Chartism and an assessment of its political potential, based on the social confrontation of workers against the bourgeoisie channelled through a proletarian movement demanding a new law:

> This proposed law is the People's Charter, which in form is purely political, and demands a democratic basis for the House of Commons. Chartism is the compact form of their opposition to the bourgeoisie. In the Unions and turnouts opposition always remained isolated: it was single working-men or sections who fought a single bourgeois. If the fight became general, this was scarcely by the intention of the working-men; or, when it did happen intentionally, Chartism was at the bottom of it. But in Chartism it is the whole working-class which arises against the bourgeoisie, and attacks, first of all, the political power, the legislative rampart with which the bourgeoisie has surrounded itself.[5]

According to Engels' assessment, however, there was an ideological limitation in English Chartism. Its political horizon was still limited by the horizon of capitalist society. On the other hand, the socialists who acted in England, although defenders of the overthrow of capitalism, were of bourgeois class origin which made action difficult in the proletarian milieu. Engels believed in the fusion between socialism and Chartism, which would strengthen a project of working-class power:

> Hence it is evident that the working-men's movement is divided into two sections, the Chartists and the Socialists. The Chartists are theoretically the more backward, the less developed, but they are genuine proletarians all over, the representatives of their class. The Socialists are more far-seeing, propose practical remedies against distress, but, proceeding originally from the bourgeoisie, are for this reason unable to amalgamate completely with the working-class. The union of Socialism with Chartism, the reproduction of French Communism in an English manner, will be the next step, and has already begun. Then only, when this has been achieved, will the working-class be the true intellectual leader of England. Meanwhile, political and social development will proceed, and will foster this new party, this new departure of Chartism.[6]

Marx was only two years older than Engels and was born in Trier, the son of a family of Jewish origin. His father, a lawyer, abandoned Judaism to broaden his professional perspectives (local law prohibited the exercise of public office by Jews). Marx tried to follow his father's career, and at the age of 18, he enrolled in law at the University of Bonn. However, in the following year, in 1837, he moved to Berlin and soon changed his course to philosophy, where he stayed until he obtained a doctorate in 1841, from the University of Jena, with his thesis on the Greek philosophers Democritus and Epicurus. In Berlin, like Engels, he also approached the "young Hegelians", who made up the most critical sector of the new university generation. His proximity to Bruno Bauer, who taught theology in Bonn, raised hopes of an academic placement, but Bauer was fired on charges of atheism and the university world was closed to Marx.

Having broken his dream of initiating a university career, from 1842 onwards, he dedicated himself to journalism, writing in Cologne for the *Rheinische Zeitung*, of which he later became editor. In that newspaper of the local bourgeoisie, Marx showed his qualities as a radical democratic propagandist. While exercising his journalistic position, he approached, for the first time in a more systematic way, the analysis of the transformations that later—especially in the chapter on the "primitive accumulation" of Capital—explained how expropriation was necessary for the creation of a class of free workers to be exploited by capital. "Free" from the ties to masters and/or land, but also because they had nothing else, except their labour power, which they then tried to sell in exchange for the wage that allowed them to stay alive.

Although using a different terminology, this is what he dealt with in a series of articles, published in 1842, in the legislative debate in the Rhine provincial assembly the previous year on "wood theft". Outraged by the legislation that illegalized not only the cutting of wood in forests protected as private property, but also the collection of fallen branches and twigs, which affected the region's poor peasants, Marx advanced a critique of the law's and State's class awareness, which was under the interests of private property and property owners. Marx found that, by criminalizing the customary rights of poor peasants, the State "is forced to lower itself to the irrational and illegal means of private property". However, by exploring the contradiction embedded in the affirmation of the private interest of the owners at the expense of the rights of all citizens, he raised the question:

> If every violation of property without distinction, without a more exact definition, is termed theft, will not all private property be theft? By my private ownership do I not exclude every other person from this ownership? Do I not thereby violate his right of ownership?[7]

The newspaper ended up attracting the attention of the authorities, who ordered its closure in 1843. Marx's life began to take new directions from this "push". He married Jenny von Westphalen, the daughter of a traditional aristocratic family in his hometown, to whom he had secretly become engaged a few years earlier. Without the workload from the newspaper, Marx dove into the studies on the *Philosophy of Right* in Hegel. Watching the political situation turn against him, he travelled to Paris and, together with Arnold Ruge, conceived a new periodical, the *Deutsch-Französische Jahrbücher*. It had only one double issue published, which included the aforementioned article by Engels and also two texts by Marx—*On the Jewish Question* and *Contribution to the Critique of Hegel's Philosophy of Right. Introduction*. In this last article, Marx presented for the first time his conclusions on the revolutionary potential of the working class. As we address below, the conclusion of that text is his first statement on the role of the proletariat as a revolutionary subject.

> Where, then, is the *positive* possibility of a German emancipation?
>
> Answer: In the formation of a class with *radical chains*, a class of civil society, an estate which is the dissolution of all estates, a sphere which has a universal character by its universal suffering and claims no *particular right* because no *particular wrong* but *wrong generally* is perpetrated against it; which can no longer invoke a *historical* but only a *human* title; which does not stand in any one-sided antithesis to the consequences but in an all-round antithesis to the premises of the German state; a sphere, finally, which cannot emancipate itself without emancipating itself from all other spheres of society and thereby emancipating all other spheres of society, which, in a word, is the *complete loss* of man and hence can win itself only through the *complete rewinning of man*. This dissolution of society as a particular estate is the *proletariat*.[8]

Such an assessment, central to the rest of Marx's writings and political activities, was not something that arose from academic impressions alone. Upon arriving in Paris in October 1843, Marx took part in meetings with different socialist groups and showed special affinity with secret societies of proletarian composition (where the dominant presence was of proletarianized artisans) that declared themselves to be communists. In a letter written to the German philosopher Ludwig Feuerbach, who at that time was his main intellectual influence, dated 11 August 1844, Marx emphasized his admiration for these French workers and stated: "You would have to attend one of the meetings of the French workers to appreciate the pure freshness, the nobility which burst forth from these toil-worn men". He then declared his certainty in the role reserved for them in the overcome of capitalism: "But in any case it is among these "barbarians" of our civilized society that history is preparing the practical element for the emancipation of mankind".[9]

At that time, in his *Critical Marginal Notes,* a critique of the article on the Silesian weavers' revolt published by Arnold Ruge under the pseudonym "a Prussian", Marx revealed both his political distancing from Ruge, who until recently had been his partner (and financier) in the *Deutsch-Französische Jahrbücher*, and his definitive adherence to the communist perspective, based on the evaluation of the revolutionary potential of the working class. As he pointed out in that text, published in two parts in the first half of August 1844, Marx was already convinced that: "A philosophical people can find its corresponding practice only in socialism, hence it is only in the proletariat that it can find the dynamic element of its emancipation".[10]

For that reason, evaluating his trajectory in the months prior to writing his first critical texts on political economy, José Paulo Netto summarizes the changes in Marx's worldview after his departure from Germany: "A communist option and the identification of the proletariat as a revolutionary subject – this is the point at which Marx, in terms of his ideological-political development, reached the end of his first semester in Paris".[11]

Considering these trajectories, around 1844, Marx and Engels had already made direct contact—participating in meetings, exchanging correspondence, politically formulating—with at least four fronts of the most advanced sectors of the European labour movement, as highlighted by Michael Löwy: the communist secret societies of Paris; the League of the Just; English Chartism; and the revolt of the Silesian weavers.[12]

It is from this participation in the working-class movement that we can better understand the initial proposition of historical materialism, comprehending the social ground of the new analytical perspective and the beginning of the overcoming of German philosophy, of classical political economy, and of the social interpretation of the "utopian socialists", to which they committed themselves in the following years. According to Löwy, this is the framework in which Marx and Engels expose, in their first joint writings and in their individual texts, "the dialectical synthesis, the transcending of the fragmentary, scattered, and partial elements, the various experiences and ideologies of the workers' movement, and the production of a coherent and rational theory appropriate to the proletariat's situation [...]".[13]

Marx and Engels therefore met the working class in its formation process. They certainly did not invent it, nor could they "invent" a concept that was already present in the vocabulary of the time and in the consciousness of that social group with which they politically identified. However, they elaborated a whole set of analyses and a method of understanding human societies in their historical dynamics, which has the category "social classes" as one of its fundamental cornerstones.

This *encounter* not only gave rise to an analytical perspective, but also led to a lifelong commitment to the struggles of the working class. In early 1848, as part of the *League of the Just* (which they proposed to turn into the embryo of an international organization, renamed the *League of Communists*), they wrote the *Communist Manifesto*. The year 1848 was marked by revolutionary eruption in much of the European continent, and Marx and Engels returned to their homeland to intervene in the German revolutionary process. Defeated, they returned to England—Marx, as an exiled for the rest of his life, dedicated himself the following years to his studies for his greatest work. Engels reluctantly returned to his father's Manchester company, seeking support for himself and so that Marx could carry out the project of the critique of political economy shared by them both. In 1864, still immersed in the research and writing work that would result in *Capital*, Marx stood at the foundation of the *International Workingmen's Association* (IWA), of which he would end up being one of the most outstanding leaders. They also followed the process of construction of a political organization in Germany which claimed their proposals, culminating in the foundation of the *Social Democratic Workers' Party of Germany*, in 1875. Engels lived longer and could intercede for a longer time in the debates of that organization, even actively participating in the creation of what came to be known as the Second International, founded in Paris, in 1889.

A Matter of Vocabulary?

Mikhail Bakhtin, a Russian Marxist thinker with a vast and relevant contribution to linguistic, literary, and cultural studies in general, places the analysis of the linguistic phenomena in the field of historically located social relations. According to him, "every ideological sign - the verbal sign included - in coming about through the process of social intercourse, is defined by the social purview of the given time period and the given social group".[14]

It is in this sense that we can understand how Bakhtin emphasizes the fact that words reflect changes in social life, but not exclusively as a reflection, since "existence reflected in sign is not merely reflected but refracted". The emphasis on refraction is an emphasis on the possibility that reality, the social being, be expressed through signs in different or even antagonistic ways, as this phenomenon falls within the framework of "an intersecting of differently oriented social interests within one and the same sign community, i.e., by the class struggle".[15]

Few words, or linguistic signs, as referred to by Bakhtin, illustrate his propositions as well as "class". The expression class refers to the idea of a specific part of a larger set, group, or category. Its use to define social groups is older, but for the aims of this work, it is enough to go back to the end of the eighteenth century, when Abbot Sieyès wrote *What is the third state?* When speaking of class, he referred to the four categories of work at the time—agriculture, industry, commerce, and services—as the term class had the meaning of categories of work, in contrast to order/estate, which designated groups defined by hierarchical, hereditary, and solidarity criteria.[16]

Throughout the nineteenth century, in French, the expression started to be referred to in terms of relations between groups based on inequalities: "dominant class", "bourgeois class", or "working class". However, for some time, most references to class made by the workers themselves used the term as a synonym for profession or trade: "class of typographers"; "class of metallurgists"; "class of miners"; etc.[17]

In England, the term working classes was widely used in the early nineteenth century, in a manner similar to the French, to designate the group of poor workers in their various professional categories. Around the 1840s, as Asa Briggs points out, the use of the expression in the singular, working class, began to expand, denoting a feeling of internal solidarity to the social group and opposition to other groups, in a new apprehension of the nature of social inequalities.[18] In Briggs' study, the relationship between words and movements is at the centre of the discussion: "The change in nomenclature in late eighteenth and early nineteenth centuries reflected a basic change not only in men's ways of viewing society but in society itself".[19]

It was precisely when the expression working class, singular, began to refer itself to a group of individuals subjected to the same social situation, that Engels and Marx noticed the transforming potential of its social action. They did not do it, as we had seen, out of theoretical or analytical clairvoyance, but because the language of class was used by a social movement—with which they identified—capable of causing a significant political impact at the time.

Marx and Engels therefore dealt with the historically existing working class, which was beginning to manifest a consciousness in itself as a class. At this point, it is necessary, in addition to historicizing vocabulary, to explain some differences in the way we treat terms referring to class in different languages. In Portuguese, like in Spanish and French, we are used to employing the expression "*classe operária*" ("*clase obrera*", "*classe ouvrière*)—sometimes synonymously with the working class and other times more narrowly (as industrial workers). In the German language of Marx and Engels, there is no equivalent expression. In the English language, which was the source of most of their readings on the subject, there is the word labourer (laborer in the North American spelling), whose use, however, is much more restricted, usually applied to manual workers (especially those from construction). Marx uses labourer to refer to all expropriated individual workers, but most of the time he is concerned with the collective subject working class or proletariat.

Considering the specificities of the term "*classe ouvrière*" in French (and we could extend it to other Neo-Latin languages), Daniel Bensaid perceived the problems of using the term in a too restrictive sense:

> In the 19th century, people talked about working classes, in plural. The German term *Arbeiterklasse* or the English expression *working class* remain extremely generic. *'Classe ouvrière'*, dominant in the French vocabulary, has a sociological connotation prone to misunderstandings. It mainly designates the industrial proletariat, excluding the wage-earner in services and commerce, which is subject to analogous conditions of exploitation from the point of view of their relationship to the private property of the means of production, their place in the division of labour or wage form of their income. Marx speaks of proletarians. Despite its apparent disuse, the term is at the same time more rigorous and broader than *'Classe ouvrière'*. In developed societies, the industrial and service proletariat represents two-thirds to four-fifths of the working population.[20]

Marx, who knew the word *ouvrière* and used it a few times when dealing with France, did not use it, as he did at other times when choosing a French term to better define expressions he considered inadequate or non-existent in German. Such a question of vocabulary is not minor. Much of the difficulty in recognizing the emancipatory potential of the proletariat as a revolutionary subject today is related to the use of too narrow a conception of what that class might be, as I will try to demonstrate below.

There are other vocabulary misunderstandings that need to be mentioned when it comes to translating concepts and reflections about work and class. Based on the English language, labour and work are two words that are usually translated into Portuguese using the same word—"*trabalho*"—but which have different meanings in their origin. Engels, in a brief footnote to an English edition of Capital after Marx's death, makes the difference clear. The footnote is a complementary comment on the very well-known fragment of Marx's text below—and is fundamental for the discussions I develop afterwards:

> On the one hand, all labour is, speaking physiologically, an expenditure of human labour power, and in its character of identical abstract human labour, it creates and forms the value of commodities. On the other hand, all labour is expenditure of human labour power in a special form and with a definite aim, and in this, its character of concrete useful labour, it produces use values.[21]

In the footnote, Engels explains:

> The English language has the advantage of possessing different words for the two aspects of labour here considered. The labour which creates Use Value, and counts qualitatively, is Work, as distinguished from Labour; that which creates Value and counts quantitatively, is Labour as distinguished from Work.[22]

In English, "labour" ended up defining not only, as a noun, "work that creates value", as Engels called it, but also served, as an adjective, to identify the social and political movements of the working class—"labour movement", "Labour Party", "labourism", etc. This adjective has also expanded to delimit the fields of study of the working class.

When it comes to history, to which the last part of this book is dedicated, the naming of a specific field as labour history says a lot: its studies, for the most part, did not turn to work in its broadest sense, which expands through various social configurations throughout history and is associated with the notion of concrete/useful labour. Rather, they concentrated their studies on labour in its typical form in capitalism, abstract wage labour, as well as on waged working-class movements and organizations. In Brazil, influenced by the British labour historiography (Hobsbawm, Thompson, etc.), we usually talk about social labour history, which refers to the fact that labour history focuses not only on labour processes and relations, but also on the working class, through their living conditions, forms of organization, and collective action.

"Labour" and "working class"; once again there may be a confusion of words when thinking about labour history or labour studies in general. After all, if labour refers not only to abstract work, but also to an adjective linked to class, it is understandable that some Marxist authors have tended to use the image employed by Marx of a capital vs. labour conflict as a synonym without mediations of class struggle between the bourgeoisie and the working class. However, the study of labour and the study of the working class may be completely intertwined when the object is capitalist social formation; they are not one and the same thing. These initial definitions, at first simple vocabulary precision, can be decisive for fundamental contemporary debates.

Class in Its Material/Economic Existence

Let us turn again to the passage from the work of Daniel Bensaid abovementioned: "Marx speaks of proletarians. (...) the term is at the same time more rigorous and broader than '*Classe ouvrière*'". How would it be possible then, in Marx's work, to find such a "broad" dimension of the concept of the proletariat/working class? As explained in the Introduction, for purely didactic reasons, the following is a brief analysis of some of Marx's passages, divided in two moments (which are actually inseparable in his writings and, even more, in the concrete reality of the working class). We shall start by dealing with class from the perspective of capitalist relations of production, which place large human collectives in different (and opposite) situations in capitalist society.

In Marx and Engels' first attempt to systematize the proposals they came up with together—the *German Ideology* manuscript, written in 1845—the role of social classes and their conflicts in social–historical processes appear to be central. They resorted to the concept of social class specially to define the terms of the transformation operated by the bourgeoisie in modern societies, who gradually shaped it according to its features—increasingly urban and mercantile—in the context of a conflict of interests with the feudal nobility. Thus, they defined:

> The separate individuals form a class only insofar as they have to carry on a common battle against another class; in other respects they are on hostile terms with each other as competitors. On the other hand, the class in its turn assumes an independent existence as against the individuals, so that the latter find their conditions of life predetermined, and have their position in life and hence their personal development assigned to them by their class, thus becoming subsumed under it. This is the same phenomenon as the subjection of the separate individuals to the division of labour and can only be removed by the abolition of private property and labour itself.[23]

In the Marxist historiography of the twentieth century, the English historian Edward Thompson was the one who took this perception of the centrality of "class struggle" in the definition of social class proposed by Marx and Engels the furthest. In an article summing up his contributions to this conceptual debate, Thompson highlighted the aspects of his interpretation of class as a "historical phenomenon" and of class struggle as a previous concept that allows one to value cultural aspects of the process of class formation, without ever taking them for "independent of objective determinations".[24]

> To put it bluntly: classes do not exist as separate entities, look around, find an enemy class, and then start to struggle. On the contrary, people find themselves in a society structured in determined ways (crucially, but not exclusively, in productive relations), they experience exploitation (or the need to maintain power over those whom they exploit), they identify points of antagonistic interest, they commence to struggle around these issues and in the process of struggling they discover themselves as classes, they come to know this discovery as class-consciousness. Class and class-consciousness are always the last, not the first, stage in the real historical process.[25]

In the next few pages, however, we focus on the dimension of the "subsumption of singular individuals to the division of labour", as defined by Marx and Engels (the structuring of society "fundamentally" through productive relations, in Thompson's words) and, consequently, of the subsumption of their class position/situation. Later, we will return to the aspect highlighted in the first sentence of the passage from the *German Ideology* and in Thompson's quote, that is, the formation of a class is not only a result of the position in life to which men (and women) are predestined by division of labour, but it is, at the same time, cause and consequence of class struggle.

The expression proletariat appears almost every time in the texts of the founders of historical materialism associated with those who possess nothing, or rather, who have no other way of surviving in a society of commodities, but to sell their labour power as a commodity. In the *Economic and Philosophic Manuscripts* of 1844, Marx criticizes the way in which the "national economy" (an expression by which Marx then referred to classical political economy) associated the worker with an animal that only receives the food necessary to survive, subsisting (existing) in order to keep working. Marx used a Latin term (from the Latin word *proletarius*, who is someone who is only defined by his own value and that of his offspring, his children) to define the "proletarian" by his lack of, as "the man who, being without capital and rent, lives purely by labour, and by a one-sided, abstract labour, is considered by political economy only as a *worker*".[26]

For this reason, the working class was defined by him in a very broad way, as the group of people who live off the sale of their labour power, primarily through wage earning. When dealing with the working class, even in his texts of critique of political economy, Marx never restricted it to the industrial working class, neither through a restrictive association with those subjected to what he called the "real subsumption" of labour to capital, nor by a definition that closed the class off to "productive labour" (which in turn also was not defined as restricted to factory workers). All these categories require some explanation.

In the *Economic Manuscripts* of 1861–1863, Marx defines formal subsumption and real subsumption of labour in relation to capital. Associating the first form with absolute surplus value and the second with relative surplus value,[27] Marx seeks to demonstrate that the process begins with the direct subordination of workers to capitalists, when they start, as owners of the means of production, to control the time and working conditions of those who were reduced to the condition of proletarians. The next step, the real subsumption, is presented as a result of the accumulation provided by the previous step and is materialized by "the large scale application of science and machinery to direct production".[28]

In the same text, Marx presents the distinction between productive and unproductive labour (and worker): "That worker is productive who performs productive labour, and that labour is productive which directly creates surplus value, i.e. valorises capital".[29] Associating the two distinctions, Marx goes on to state that with the development of real subsumption, "it is not the individual worker but rather the socially combined labour capacity that is more and more the real executor of the labour process as a whole", making it senseless, therefore, to seek the productive worker only among those who perform direct manual tasks.[30]

Going further, it is not the content of the labour performed, nor the sector of the economy in which that labour is performed that defines the productive character of the labour or the worker. That is why Marx insists on exemplifying productive work, with figures such as the artist or the teacher, while recognizing that they were examples in which the subsumption of capital was still formal.

> A singer who sings like a bird is an unproductive worker. If she sells her singing for money, she is to that extent a wage labourer or a commodity dealer. But the same singer, when engaged by an entrepreneur who has her sing in order to make money, is a productive worker, for she directly produces capital. A schoolmaster who educates others is not a productive worker. But a schoolmaster who is engaged as a wage labourer in an institution along with others, in order through his labour to valorise the money of the entrepreneur of the knowledge-mongering institution, is a productive worker.[31]

If the productive character of labour and the worker is not defined by employment in large industry (nor, therefore, by real subsumption), then neither is the working class restricted to only those who carry out productive labour. On the contrary, it is the proletarian condition and wage-earning that define it. Marx recalls, in that same text, that not all waged workers are productive, but that even those who exercise professions previously associated with a halo of autonomy (such as doctors and lawyers) increasingly saw themselves reduced to wages. Consequentially, the prices of these activities were subjected—"from the prostitute's to the king's"—to the laws that govern the price of wage labour.[32]

In this same direction, Alex Callinicos's approach to a passage from *Capital* is useful to defend that for Marx the concept of the proletariat, or working class, is quite broad.[33] The passage is the one in which Marx notes that

> the extraordinary productiveness of modern history, accompanied as it is by both a more extensive and a more intense exploitation of labour power

in all spheres of production, allows for the unproductive employment of a larger and larger part of the working class.[34]

For Callinicos, the passage suggests that:

Marx did not identify the working class with any particular set of occupations, for example, those in manufacturing industry: domestic servants are 'part of the working class', albeit an unproductive portion in the sense of not creating surplus value. In line with Marx's general relational understanding of class, the proletariat is best defined as all wage-labourers

(1) compelled by lack of access to the means of production to sell their labour-power; and

(2) the use of whose labour-power within the process of production is subject to the supervision and control of capital and its agents. By these criteria, the working class has grown considerably in the present century [20th century].[35]

In Capital, Marx did not complete his work with regard to definitions of the concept of social class. The last part of the manuscript incorporated into volume 3 by the editing work of Engels ("Classes"—Chapter 52 of Part VII of the book) closes after presenting capitalists, landowners and wage workers as the three fundamental classes of capitalist society, but it does so before the author develops the answer to the question he formulated: "What constitutes a class?"[36]

This does not mean, however, that Marx did not advance the discussion of social classes in his main book. Quite the opposite. Alex Callinicos draws attention to the centrality of the discussion about labour and the working class in *Capital*:

Capital is in some very obvious sense about labour. For Marx, abstract labour is the substance of value, hence living labour is the source of new value, and the surplus value appropriated from this new value represents surplus labour performed by wage workers.[37]

Daniel Bensaid analyses the different dimensions of the concept of class in *Capital*, associating them with the development of the whole book to explain the different faces of the process of capitalist accumulation.[38] Taking the understanding of class in Marx as "a relational totality"—"Class exists only in a conflictual relationship with other classes"[39]—and not as a simple sum of the units that compose it. Bensaid follows the rhythm of the exposition in *Capital* to point out that in volume 1: "the class relation took the form of an antagonistic relation of exploitation between the worker as producer and the capitalist as industrial capitalist, as a division between necessary labour and surplus labour".[40] A similar definition of the aims of volume 1 appears in Ernest Mandel's words, in his Introduction to *Capital*:

> Volume 1 of *Capital* is centred around Marx's basic discovery, the explanation of the 'secret' of surplus-value. There exists one commodity, to wit labour-power, whose use-value for the capitalist is its ability to produce new value larger than its own exchange-value. The 'process of production' which Marx analyses in Volume 1 is, therefore, essentially the process of production of surplus-value.[41]

Thus, in volume 1, Marx deals with the labour process, to explain "the expansion of value" that characterizes the "no limits movement" of capital and, therefore, "this passionate chase after exchange value" that is common to capitalists, as "personified capital".[42] In this sense, as we have seen, it defines the labour process in general, common to all social formations, concrete or useful labour, such as:

> So far therefore as labour is a creator of use value, is useful labour, it is a necessary condition, independent of all forms of society, for the existence of the human race; it is an eternal nature-imposed necessity which there can be no material exchanges between man and Nature, and therefore no life.[43]

However, he is especially concerned with demonstrating how the specific characteristics assumed by wage labour relations in capitalist society give it a different form, which explains the "valuing of value". For that, he demonstrates how, while selling their labour power to the capitalist, the worker sells it (as any commodity is sold) at its value, measured by the cost of reproduction of this labour power (or capacity), defined as "the aggregate of those mental and physical capabilities existing in a human being, which he exercises whenever he produces a use value of any description".[44]

But labour power is a very specific commodity, because, on the one hand, its value "like that of every other commodity, is already fixed before it goes into circulation, since a definite quantity of social labour has been spent upon it". However, "its use value consists in the subsequent exercise of its force".[45]

As a process of consumption of labour power by the capitalist, this externalization reveals two characteristic phenomena. Under the full control of the capitalist, the worker will consume the means of production that the former has purchased in a way that neither wastes raw materials nor necessarily wears out the means of work. The capitalist, however, does not control the commodity labour power according to the same consumption rules as the other commodities that enter the production process:

> To the purchaser of a commodity belongs its use, and the seller of labour power, by giving his labour, does no more, in reality, than part with the use value that he has sold. From the instant he steps into the workshop, the use value of this labour power, and therefore also its use, which is labour, belongs to the capitalist. By the purchase of labour power, the capitalist incorporates labour, as a living ferment, with the lifeless constituents of the product. From his point of view, the labour process is nothing more than consumption of the commodity purchased, i. e., of labour power; but this consumption cannot be effected except but supplying the labour power with the means of production. The labour process is a process between things that the capitalist has purchased, things that have become his property. The product of this process belongs, therefore, to him.[46]

Thus, just as much as the raw materials and the tools needed to work them, labour power is a commodity with a measurable cost, corresponding to its reproduction. However, unlike other goods purchased by the capitalist, this live labour creates more value throughout the production process (surplus value). That is because the payment of labour power for its exchange value (necessary for its subsistence) is not equivalent to its use value, that is, the amount of value that this labour power adds to the production process by working, as Marx explains:

> the means of subsistence that are daily required for the production of labour power, cost half a day's labour. But the past labour that is embodied in the labour power, and the living labour that it can call into action; the daily cost of maintaining it, and its daily expenditure in work, are two totally different things. The former determines the exchange value of the labour power, the latter is its use value. The fact that half a day's labour is necessary to keep the labourer alive during 24 hours, does not in any

> way prevent him from working a whole day. Therefore, the value of labour power, and the value which that labour power creates in the labour process, are two entirely different magnitudes; and this difference of the two values was what the capitalist had in view, when purchasing the labour power.[47]

Therefore, the capitalist's ultimate aim will always be to extract the maximum from this capacity of labour power to generate surplus value in the production process. Thus, the "rate of surplus value is therefore an exact expression for the degree of exploitation of labour power by capital, or of the labourer by the capitalist".[48] Labour power—and its sellers, the working class—and capital (personified in capitalists) are, therefore, as explained in volume 1, in objectively antagonistic positions in the productive process, explained by Marx in terms of the vital impulse of capital to self-expand, draining as much as possible from the labour power that it bought from workers:

> The capitalist has bought the labour power as its day rate. To him its use value belongs during one working day. He has thus acquired the right to make the labourer work for him during one day. But, what is a working day?
>
> At all events, less than a natural day. By how much? The capitalist has his own views of this *ultima Thule*, the necessary limit of the working day. As capitalist, he is only capital personified. His soul is the soul of capital. But capital has one single life impulse, the tendency to create value and surplus value, to make its constant factor, the means of production, absorb the greatest possible amount of surplus labour.
>
> Capital is dead labour, that, vampire-like, only lives by sucking living labour, and lives the more, the more labour it sucks. The time during which the labourer works, is the time during which the capitalist consumes the labour power he has purchased of him.[49]

Although, as we shall later see, Marx discusses the working class much further in volume 1 of *Capital*, we can first return to the association made by Daniel Bensaid between the passages of *Capital* and the discussion about the working class. The French philosopher points out that in volume 2, where Marx explores the cycle of the metamorphosis of capital, "this process is a succession of acts of buying and selling. The relation of exploitation emerges here as that between the worker as wage-labourer selling his labour-power and the capitalist as possessor of money-capital". At this point in Marx's discussion, the argument is no longer guided by the question of the "division of labour-time, but of conflictual negotiations over labour-power as a commodity".[50] In the formulation expressed by Marx in volume 2, when dealing with the cycle of metamorphoses in the forms of capital:

> Capital here appears as a value which goes through a series of interconnected, interdependent transformations, a series of metamorphoses which form just as many phases, or stages, of the process as a whole. Two of these phases belong in the sphere of circulation, one of them in that of production. In each of these phases capital value has a different form for which there is a correspondingly different, special function. Within this movement the advanced value does not only preserve itself but grows, increases in magnitude. Finally, in the concluding stage, it returns to the same form which it had at the beginning of the process as a whole. This process as a whole constitutes therefore the process of moving in circuits.[51]

When explaining each of the forms taken by capital in this cyclical process, Marx differentiates between "money capital", "commodity capital", and "productive capital", understanding each of these forms as a function performed in the complete cycle of what he defines there as industrial capital. It is important to highlight that these expressions gain specific meanings in Marx's work, different than those which we are commonly used to:

> The two forms assumed by capital value at the various stages of its circulation are those of money capital and commodity capital. The form pertaining to the stage of production is that of productive capital. The capital which assumes these forms in the course of its total circuit and then discards them and in each of them performs the function corresponding to the particular form is industrial capital, industrial here in the sense that it comprises every branch of industry run on a capitalist basis.
>
> Money capital, commodity capital, and productive capital do not therefore designate independent kinds of capital whose functions form the content of likewise independent branches of business separated from one another. They denote here only special functional forms of industrial capital, which assumes all three of them one after the other.[52]

Since the aim of industrial capital—which corresponds to the cycle of metamorphoses of forms of capital—is not only the appropriation, but also the creation of surplus value, a mode of production marked by this logic of accumulation necessarily generates social antagonisms, as Marx explains:

> Industrial capital is the only mode of existence of capital in which not only the appropriation of surplus value, or surplus product, but simultaneously its creation is a function of capital. Therefore with it the capitalist character of production is a necessity. Its existence implies the class antagonism between capitalists and wage labourers.[53]

The antagonism between capitalists and workers, according to the argument presented by Marx in volume 2, however, goes beyond the creation and appropriation of surplus value in the production process. As labour power sellers and consumers of goods, necessary for the reproduction of their only commodity available for sale, the worker also enters the sphere of circulation in a conflicting manner in relation to the capitalist. In it, the wage spent by the collective worker (as a class) to reproduce their labour power returns to the collective capitalist (as a class). Resuming Marx's argument:

> as a buyer of commodities maintains and reproduces his labour power, this being the only commodity which he has to sell. Just as the money advanced by the capitalist in the purchase of his labour power returns to him, so labour power returns to the labour market in its capacity of a commodity exchangeable for money.[54]

The cycle of reproduction of capital can thus be resumed. In the sphere of circulation, capitalists and workers are equal consumers of goods, but this is far from making them equals. For the worker, the purchase and consumption of goods—regardless of historical variations in living standards, which can be significant—can be reduced to the basic needs to reproduce the labour power that will continually be sold to the capitalist in order to survive. For the capitalists, as we are well aware, the possibilities of consumption are substantially superior to the simple maintenance of subsistence. For the capitalist, who is antagonistically positioned in a collective (class) point of view, to that of the worker, the process is described by Marx as follows:

> During all these transformations capitalist I continually holds the variable capital in his hands; 1) to start with as money capital; 2) then as an element of his productive capital; 3) still later as a portion of the value of his

> commodity capital, hence in the form of commodity value; 4) finally once more in money which is again confronted by the labour power for which it can be exchanged. During the labour process the capitalist is in possession of the variable capital as active value-creating labour power, but not as a value of a given magnitude. But since he never pays the labourer until his power has acted for a certain length of time, he already has in hand the value created by that power to replace itself plus the surplus value before he pays him.[55]

Finally, in volume 3, the question of class reappears in the framework of global reproduction. From there, Marx presents an analytical perspective that, according to Bensaid, could never restrict the study of class to the simple opposition of interests between capital and labour in production. The determining feature of the contradictory class relationship is now understood in the expanded dimension of the logic of capitalism:

> When it comes to production and reproduction as a whole, classes are no longer exclusively determined by the extraction of surplus-value, or by the categories of productive and unproductive labour. They are determined by the combination of the relation of exploitation in production, the wage relation and the productivity / non-productivity of labour in circulation, and the distribution of revenue in reproduction as a whole.[56]

This is how, for example, in volume 3, when explaining one of the central formulations of his work, the law of the falling tendency of the rate of profit, Marx reintroduces the discussion on the ways of extracting surplus-value as components (resulting from and also as cause) of the contradictory dynamics of reproduction of capital on a larger scale. Having explained the relationship between capitalist profit and the extraction of surplus value in volume 1, where he also outlined the so-called general law of capitalist accumulation (which we refer to later), in volume 3 Marx is able to explain how the same rate of surplus-value can generate very different rates of profit as the "organic composition of the capital" varies, that is, according to the proportion of constant capital (means of production) in relation to variable capital (labour power), applied in each company or sector of the economy. It is from this relationship that Marx concludes that "the gradual growth of constant capital in relation to the variable capital must necessarily lead to the gradual fall of the general rate of profit, as long as the rate of surplus value, or the intensity of exploitation of labour by capital".[57]

The whole explanation of the process that leads capitalists to try to make up for and bypass this tendency to falling rates of profit—including the discussion on the "counteracting influences" to this law and Marx's most important considerations on capitalist crises—presented in volume 3 of *Capital*, is associated with labour exploitation and, hence, to the relations between classes.

Thus, we can only agree with Callinicos' assumption, already mentioned, that "*Capital* is in some very obvious sense about labour". Following the path suggested by Bensaid to show how the discussion about the working class and its relations with capitalists goes through the three volumes of *Capital*, we can now draw attention, to conclude this section, to two moments in volume 1, from which it is possible to find important references both for the discussions about the working class in face of the recent (re)configurations of the capitalist economy and to its origins and historical specificities. These are important for realizing that Marx had an overview of the totality of the general laws of capitalist accumulation, preceding the organization of the exposition of his major work.

The chapter of *Capital* on "The General Law of Capitalist Accumulation" is one of those moments in which the totalizing understanding that runs throughout the work as a whole is made explicit, even if Marx did not complete it. Usually quoted for the definition of "relative surplus population" or "industrial reserve army", it is also one of the passages of *Capital* in which Marx best discusses several fundamental arguments for understanding issues such as composition, concentration, and centralization of capital. These are decisive aspects for understanding not only the dynamics of expanding value, as explored in volume 1, but also for the subsequent discussions of volumes 2 and 3, which were quickly highlighted here.

To get to the "general law", the chapter presents a very rich exposition. In the first part, Marx demonstrates the growing labour demand for capital accumulation, by explaining the question of the composition of capital:

> The composition of capital is to be understood in a twofold sense. On the side of value, it is determined by the proportion in which it is divided into constant capital or value of the means of production, and variable capital or value of labour power, the sum total of wages. On the side of material, as it functions in the process of production, all capital is divided into means of

> production and living labour power. This latter composition is determined by the relation between the mass of the means of production employed, on the one hand, and the mass of labour necessary for their employment on the other. I call the former the value composition, the latter the technical composition of capital. Between the two there is a strict correlation. To express this, I call the value composition of capital, in so far as it is determined by its technical composition and mirrors the changes of the latter, the organic composition of capital. Wherever I refer to the composition of capital, without further qualification, its organic composition is always understood.[58]

The relationship between means of production (constant capital) and labour power (variable capital), which constitutes this composition of capital, cannot be explained by simple laws of supply and demand. After all, the incorporation of new masses of workforce is a result of the incorporation of new areas of social life under the dictates of capital (generating expropriations) and a need for the accumulation process—"accumulation of capital is, therefore, [the] increase of the proletariat".[59] The growth of capitalist demand for labour could be faced with an insufficient supply, which would eventually generate greater bargaining power and, consequently, a progressive improvement in the wage and life conditions of the working class under capitalism. For most of the explanations by political economists criticized by Marx, the regulation of this trend is given by the population dynamics itself and the long-term result leads to a balance between supply and demand of labour which would guarantee capitalist profits and a decent living standard for the proletariat. Marx, however, explains that the demand for labour is increasing when accumulation takes place under a constant "organic composition of capital", a condition that does not correspond to the real dynamics of capitalist accumulation. In the latter, the logic of surplus value extraction prevails, in which

> labour power is sold to-day, not with a view of satisfying, by its service or by its product, the personal needs of the buyer. His aim is augmentation of his capital, production of commodities containing more labour than he pays for, containing therefore a portion of value that costs him nothing, and that is nevertheless realized when the commodities are sold. Production of surplus value is the absolute law of this mode of production.[60]

Therefore, the growing demand for labour is counterbalanced by the fact that capitalist accumulation leads to the concentration and centralization of capital, as a result of a process of change in the organic composition of capital, the subject of the second part of the chapter. At the beginning of Marx's explanation is the discussion of the increase in labour productivity—expressed in the "relative extent of the means of production that one labourer, during a given time, with the same tension of labour power, turns into products"[61]—which is related to the growing incorporation of technology to the production process. Thus, "whether condition or consequence, the growing extent of the means of production, as compared with the labour power incorporated with them, is an expression of the growing productiveness of labour".[62]

A reflex of this process of growing productivity is, therefore, the increase in the fraction of constant capital (value of the means of production) in relation to that of variable capital (value of labour power) in the composition of capital. Marx continues his exposition, explaining how, after the first drive given by the process of "primitive accumulation" (detailed below), competition and the credit system promote the concentration of capital in ever-increasing volumes (larger companies absorbing smaller companies and/or occupying larger market shares). He also explains the process that leads capital holders who have an increasing labour productivity capacity and can obtain higher rates of surplus value to continue incorporating more space in the market and/or ownership of other companies, pointing to capital centralization. In a synthesis paragraph, Marx explains how concentration and centralization are reached from the competition between many capitalists at the beginning of the accumulation process:

> This splitting-up of the total social capital into many individual capitals or the repulsion of its fractions one from another, is counteracted by their attraction. This last does not mean that simple concentration of the means of production and of the command over labour, which is identical with accumulation. It is concentration of capitals already formed, destruction of their individual independence, expropriation of capitalist by capitalist, transformation of many small into few large capitals. This process differs from the former in this, that it only presupposes a change in the distribution of capital already to hand, and functioning; its field of action is therefore not limited by the absolute growth of social wealth, by the absolute limits of accumulation. Capital grows in one place to a huge mass in

a single hand, because it has in another place been lost by many. This is centralization proper, as distinct from accumulation and concentration.[63]

Considering that the increase in labour productivity is a requirement and, increasingly, a consequence of this process, with centralization we can see "the diminution of the mass of labour in proportion to the mass of means of production moved by it".[64] A necessary consequence of centralization is, therefore, the proportional decrease in the demand for labour. This is the necessary context for Marx to explore further, in the third part of the chapter, the question of the "relative surplus population" or "industrial reserve army".

After explaining how "with the advance of accumulation, [...], the proportion of constant to variable capital changes", Marx draws attention to the fact that, "since the demand for labour is determined not by the amount of capital as a whole, but by its variable constituent alone, that demand falls progressively". But the process of capitalist accumulation itself ends up producing an additional, "relatively superfluous"[65] worker population, by expanding into new territories—both physical and social. This leads to the enunciation of what Marx calls the "absolute general law of capitalist accumulation":

> The greater the social wealth, the functioning capital, the extent and energy of its growth, and, therefore, also the absolute mass of the proletariat and the productiveness of its labour, the greater is the industrial reserve army. The same causes which develop the expansive power of capital, develop also the labour power at its disposal. The relative mass of the industrial reserve army increases therefore with the potential energy of wealth. But the greater this reserve army in proportion to the active labour army, the greater is the mass of a consolidated surplus population, whose misery is in inverse ratio to its torment of labour. The more extensive, finally, the lazarus-layers of the working class, and the industrial reserve army, the greater is official pauperism. This is the absolute general law of capitalist accumulation. Like all other laws it is modified in its working by many circumstances, the analysis of which does not concern us here.[66]

This "relative surplus population", which is a "necessary product" of accumulation, also constitutes a "lever" to capitalist accumulation, as it represents an "industrial reserve army", available to be exploited by capital, regardless of population increase.[67] With every new sector of the economy or region of the globe opened up by capitalist expansion, this army will be available to produce surplus value, as its abundance grants capital the possibility of keeping the wages of those effectively employed at a level low enough that the cyclical processes of variation in the rate of profit do not mean a definitive brake in accumulation. At the end of this explanatory journey, Marx is ready to move forward, demonstrating that "the whole form of the movement of modern industry depends, therefore, upon the constant transformation of a part of the labouring population into unemployed or half-employed hands".[68]

At this point, Marx presents a synthesis, by introducing the element of workers' consciousness of the logic of this intensified exploitation to which they are subjected, and thereby, introduces the importance of class struggle in explaining the whole process. He also presents one more critique of political economists who, in their inability to explain the issue of relative surplus population, do not hide the class position from which they defend the "free" negotiation of labour power. Given the importance of argumentation, it is worth including a longer quote:

> Capital works on both sides at the same time. If its accumulation, on the one hand, increases the demand for labour, it increases on the other the supply of labourers by the "setting free" of them whilst at the same time the pressure of the unemployed compels those that are employed to furnish more labour, and therefore makes the supply of labour, to a certain extent, independent of the supply of labourers. The action of the law of supply and demand of labour on this basis completes the despotism of capital. As soon, therefore, as the labourers learn the secret, how it comes to pass that in the same measure as they work more, as they produce more wealth for others, and as the productive power of their labours increases, so in the same measure even their function as a means of the self-expansion of capital becomes more and more precarious for them, as soon as they discover that the degree of intensity of the competition among themselves depends wholly on the pressure of the relative surplus population; as soon as, by Trades' Unions, &c., they try to organize a regular co-operation between employed and unemployed in order to destroy or to weaken the ruinous effects of this natural law of capitalistic production on their class, so soon capital and its sycophant, political economy, cry out at the infringement of the "eternal" and so to say "sacred" law of supply and demand. Every combination of employed and unemployed disturbs the "harmonious" action of this law.[69]

In the fourth part of the chapter, before stating the "general law", aforementioned, Marx presents his well-known taxonomy of "every possible form" of "relative surplus population". There are basically three forms: the floating, the latent, and the stagnant. The first form corresponds to the continuous flow of attraction and repulsion of workers to the "centres of modern industry - factories, manufactures, iron-works, mines, &c".[70] The second form, the latent, corresponds to the constant availability of rural workers, proletarianized by the advance of properly capitalist agriculture, generating a latent surplus population in the countryside, whose flow to urban centres turns out to be—when possible—a very strong compulsion in face of very low wages and rural pauperism. Finally, the third category—the stagnant—is composed of the active sector of the working class that occupies the most irregular occupations, such as domestic labour and day labourer.

Marx adds to these three forms a "lowest sediment", which inhabits "pauperism". Pauperism is also divided into three categories: those able to work; orphans and pauper children (candidates for the industrial reserve army); and, thirdly, the "the delayed and ragged, and those unable to work". Such layers of pauperism are, however, distinct from the lumpenproletariat (a category that Marx had dealt with politically in his trilogy on post-1848 France), here presented in a more "occupational" sense as the "vagabonds, criminals, prostitutes".[71]

Commentators, in general, highlight these taxonomies of "relative surplus population" and their pauper sediments and try to relate them to concrete situations in the capitalist labour market, which is interesting (and in a way we will also do that further in this text). However, it is worth noting that Marx does not present a classification of distinct strata of the working class, nor of homogeneous and stable portions of this class. On the contrary, he points out that such forms (or experiences, we might say) are a constitutive part of the existence of the class, a dynamic existence, in which individual workers can live through several of these experiences over the course of a lifetime. Thus, the stagnant form of relative surplus population constitutes, according to him, "at the same time a self-reproducing and self-perpetuating element of the working class, taking a proportionally greater part in the general increase of that class than the other elements".[72]

Another central passage in volume 1 of Capital for the discussion we intend to develop in this book is the section on "The Secret of Primitive Accumulation", from which we can access Marx's interpretation of the historical process that generated the fundamental social relation between capitalists and the working class, especially in England. The result of the process was the availability of labour for the exploitation by capital, through the multiplication of "free labourers", defined by Marx as:

> Free labourers, in the double sense that neither they themselves form part and parcel of the means of production, as in the case of slaves, bondsmen, &c., nor do the means of production belong to them, as in the case of peasant proprietors; they are, therefore, free from, unencumbered by, any means of production of their own.[73]

In order to explain how this situation came to be, denaturalizing the opposition between rich and poor so present in common knowledge, and even to some extent in classical political economy, Marx develops a historical analysis of the expropriation of direct producers (proletarianization) in the fifteenth century. With this, he seeks to turn to "the pre-historic stage of capital and the mode of production corresponding with it", explaining that:

> The capitalist system presupposes the complete separation of the labourers from all property in the means by which they can realise their labour. As soon as capitalist production is once on its own legs, it not only maintains this separation, but reproduces it on a continually extending scale. The process, therefore, that clears the way for the capitalist system, can be none other than the process which takes away from the labourer the possession of his means of production; a process that transforms, on the one hand, the social means of subsistence and of production into capital, on the other, the immediate producers into wage labourers. The so-called primitive accumulation, therefore, is nothing else than the historical process of divorcing the producer from the means of production.[74]

Hence, the chapter is largely devoted to demonstrating how the assertion of capitalist private property was only possible with the complete destitution of the majority of direct producers of any property they might own, other than their labour power. Let us remember the aforementioned essay on the criminalization of firewood collection by the Rhineland assembly, which Marx had written in 1842, where he asked: "by my private ownership do I not exclude every other person from this ownership?".[75] For it is exactly this process that he now explains in much more depth by defining primitive capital accumulation as an expropriation:

> What does the primitive accumulation of capital, i.e., its historical genesis, resolve itself into? In so far as it is not immediate transformation of slaves and serfs into wage labourers, and therefore a mere change form, it only means the expropriation of the immediate producers, i.e., the dissolution of private property based on the labour of its owner.[76]

With capitalism what is affirmed is not private property in its broad sense, but a specific kind of private property, one that excludes the direct worker from ownership of the means of production that allowed him to work directly to reproduce his and her living conditions, be they land or work tools. For this to be possible, the expropriation of artisans and peasants, which begins due to transformations in rural production, required a direct intervention of the State to be completed, through a wide range of legal/repressive mechanisms. Marx highlights all the legislation that, since the restoration of the Stuarts, with the so-called glorious revolution, in late seventeenth-century England, made the expulsion of small producers official—regardless of their subjection to relationships of personal dependence—from the lands where they used to work or the corporations to which they were linked, in the case of artisans. He also approaches the private appropriation of common lands, with the enclosures and the generalized commodification of the means of survival of these direct producers, as well as explains its necessary consequence: a legal apparatus that, since the sixteenth century, has sought to subordinate ever-larger contingents of dispossessed/proletarianized workers to the market for the purchase and sale of labour, under penalties of the law for those who refused, or were unable to fulfil such a destiny, henceforth treated as vagabonds. Contradictorily (at least in appearance), this "liberation" of workers, accompanied by the imposition of "market rules" for the sale of labour power, was done through repressive measures that amounted to the imposition of direct slavery, such as in the example of a 1547 law, commented by Marx:

> If it happens that a vagabond has been idling about for three days, he is to be taken to his birthplace, branded with a redhot iron with the letter V on the breast and be set to work, in chains, in the streets or at some other labour. If the vagabond gives a false birthplace, he is then to become the slave for life of this place, of its inhabitants, or its corporation, and to be branded with an S.[77]

"Free labour" and slavery, by the way, are a constitutive pair of primitive accumulation also because Marx, although paying greater attention to the history of the first capitalist economy to reach the industrial stage—England—approaches this historical genesis of capitalism in reference to its global dimension. For this very reason, the colonization of the "Indies", especially the "Western Indies" (the Americas), with the consequent modern commercial slavery, is also highlighted in the chapter. On the one hand, the slave trade itself was one of the levers of primitive accumulation, through trade in a monopoly system:

> England thereby acquired the right of supplying Spanish America until 1743 with 4,800 negroes yearly. This threw, at the same time, an official cloak over British smuggling. Liverpool waxed fat on the slave trade. This was its method of primitive accumulation. [...] Liverpool employed in the slave trade, in 1730, 15 ships; in 1751, 53; in 1760, 74; in 1770, 96; and in 1792, 132.[78]

On the other hand, the connection between English capitalist production and American slavery extends beyond the period of primitive accumulation, as the main supply source of the main raw material for the English textile industry—flagship of the industrial revolution—was the slave South of the United States. Emphasizing the cruellest faces of the exploitation of child labour at one end and African slavery on the other in the Atlantic, Marx explains:

> Whilst the cotton industry introduced child slavery in England, it gave in the United States a stimulus to the transformation of the earlier, more or less patriarchal slavery, into a system of commercial exploitation. In fact, the veiled slavery of the wage workers in Europe needed, for its pedestal, slavery pure and simple in the new world.[79]

In his synthesis of the process, Marx once again criticizes in a devastating way the classical political economy for its naturalization of capitalist social relations, stressing that the split between capital and workers is the product of history. A very bloody history, by the way, as "capital comes dripping from head to foot, from every pore, with blood and dirt".[80]

> the transformation of the individualized and scattered means of production into socially concentrated ones, of the pigmy property of the many into the huge property of few, the expropriation of the great mass of the people

> from the soil, from the means of subsistence, and from the means of labour, this fearful and painful expropriation of the mass of the people forms the prelude to the history of capital. [...] The expropriation of the immediate producers was accomplished with merciless vandalism, and under the stimulus of passions the most infamous, the most sordid, the pettiest, the most meanly odious. Self-earned private property, that is based, so to say, on the fusing together of the isolated, independent labouring individual with the conditions of his labour, is supplanted by capitalistic private property, which rests on exploitation of the nominally free labour of others, i.e., on wage labour.[81]

The value judgement inherent in this assessment—which does not by far direct the analysis, which Marx based on the concrete study of concrete forms of expropriation—is, however, one of the constitutive elements of the political project to overcome this social order constructed and supported by the blood of those expropriated by capital. Therefore, it is at the end of this chapter, after briefly re-presenting the issue of the centralization of capital—"the expropriation of many capitalists by few"—that Marx returns to the political dimension of his work. The contradictions of such a process are evident, which is why Marx maintains that the dynamics of capital accumulation engenders the possibility of "negation of negation".

After all, "the capitalist mode of appropriation, the result of the capitalist mode of production, produces capitalist private property. This is the first negation of individual private property, as founded on the labour of the proprietor". However, "with the constantly diminishing number of the magnates of capital, who usurp and monopolise all advantages of this process of transformation, grows the mass of misery, oppression, slavery, degradation, exploitation; but with this too grows the revolt of the working class". From the point of view of the correlation of demographic forces, such centralization made it "simple" to overcome capital. Once "the knell of capitalist private property sounds", the expropriation will take place at an inverse pole, because of the scale of socialization of production achieved by large industry, objective conditions were created to overcome capitalist contradictions, through a new social formation erected "on co-operation and the possession in common of the land and of the means of production". If in the historical process of primitive accumulation and in the later development of proper capitalist accumulation "we had the expropriation of the mass of the people by a few usurpers", from now on we will be faced with the challenge of "the transformation of scattered private property, arising from individual labour, into capitalist private property [which] is, naturally, a process, incomparably more protracted, violent, and difficult, than the transformation of capitalistic private property, already practically resting on socialised production, into socialised property. In the former case, we had the expropriation of the mass of the people by a few usurpers; in the latter, we have the expropriation of a few usurpers by the mass of the people".[82]

There is a double aspect to the richness of the Marxian discussion on primitive accumulation. On the one hand, it is a historical perspective that allows an understanding of the constitutive bases of capitalism, taken not as a presupposition, but as a process of social transformations over centuries. Through such a discussion, Marx demonstrates the vitality of the method he had proposed in the Introduction of his *Grundrisse*, as after all the effort throughout volume 1 of *Capital* to reach the "simplest determinations" through "abstractions", he now took the "return journey" to real/concrete, which can already be perceived as a "rich totality of many determinations and relations".[83] The chapter reconstructs that historical period analytically with the dramatic intensity proper to a process of capitalist genesis bathed in blood and mud. The process of primitive accumulation, as a historical epoch, marked the creation of conditions for capitalist accumulation to take place in its industrial form, since, as Callinicos highlights, "the self-expansion of capital can only become an autonomous process when it succeeds in separating the direct producers from the means of production, a historical transition that is constantly reproduced through the process of exploitation".[84]

On the other hand, the subordination of labour power to capital, through expropriation, cannot be taken only as a "stage" won by capital. As Callinicos recalls, this subordination is "a historical result that presupposes capital's continually renewed success in denying it [labour capacity] direct access to the means of production".[85] The automatism of capital in its self-expansion will lead to the continued reproduction of expropriations, in other regions of the globe or in other areas of human activity. Thus, it will carry and multiply its contradictions in this way, enhancing the "negation of negation". Capital, however, despite its contradictions, will not overcome itself. As Marx pointed out, the expropriation of the expropriators will come from "the revolt of the working class", which implies understanding it not only as a product of the expropriation process—and a social group subjected to exploitation—by capital, but also as a historical subject.

Class Consciousness

By now, it should be evident that the material/objective dimension of existence of the working class in capitalism is far from being an issue treated in a simplified way by Marx. Marx, however, does not think of this class only in terms of its objective dimension, but also in terms of its collective subjectivity. A subjectivity which we can understand in a double dimension, completely combined in practice: on the one hand, subjectivity is a term associated with class consciousness; on the other hand, not dissociated from the first dimension, the working class is a social–historical subject, a conscious subject, who can change the course of history through its praxis. This combination of objective conditioning and subjective potential appears in many texts by Marx and Engels, as in the Marxian analysis of the French political process after the 1848 Revolution, notably in *The Eighteenth Brumaire of Louis Bonaparte* (1852). Quoting one of its most famous passages: "Men make their own history, but they do not make it just as they please; they do not make it under circumstances chosen by themselves, but under circumstances directly encountered, given and transmitted from the past".[86]

This materialist combination of analysis of the transforming action of human collectivities, as well as the historical circumstances that condition them, is the distinctive feature of all Marxian work. Thus, already in the 1840s Marx's construct could overcome previous materialisms—which he defined as mechanical—precisely because it highlighted the importance of the subjective element in the activity of men in society. In the words of Raymond Williams:

> Thus Marx's critique, of the materialism hitherto described, accepted the physical explanations of the origin of nature and of life but rejected the derived forms of social and moral argument, describing the whole tendency as *mechanical* materialism. This form of materialism had isolated objects and had neglected or ignored *subjects* (...) and especially human activity as *subjective*. Hence his distinction between a received **mechanical materialism** and a new **historical materialism**, which would include human activity as a primary force.[87]

Williams' synthesis starts from the critique developed by Marx and Engels of German philosophy after Hegel, especially of the apparently radical young Hegelians, such as Bauer and Stirner (and subsequently Feuerbach) in *The German Ideology*. In this unfinished work, recognized as the foundation of historical materialism, the starting point was precisely the criticism of the limits of a materialism still stuck to Hegelian idealist dictates, mainly due to its inability to perceive how ideas and objects interact in reality, constituted by human subjects, in their praxis. According to Marx's notes, known as *Theses on Feuerbach*:

> The chief defect of all previous materialism (that of Feuerbach included) is that things [*Gegenstand*], reality, sensuousness are conceived only in the form of the *object, or of contemplation*, but not as *sensuous human activity, practice*, not subjectively. Hence, in contradistinction to materialism, the active side was set forth abstractly by idealism – which, of course, does not know real sensuous activity as such. Feuerbach wants sensuous objects, really distinct from conceptual objects, but he does not conceive human activity itself as *objective* activity.[88]

Thus, the valorization of the interaction between subjectivity and material life in human activity—an "objective activity", in the sense that it is oriented towards the creation of objects from a planned intervention—reappears in passages of *Capital*, such as some already mentioned and others in which Marx defines labour (concrete, which creates use values) as: "human action with a view to the production of use values", "appropriation of natural substances to human requirements", "condition for effecting exchange of matter between man and nature".[89]

Furthermore, historical materialism, as presented since the 1840s, was also defined by the denial of the autonomy or independence of the subjective/ideal element. Rather, it is considered socially and historically determined. Far from the "free will" of the protestant/liberal conception, or from the idealist vision of a constituent subjectivity of social reality, Marx integrates material life and subjectivity in his analysis through the determination of a broader concept, which refers to his objective of a totalizing understanding of the social, the mode of production. Thus, as summarized in the "Preface" to *A Contribution to the Critique of Political Economy* (1859): "The mode of production of material life conditions the general process of social, political and intellectual life. It is not the consciousness of men that determines their existence, but their social existence that determines their consciousness".[90]

The distance between Marx's assertion of material determination and economic determinism is evident there. Firstly, because the mode of production is a much broader category and not a simple synonym for economics (which in the sense of classical political economy from which Marx's critique developed was also a much broader term than in the dominant sense among economists today). And the mode of production of material life, even in this passage so often invoked in its 1859 preface, appears to "condition" social, political, and intellectual life. It is to the broader philosophical category, "social existence"—social being—that Marx resorts to properly explain the determination of consciousness. The idea of determination is related to what is prior to human praxis, as well as to the limits and pressures that act on human subjectivity within this social praxis. This sense is evident in another well-known passage in the same "Preface":

> No social formation is ever destroyed before all the productive forces for which it is sufficient have been developed, and new, superior relations of production never replace older ones before the material conditions for their existence have matured within the framework of the old society. Mankind thus inevitably sets itself only such tasks as it is able to solve, since, closer examination will always show that the problem itself arises only when the material conditions for its solution are already present or at least in the course of formation.[91]

The limits imposed by the determination of the social being, in turn, condition men's ability to apprehend reality and, therefore, to intervene in it (their potential as subjects of history). Such limits are presented at different moments in the work of Marx and Engels, especially through one concept: ideology. Developed from the aforementioned critique of the German philosophy of their time, pointing out the strength of the ever-present idealist matrix in the "materialism" of his contemporaries, as well as the class pressures—bourgeois—from which its radicalism was not freed, in *The German Ideology*, Marx and Engels demonstrated how "the ruling ideas are nothing more than the ideal expression of the dominant material relations, the dominant material relations grasped as ideas". The inability to perceive this produces ideology, an inverted version of reality: "If in all ideology men and their relations appear upside-down as in a camera obscura, this phenomenon arises just as much from their historical life-process as the inversion of objects on the retina does from their physical life-process".[92]

In this sense, ideology is not simply a projection that freely inhabits the level of ideas, nor is it a mere specular illusion, as it comes from the same historical process that differentiates humanity into social classes. Hence, the overcoming of a given ideological expression does not take place autonomously on the level of ideas, having to be faced from the material terrain. None of this happens as an immediate and mechanical consequence, as Marx's concept of ideology also has a sense, not contradictory to the abovementioned and often complementary to it, which enabled some Marxists to use it as a set of ideas, values, or worldview of a given social class. In the aforementioned *Preface*, when explaining the changes "of the whole immense superstructure" he says:

> it is always necessary to distinguish between the material transformation of the economic conditions of production, which can be determined with the precision of natural science, and the legal, political, religious, artistic or philosophic—in short, ideological forms in which men become conscious of this conflict and fight it out.[93]

One of the Marxists who most contributed to the debate on the ways in which human groups gain consciousness of conflicts was the revolutionary leader, Antonio Gramsci. Jan Rehmann noted that the translation exercises that Gramsci performed in his prison writings began precisely with the *Theses on Feuerbach* and the *Preface* just quoted. In an interesting change in translation, he translated "the ideological forms in which men become conscious" as "the ideological forms on which terrain men become conscious", emphasizing the materiality of the ideological "terrain".[94]

Following the path opened by Marx in the *Theses on Feuerbach*, Gramsci was a philosopher whose aim was to transform the world. In this sense, the problem that arose, both in his work and in his obviously inseparable political action, was that of revolution. No wonder Gramsci defined Marxism as the philosophy of praxis. Thinking about the revolution in his time posed him several problems associated with the subjective face of social life. For example, he understood the forms of class domination based not only on their economic traits, or the aimed policy in a State presented as a simple coercive instrument of bourgeois power. This challenge led Gramsci to seek to understand how a dimension of consensus crossed domination and, to understand it, how it was necessary to understand the ideological mechanisms through which the ruling class managed to present its project of society and its worldview as bearers of universal validity.

Hegemony is a relationship of domination in which the element of force is not absent, but is also sustained by: the consensus created among the subordinate classes; the role of intellectuals in creating the conditions for such a form of domination (or the conditions favourable to its overcoming) through intellectual and moral reform; common sense as a terrain on which dominant ideologies act; the existence of a solid national-popular project (visible, for example, in the literary manifestations of a time), as a condition for the full exercise of hegemony, among so many other issues present in Gramsci's writings, thus constituting a fertile ground for the debate on ideology and conscience.[95] Gramsci's starting point for discussing all these questions was always the work of Marx and Engels. He resumes, in his *Prison Notebooks*, the *Theses on Feuerbach*'s considerations to define the way in which the determination of the social being on social conscience is socially and historically manifested:

> The 'nature' of man is the set of social relations, which determines a historically defined consciousness (...) Furthermore: the set of social relations is contradictory at every moment and is in continuous development, so that the 'nature' of man is not something homogeneous for all men at all times.[96]

It is from this point that Gramsci tackles the problem of explaining the challenges facing the construction of an autonomous consciousness among the dominated or, as he prefers to call it, among the subalterns, from a perspective that highlights the contradictory dynamics of the relations between the fundamental social classes, that is, class struggle throughout history:

> Once we find that, as the set of social relations is contradictory, the conscience of men cannot but be contradictory, the problem arises of how such a contradiction manifests itself and how unification can be progressively achieved: it manifests itself throughout the whole social body, with

> historical group consciousness (with the existence of stratifications corresponding to different phases of the historical development of civilization and with antitheses in groups that correspond to the same historical level) and manifests itself in particular individuals as a reflection of such 'vertical and horizontal' disaggregation. In subaltern groups, because of the lack of autonomy in the historical initiative, disaggregation is more serious and the struggle to free themselves from imposed and not proposed principles is stronger, in order to obtain an autonomous historical consciousness.[97]

The answer formulated by the Sardinian revolutionary to the problem of going beyond the limits imposed by class domination on the ideological plane, towards an emancipated and emancipatory class consciousness, is nourished by another concept, that of common sense. The possibility of this take over will depend fundamentally, according to Gramsci, on the capacity of the philosophy of praxis (Marxism) to present itself as a critique and overcoming of the common sense of an era. This is defined, in negative terms, as opposed to "critical sense" (a "philosophy", in the sense of an autonomous conception of the world). Thus, common sense is presented as an amalgama of "diffuse, uncoordinated features of a generic form of thought common to a particular period and a particular popular environment".[98] However, there is also, in this same common sense, a "healthy nucleus (…) the part of it which can be called ' good sense' and which deserves to be made more unitary and coherent".[99] For this reason, its overcoming by the philosophy of praxis "must be a criticism of 'common sense', basing itself initially, however, on common sense in order to demonstrate that 'everyone' is a philosopher and that it is not a question of introducing from scratch a scientific form of thought into everyone's individual life, but of renovating and making 'critical' an already existing activity".[100]

Gramsci's proposal recognizes the potential of the proletariat as a social subject of human emancipation but highlights the challenges for an emancipatory critical philosophy, such as Marxism, to contribute to overcoming the ideological traps that have been created for centuries and are contemporarily fed by class domination, which tend to link the class consciousness of the "subalterns" to the dictates of passivity that dominate common sense.

Turning to Marx, another way of facing the limits imposed on social consciousness by the determination of the social being, or another way of understanding the prevalence of the mode of production and the social relations engendered in it in understanding the limits of human subjectivity, appears through the Marxian category of alienation.[101] It is in the very materiality of labour (and exploitation) relations that men lose control over what they produce, how they produce, and why they produce. And, until they regain this control, they will not be able to give full meaning to labour—which, as we have seen, is understood by Marx, in its concrete sense, as the mediation of their relations with nature and with other men—and, therefore, life. Turning again to Raymond Williams:

> In Marx the process is seen as the history of labour, in which man creates himself by creating his world, but in class-society is alienated from this essential nature by specific forms of alienation in the division of labour, private property and the capitalist mode of production in which the worker loses both the product of his labour and his sense of his own productive activity, following the expropriation of both by capital. The world man has made confronts him as stranger and enemy, having power over him who has transferred his power to it.[102]

István Mészáros considers that the introduction of the concept of "alienated labour" in Marx's work (particularly in the *Manuscripts* of 1844) was fundamental to the Marxian program of achieving the unity of theory and practice. Such a program translates into transcendence, understood as "the negation and supersession of 'labour's self alienation'".[103] Synthesizing the *Manuscripts*, Mészáros observes that the complex key concept of alienation has, in Marx's work, four main aspects: "a) man is alienated from nature; b) he is alienated from himself (from his own activity); c) from his 'species-being' (from his being as a member of human species); d) man is alienated from man (from other men)".[104]

Using Marx's own texts, especially the *Economic and Philosophic Manuscripts*, we realize that the point at which he seeks to distinguish himself from classical political economy, in this first critical approach, lies in his quest to explain elements such as private property from facts present in concrete social life, avoiding dealing with them as given, or avoiding explanations of concrete reality through artifices such as creating an imaginary primitive state. It is in the terrain of facts that he places his analysis on labour, as a (in Mészáros's words, first order) mediation of the relationships between men and nature and between men. Thus, the sense of alienation is presented in the context of the analysis of a historical process:

> The worker becomes all the poorer the more wealth he produces, the more his production increases in power and size. The worker becomes an ever ceaper commodity the more commodities he creates. The devaluation of the world of men is in direct proportion to the increasing value of the world of things. Labour produces not only commodities: it produces itself and the worker as a commodity— and this at the same rate at which it produces commodities in general.
>
> This fact expresses merely that the object which labour produces—labour's product—confronts it as something alien, as a power independent of the producer. The product of labour is labour which has been embodied in an object, which has become material: it is the objectification of labour. Labour's realisation is its objectification. Under these economic conditions this realisation of labour appears as loss of realisation for the workers; objectification as loss of the object and bondage to it; appropriation as estrangement, as alienation.[105]

In *Capital*, Marx develops this analysis by discussing the fetishistic character of the commodity. For this, he used the image of a mystery that involves the products of human labour in capitalist society, evaluated not by their use value, but by some kind of metaphysical characteristic that escapes common sight. Marx attributes the difficulty in understanding man-made objects for what they really are precisely to the fact that they become commodities. Thus,

> A commodity is therefore a mysterious thing, simply because in it the social character of men's labour appears to them as an objective character stamped upon the product of that labour; because the relation of the producers to the sum total of their own labour is presented to them as a social relation, existing not between themselves, but between the products of their labour.[106]

The things seem to dominate the world of men, which no longer feel that they dominate the world of things, but are reified by the latter: "There it is a definite social relation between men, that assumes, in their eyes, the fantastic form of a relation between things".[107] Something that stems precisely from the nature of labour relations in a class society—abstract, estranged—or as Marx says: "This Fetishism of commodities has its origin, as the foregoing analysis has already shown, in the peculiar social character of the labour that produces them".[108]

Again, as in the debate on the ideological "terrain", the situation of alienation, therefore, can only be understood as phantasmagoria, or fetish, according to Marx, because such commodity fetishism gains real existence from the way in which labour relations and the exploitation of the work-force by capital are structured in the "commodity world" in which we live. Also in this case, the emancipatory project proposed by Marx cannot be carried out by the simple unveiling of fetish but demands the overcoming of the class relation that organizes the exploitation of labour. Despite all the intricate labyrinths interposed between objective reality and the forms of refraction of that reality in the consciousness of large human groups, Marx and Engels found, as we have seen, collective movements of the working class that denoted conscious action towards this emancipatory objective.

The proletariat's consciousness of its social place, and particularly the construction of an emancipatory project that could overcome this subalternization, was perceived by Marx and Engels, since the 1840s. However, the transition from a collective worldview limited by dominant ideology and by all the fetishes of alienation was not a simple social process, nor an easily explained phenomenon.

In the critique of Proudhon presented in *Misery of Philosophy*, Marx analysed the growth in the number of strikes and associations of the working class, especially in England. In his perception, such struggles began with a localized confrontation with the bosses for salary improvements, which generated the need to form temporary coalitions. Over time, the bosses organized themselves to face strikes and mobilizations of workers with direct repression and anti-association laws, while temporary coalitions were converted into permanent ones, that is, unions (trade unions, in the English case). Coalitions, strikes, and trade unions, according to Marx, "went on simultaneously with the political struggles of the workers, who now constitute a large political party, under the name of *Chartists*".[109] Then, it was no longer just a matter of demanding better wages, but of defending the right to association, and that is why Marx says that "once it has reached this point, association takes on a political character".[110] Following that text, Marx expressed the difference between the material existence of the working class and its development of consciousness, within class struggle itself, using images that would later be taken by most Marxists as a pair defining two distinct moments: "class in itself"/"class for itself". In Marx's terms, which are not exactly those that Marxists would later establish:

> Economic conditions had first transformed the mass of the people of the country into workers. The domination of capital has created for this mass a common situation, common interests. This mass is thus already a class as against capital, but not yet for itself. The interests it defends become class interests. But the struggle of class against class is a political struggle.[111]

Marx kept this conception of class formation as a process throughout his later reflection, in which consciousness does not immediately result from economic conditions, but develops amidst class struggle, which acquires a political dimension, even if he didn't resort to the expression "class for itself" anymore. He approached the question again in his investigations of France, particularly in *The Eighteenth Brumaire of Louis Bonaparte*.[112] In that work, the study of classes, confronted with a concrete case, gained much more shades. The analysis operates through a continuous shift from the terrain of parliamentary-party struggle to the terrain of class struggle, with no reductionisms, as in addition to the bourgeoisie and the proletariat Marx locates on the political scene peasants, landowners, the urban petty bourgeoisie, the lumpenproletariat, and even the role of bureaucratic strata and institutions such as the church, setting a complex and changing chessboard as clashes were polarized by the antagonistic positions of the fundamental social classes, in a revolutionary situation.

Analysing the role of classes, from the point of view of political action at the crucial moment of the 1848 Revolution and the conjuncture that followed it, Marx returns to the question of the level of consciousness they could or could not develop. While acknowledging the struggle that the Parliamentary Republic had established, especially in rural French areas, between a "modern consciousness" (represented by the schoolmasters) and a "traditional consciousness" (represented by the priests), Marx observed the victory of the latter. He noticed in his analysis that French peasants, small-holding peasants, given the isolation conditions of their mode of production, did not develop multiple relations among themselves, especially on the political level, which, in that national and conjunctural framework, contributed to a situation marked by the incompleteness of their constitution as a class. In this work, instead of using the expression class for itself, he chose to affirm, dialectically, that peasants formed and did not form a class:

Insofar as millions of families live under economic conditions of existence that separate their mode of life, their interests and their culture from those of the other classes, and put them in hostile opposition to the latter, they forma a class. Insofar as there is merely a local interconnection among these small-holding peasants, and the identity of their interests begets no community, no national bond and no political organization among them, they do not form a class.[113]

Other concrete moments of the European class struggle and other revolutions, even when defeated, pushed Marx to resume this kind of reflection on the class consciousness of the proletariat. In a well-known passage from a letter to Friedrich Bolte, dated November 1871, six months after the defeat of the Paris Commune, while explaining the history of the *International Workingmen's Association*, Marx assessed the degree of development of the workers' class consciousness (treated as a "maturation"). Again, the central issue is the political character—"that's to say, a movement of the class"—of those movements that make the class struggle explicit, as they put at stake the interests of the workers as a whole against the interests of the ruling class:

The political movement of the working class naturally has as its final object the conquest of political power for this class, and this requires, of course, a previous organisation of the working class developed up to a certain point, which arises from the economic struggles themselves.

But on the other hand, every movement in which the working class comes out as a class against the ruling classes and tries to coerce them by pressure from without is a political movement. For instance, the attempt in a particular factory, or even in a particular trade, to force a shorter working day out of the individual capitalists by strikes, etc., is a purely economic movement. The movement to force through an eight-hour law, etc., however, is a political movement. And in this way, out of the separate economic movements of the workers there grows up everywhere a political movement, that is to say a movement of the class, with the object of achieving its interests in a general form, in a form possessing general, socially binding force. Though these movements presuppose a certain degree of previous organisation, they are in turn equally a means of developing this organisation.[114]

There is another fundamental aspect to consider: from the conception of class consciousness, developed in his analysis of the class struggles of his time, Marx defends that the working class has, in capitalism, a revolutionary potential. Its “final object”, to use the words in the letter to Bolte, is the conquest of political power. It should be noted that this potential is not directly and immediately explicit in the economic struggle and even when defining the “mature” class consciousness, as in that letter. The example chosen by Marx to speak of a political class consciousness is that of a struggle within the limits of legality: the struggle for a law to reduce working hours. Thus, we can deduce that not all class consciousness, even if political, therefore, mature, immediately points to the revolutionary “final object”. In any case, if the discussion on class consciousness permeates all Marxian reflection, this is explained by its centrality to the proposition about the revolutionary potential of the working class. But how to explain the transition from the “purely economic movement” to the conscious “political movement” and, in this, to the revolutionary moment?

We can turn again to Gramsci and another central moment for this discussion on the process of formation of class consciousness. When, in his Notebooks, he dealt with the balance of forces in situations in which the hegemony of a dominant social group over the dominated groups is built,[115] Gramsci translated the issue of class consciousness into the terrain of political struggle in its broadest sense and exemplified his analysis with the construction of the hegemonic domination of the bourgeoisie in contemporary capitalist societies. Gramsci spoke of the bourgeoisie, but aimed directly at the question of the class consciousness of the proletariat, presenting a distinction between a first correlation of forces—which he calls “social”, more directly linked to economic structures—and a more properly political one, thus synthesized in a famous passage:

> A subsequent moment is the relation of political forces; in other words, an evaluation of the degree of homogeneity, self-consciousness, and organisation attained by the various social classes. This moment can in its turn be analysed and differentiated into various levels, corresponding to the various moments of collective political consciousness, as they have manifested themselves in history up till now. The first and most elementary of these is the economic-corporate level: a tradesman feels obliged to stand by another tradesman, a manufacturer by another manufacturer, etc., but the tradesman does not yet feel solidarity with the manufacturer; in other words, the members of the professional group are conscious of its unity and homogeneity, and of the need to organize it, but in the case of the

> wider social group this is not yet so. A second moment is that in which consciousness is reached out of the solidarity of interests among all the members of a social class-but still in the purely economic field. Already at this juncture the problem of the State is posed-but only in terms of winning politico-juridical equality with the ruling groups: the right is claimed to participate in legislation and administration, even to reform these but within the existing fundamental structures. A third moment is that in which one becomes conscious that one's own corporate interests, in their present and future development, transcend the corporate limits of the purely economic class, and can and must become the interests of other subordinate groups too.[116]

Distinguishing "levels" related to "moments" of the correlation of forces (and therefore of the dynamics of class struggle), Gramsci seeks to capture both the possible diversity of forms of class consciousness and the procedural nature of its formation. A very fruitful development of proposals such as those expressed by Marx in his letter to Bolte in 1871. Gramsci's "third moment" (the struggle for hegemony), with the sense of building legitimizing and cohesive consensus in the struggle for the conquest of political power, finds a parallel in that excerpt quoted from Marx's letter right at the beginning. In the letter to Bolte, what Gramsci called the "economic-corporate" moment appeared as a "purely economic movement". The second moment of the correlation of political forces in Gramsci's discussion—in which the economic claims of the social group are translated into political claims, causing "the problem of the State" to be considered—appears in Marx as a "political movement", therefore, a "movement of the class".

Another attempt to contribute to the understanding of this process of constitution of class consciousness was presented by E. P. Thompson. The most important specific contribution outlined by the English historian was the elaboration of an analysis that proposes the mediation and/or junction, always procedural, between the determinations of the objective existence of the class (the social being) and its social conscience, through the category "experience". Through it, Thompson believed he was able to demonstrate how:

> men and women also return as subjects, within this term – not as autonomous subjects, 'free individuals', but as persons experiencing their determinate productive situations and relationships, as needs and interests and as antagonisms, and then 'handling' this experience within their

> consciousness and their culture (...) in the most complex (...) ways, and then often but not always through the ensuing structures of class) acting upon their determinate situation in their turn.[117]

Dealing with subjects who act on a determined situation, we can thus return to the question of the historical subject of social transformation. We saw how, at the turn of 1843 to 1844, in the *Contribution to the Critique of Hegel's Philosophy of Right - Introduction*, Marx found that the bourgeoisie no longer had the potential to play a progressive role in the German case (but not only), nor to carry out the revolution towards human emancipation, nor to advance philosophical thought towards demystifying knowledge. Hence, instead of trying to repeat the French revolutionary process of the previous century, driven by a bourgeoisie eager to break the limits imposed by the Ancién Regime, it would be necessary to find another social subject that, because of its objective conditions, could play a leading role in the process of social emancipation. In the passage quoted above, we see that Marx poses the question: "Where, then, is the positive possibility of a German emancipation?" and also the answer. There was only one class capable of fulfilling such a role: "the proletariat".[118] The proletariat is a class that forms and is formed by "radical chains" and its potential to emancipate itself from these chains is determined (limited and pressured/enabled) by the need to emancipate all social spheres.

In that work, Marx aimed to distance himself from a conception that overvalues the role of philosophy as transforming "enlightenment" and presents the necessary material basis for any emancipatory project by assigning it a concrete social subject: the working class. Although the article thus contains Marx's clear intention to break with the idealist bases of Hegelian Philosophy, some commentators interpreted it as a text marked by a conception of the proletariat as an inert element, to be fertilized by philosophical thought so that its transformation potential is activated.[119] Even so, the key point of the conclusion reached by Marx at that moment is the necessary link between revolutionary social theory and a social class emerging from social existence that predisposes it to transformative action. There is, in fact, an appreciation of the role of the philosopher/critic in the demystification of the social world and in the construction of the emancipatory project, as a part of Marx's reflection. However, this role is subordinated to an objective/subjective social bond, a class bond: "as philosophy finds its *material* weapons in the proletariat, so the proletariat finds its *spiritual* weapons in philosophy. And once the lightning of thought has squarely struck this ingenuous soil of the people the emancipation of the *Germans* into *human beings* will take place".[120]

Marx had the opportunity in many other occasions to present his position in defence of the revolutionary potential of the proletariat, although differently from the first idea that an "ingenuous soil" would be fertilized by the "spiritual weapons" of revolutionary philosophy. In the debate with Proudhon in *The Poverty of Philosophy*, commented earlier, Marx recalls that "an oppressed class is the vital condition for every society founded on the antagonism of classes" and that "the emancipation of the oppressed class thus implies necessarily the creation of a new society". But, to the question "Does this mean that after the fall of the old society there will be a new class domination culminating in a new political power?", he answers negatively. Thinking about the revolutionary specificity of the proletariat, he states that: "the condition for the emancipation of the working class is the abolition of all classes, just as the condition for the emancipation of the third estate of the bourgeois order, was the abolition of all estates and all orders".[121]

Around twenty years later, when the *International Workingmen's Association* was created in 1864, the "Provisional Rules" written by Marx, opened by affirming the revolutionary potential of the proletariat as a subject of social transformation: "the emancipation of the working classes must be conquered by the working classes themselves".[122]

For this very reason, the affirmation of the proletariat as a revolutionary subject cannot be taken as a Hegelian "remnant" of the young Marx, to be later overcome by the mature Marx of the "critique of political economy". Thirty years after the criticism of Hegel, in the afterword to the second German edition of *Capital*, in 1873, we find Marx's assessment of his book as a philosophical elaboration originating from the working class. The interaction between theory and class was formulated there in a more organic way:

> The appreciation which *Das Kapital* rapidly gained in wide circles of the German working class is the best reward of my labours. Herr Mayer, a Vienna manufacturer, who in economic matters represents the bourgeois point of view, in a pamphlet published during the Franco-German War aptly expounded the idea that the great capacity for theory, which used to be considered a hereditary German possession, had almost completely disappeared amongst the so-called educated classes in Germany, but that

amongst its working class, on the contrary, that capacity was celebrating its revival.[123]

While explaining this association, Marx completes the reasoning about the class bond of his theoretical critique, explaining once again his affirmative perspective on the potential of the proletariat as the subject of the socialist revolution for which he had been fighting for nearly three decades:

> The peculiar historical development of German society therefore forbids, in that country, all original work in bourgeois economy; but not the criticism of that economy. So far as such criticism represents a class, it can only represent the class whose vocation in history is the overthrow of the capitalist mode of production and the final abolition of all classes –the proletariat.[124]

It is important to emphasize that the idea that the proletariat has a "vocation in history" cannot be understood, at least in Marx, in the sense that its very existence is a sufficient condition for it to behave as such. According to him, the revolutionary result of the class struggle is not an inevitable consequence of this struggle. On the contrary, there is a revolutionary potential in the contradictions inherent to capitalism; however, such potential depends on the subjectivity (class consciousness and action as a historical/social revolutionary subject) of the working class.

There is nothing better to illustrate this non-deterministic complexity of their proposal of interpretation and social intervention than the most "propagandistic" and best-known work by Marx and Engels. In the introductory text commissioned by the newly created League of Communists, *The Communist Manifesto*, Marx and Engels made public that proposal they had elaborated in *The German Ideology* to highlight the central role of class struggle in historical dynamics. Again, relating classes to the process of social division of labour, Marx and Engels sought to clarify the foundations of the social structure in capitalism. By demonstrating that class as a social phenomenon was only constituted in opposition to the interests of other class(es) and, therefore, by growing conscious of one's social position, which could be the starting point for a political project of transformation, they sought to lay the foundations for a theory of social dynamics, clearly asserting the central role of class struggle.

Therefore, they stated: "The history of all hitherto existing society is the history of class struggles".[125] Through the association between the categories of analysis of class and class struggle, both the foundations of the economic-social division of capitalist society and the nature of the social conflict characteristic of most of the history of human societies became possible to understand. This was the way to present their certainties about the revolutionary potential of the proletariat as a subject of history capable of leading to the emancipation of humanity.

However, even in *The Communist Manifesto*'s most famous passage on class struggle and revolution, the revolutionary outcome is not the only possible outcome of class struggle, which can also lead to mutual defeat:

> Freeman and slave, patrician and plebeian, lord and serf, guild-master and journeyman, in a word, oppressor and oppressed, stood in constant opposition to one another, carried on an uninterrupted, now hidden, now open fight, a fight that each time ended, either in a revolutionary re-constitution of society at large, or in the common ruin of the contending classes.[126]

Up to now, we have dealt with this social subject in terms of one working class, which seems correct and consistent with the perspective developed by Marx and Engels. However, this "unity" of the class is built amidst social relations that, in addition to engendering the opposition of objective interests between capitalists and proletarians as a result of the exploitation of the latter by the former, also engender intra-working-class differences, either because of the complexity of tasks division posed by the cooperation of labour in large industry, or through ideological forms and alienating mechanisms that cut across the collective subjectivity of the class. Neither are the objective conditions of exploitation identical for the whole class, nor do the collective identifications of its consciousness always work in a convergent way. In the case of "objective conditions", Marx drew attention, in *Capital*, to the need of wage earners who perform management tasks in complex modern productive units, exercising, as he explains through the metaphor of the army, a role of command and representation of capital itself:

> Just as at first the capitalist is relieved from actual labour so soon as capital has reached that minimum amount with which capitalist production, as such, begins, so now, he hands over the work of direct and constant supervision of the individual workman, and groups of workmen, to a special kind

> of wage labourer. An industrial army of workman, under the command of a capitalist, requires, like a real army, officers (managers), and sergeants (foremen, overlookers), who, while the work is being done, command in the name of the capitalist.[127]

Dealing with the heterogeneity that crosses class, which even pushes forms of prejudice and oppression, is an inevitable challenge for those who support the analytical validity of the concept of working class and as much or more for those who entrust the transformative potential of this historical subject.

New Subjects?

A recurrent problem of Marxist analysis has been trying to avoid problematizing the meanings of the working class's heterogeneity and its different historical experiences of oppression and alienation, which are combined with exploitation in different ways, through a simple statement of existence of an analytical priority of the concept of class over others, such as gender or race. If the Marxist perspective implies understanding capitalism as a dynamic and contradictory totality, the challenge for us is to engage in analyses and devise strategies that consider the complex relationships within this totality.

From the point of view of gender oppression,[128] it must be recognized that the relations between gender and class, or, to put it another way, between capitalism and patriarchy/oppression of women were often neglected or overlooked by Marxist analyses, as well as by socialist organizations, contributing to the predominance of a divorce between most social analyses and the perspectives of struggle of Marxists and feminists.[129] Recognizing this weakness of the Marxist perspective and of socialist organizations does not necessarily mean denying their potential to explain the complexity within the relations between class and gender and to intervene in transforming them.

The first explanatory element, in this sense, must start from the observation that patriarchal forms of gender oppression long preceded capitalism, but survived its emergence and combined with capitalist social relations in a very unique way. In modes of production prior to capitalism, especially in relations of production based on the family unit, which were focused primarily on subsistence, the subordination of women (and children) to patriarchal power organized the production process to a great extent. Marx and Engels were among the first to try to understand this process.

In the *Communist Manifesto*, they ridiculed the bourgeois fear that communism would introduce the "community of women" and explained this fear: "The bourgeois sees in his wife a mere instrument of production. He hears that the instruments of production are to be exploited in common, and, naturally, can come to no other conclusion than that the lot of being common to all will likewise fall to the women". In the following paragraphs, they do a bad joke on the infidelity of the bourgeoisie and such a "community of women", but the founders of historical materialism categorically affirm the communist objective of suppressing the material subordination of women: "[The bourgeois] has not even a suspicion that the real point aimed at is to do away with the status of women as mere instruments of production".[130]

This denunciation of the oppressive character of relations between men and women appears again in several other texts by the two authors. Regarding the historical sense of patriarchy, Engels, in *The Origin of the Family, Private Property and the State*, recalled the statement he and Marx wrote in the *German Ideology*, almost 40 years before Engel's work, saying that "the first division of labour is that between man and woman for child breeding", and added "the first class antithesis which appears in history coincides with the development of antagonism between man and woman in monogamian marriage, and the first class oppression with that of the female sex by the male".[131] In that book, he linked the emergence of male dominance to the origin of private property and class society, when men imposed monogamous marriage over group marriages and forced the male lineage over matriliny to ensure male children's control over inheritances. Although Engels encountered the limits of the anthropological studies of the time, in which he based himself, and as a result he incurred some confusion—such as the direct association between matrilineality (lines of family descent in which the children belong to the mother's extended family/clan) and matriarchy (a supported female social domain)—his perspective of inserting patriarchy in the historical dynamics of transformations in social relations remains a central methodological reference for Marxism in addressing the issue, as it allows us to realize that the oppression of women is not "natural" and did not always exist, but emerged as a result of historical-social processes.

The primitive accumulation of capital, however, was a process of expropriation which, as we saw from Marx's analysis, marked the separation of the now proletarians from the means of production necessary to supply their subsistence, casting them onto the market. For this reason, it consisted, to a large extent, of breaking down the different forms of relations of production organized by patriarchal power in family units. However, the patriarchal logic survived, was transformed, and incorporated by capitalism. This permanence can only be adequately explained if we are able to go beyond deterministic or essentialist views. It is not, of course, an essential differentiation between the biological nature of men and women that explains the permanence of gender hierarchies, because if biological differences exist, the solutions for them have been different throughout history and continue to be different according to distinct social positions. On the other hand, the perspectives that affirm the survival of patriarchy due to its purely economic characteristics are deterministic, as well as those that start from its supposed immutable or autonomous cultural characteristics in relation to the whole of social relations.

It is up to us to explain how the survival of the patriarchal ideology, combined with the valorization of the monogamous family model as a norm, gains materiality in different modalities of control of female behaviour and in the establishment of heteronormative standards by men, ranging from psychological pressure to the cruellest forms of direct violence. All of this plays an important role in the legitimization and organization of capitalist social relations that subordinate women's labour twice (and their social position in general). On the one hand, capital in its growth destroys relations of production based on the family unit, and on the other hand, capitalism does not dispense with the family—and here we are dealing particularly with women, but also with children and the elderly (again with emphasis female individuals)—as a prime unit in the execution of a series of kinds of work essential for the reproduction of the workforce.

Reproductive labour—involving not only biological reproduction, but also feeding, cleaning, caring for children (new generations of workers) and the sick, etc.—performed by women, as domestic labour, in the proletarian "home" (and also outside it) has an impact on the cost of the labour power in general, as transferring all these activities to the "public sphere", governed by market norms, could have an excessive cost to capital. In certain social–historical circumstances, the concentration of reproductive labour in the domestic sphere may allow capital to remunerate the labour power (whose value, Marx explained, is that of its reproduction, a variable value according to historical circumstances) with a wage lower than what would be necessary if all these conditions essential for survival were to be bought in the market.

Thus, even if many of the people, women in particular, who carry out unpaid domestic labour are also (part-time or full-time) waged workers outside their family's domestic space, a portion of their labour power is used outside the direct circuit of capital expansion, to lower the cost of reproduction of the labour power in general. This is because reproductive labour is, insofar as it does not produce value (in the sense of productive labour, as the category is used by Marx), unproductive labour and the female workers who perform it are, at least at the time they exercise it, often not paid.

The association between the oppression of women and their confinement to the home and domestic labour already appeared in the debate between Marxists and socialists in the turn of the nineteenth century to the twentieth century. In revolutionary experiences that sought to go beyond the domain of capital, as in the first years after the 1917 Revolution in Russia, the alternative of the socialization of reproductive labour, with most of its execution being carried out by public services with universal access, outside the private/family sphere, has been partially experimented—albeit for a short period of time—and has had very interesting results.[132]

In any case, it is worth noting that Marx demonstrates, as we have already commented here, that capitalist accumulation makes it possible to employ increasingly larger contingents of workers in unproductive labour. The recognition of the specificity and importance of this type of reproductive labour, essential for the reproduction of the commodity that guarantees the expansion of capital—labour power—bring with it the need to understand that the working class is not composed only of male workers and female workers who are waged or occasionally unemployed, but also by women who carry out domestic labour, who are also part, as Lise Vogel reminds us, of the totality of the "past, present, and potential wage-labour force, together with all those whose maintenance depends on the wage but do not or cannot themselves enter wage-labour".[133] Vogel rescues Marx's discussion in *Capital* about the capitalist relation of labour exploitation and the reproduction of the labour power, to go beyond the argument explained by Marx, advancing in the analysis of the specificity of gender oppression associated with domestic/reproductive labour:

> it is the responsibility for the domestic labour necessary to the capitalist social reproduction – and not the sex division of labour or the family per se – that materially underpins the perpetuation of women's oppression and inequality in capitalist society.[134]

However, not all domestic labour is unpaid, and the patriarchal ideology also legitimizes the incorporation of women into the waged labour market in subordinate positions and/or with lower wages. After all, as Marx recalls, "in contradistinction therefore to the case of other commodities, there enters into the determination of the value of labour power a historical and moral element".[135] From women and children in textile factories in the early days of industrial expansion, discussed by Marx in *Capital*, to highly skilled workers in strategic ventures for capital today (and at the intersections that continue to exist between these two poles and beyond), female labour has always been paid below and treated in a discriminatory manner in relation to male labour. In addition, the patriarchal ideology reinforces the priority allocation of women in the waged labour market to positions related to "care" (social reproduction), such as services in the areas of education, health, food, and cleaning. In the positions with the lowest remuneration and considered to be less "qualified", racialized women predominate, inseparably combining oppressions of different origins, as we will return to below. Moreover, in all these cases, the division within the working class, legitimized by patriarchal ideology, is functional as a way of lowering the average cost of the labour power and hierarchizing fractions of the working class.

In the last decades, Marxists-Feminists have invested in the development of a Social Reproduction Theory, based on "unitary" conceptions such as that of Lise Vogel. Building on Marx's critique of political economy, especially his analysis of "the pivotal role played by labour power" and his characterization of labour power as "singular in the sense that it is not produced capitalistically", but noticing the silences in Marx's work regarding the relationship between this singularity and the oppression of women, this theory advanced the perception of the relationship between "labour that produce[s] commodities and labour dispensed to produce people as part of the systemic totality of capitalism".[136]

Still considering this field of analysis, Cinzia Arruzza highlights how such a conception of social reproduction is distinct, but not opposite, from the use of the category by traditional Marxist analysis, which "usually indicates the process of reproduction of a society in its totality".

In the terrain of Marxist feminism, however, social reproduction means something more precise:

> the maintenance and reproduction of life, at the daily or generational level. In this context, social reproduction designates the way in which the physical, emotional, and mental labor necessary for the production of the population is socially organized: for example, food preparation, youth education, care for the elderly and the sick, as well as questions of housing and all the way to questions of sexuality...[137]

This reading of the category goes even further, as Arruzza emphasizes the exclusive focus on domestic labour, including "a series of social practices and types of labor", also enabling one "to locate more precisely the mobile and porous quality of the walls of the home: in other words, the relation between, on the one hand, domestic life within the home, and the phenomena of commodification, the sexualization of the division of labor, and the policies of the welfare-state on the other".[138]

Therefore, it is important to understand how the forms acquired by gender oppression cross the working class—in family relationships and in the labour market—and guarantee advantages and privileges to working men in relation to women, reinforcing the process. Even so, it is inevitable to realize that overcoming gender oppression is impossible under the logic of capital, which integrated it in a complex and nonlinear manner with labour exploitation, and is, therefore, inseparable from the emancipation of the entire working class. In the words of Cínzia Arruzza:

> Recognizing that in this context men, including working-class men, enjoyed and continue to enjoy a relative benefit from gender oppression does not mean viewing men as an exploiter class, but understanding the complexity with which capitalism integrates and employs pre-capitalist power relations to create hierarchies of exploited and oppressed, digging trenches and raising barriers.[139]

A similar challenge lies in the ability to understand that if gender oppression cuts across classes, class divisions also cut across gender positions. All women do not experience gender oppression homogeneously, although they are collectively subjected to oppressive patriarchal power. Differences in class, civil status, ethnicity, and race generate different forms of subjectivity. Thus, more than establishing a "primary" identity that guides a homogeneous and autonomous collective subject, gender positions interact with those of class and race, acting complexly to determine the specific—and hierarchical—ways in which oppressions are subjectively experienced.[140]

Unlike gender oppressions, whose basis in patriarchy predates capitalism, oppressions ideologically justified by racial criteria arise together with capitalism, directly associated with the ideological legitimation of modern slavery, especially from the moment when the struggles against slavery threaten to question the continuity of slave institutions.[141]

Forms of prejudice (which we would define today as "ethnic prejudice", or racism) in periods prior to the phase of primitive accumulation of capital were associated much more with cultural and religious factors than with supposed innate biological characteristics, although they could involve negative characterizations regarding the physical aspect of the discriminated peoples.[142] The justifications for the modalities of enslavement prior to the modern period were also different. Even during the first phases of primitive capital accumulation, the enslavement—temporary or for an indefinite period—of expropriated workers, "whites" and English natives, was provided by English penal legislation, as Marx recalled in aforementioned passages from the chapter on primitive accumulation of *Capital*.[143]

The concept of race based on assumed biological determinations (identifiable by blood criteria or by phenotypic characteristics) of human populations is completely impregnated with the ideological effort to legitimize the institution of modern slavery, which arose from the option for a mercantile colonization of the "New World", by European peoples from the sixteenth century. Faced with the open border characteristic of the conquered territories, the distinct possibilities and limits for the subjugation and exploitation of the indigenous peoples and the unavailability/incompatibility of European wage-earning "free" workers for mercantile production in the new colonies, different colonizing peoples turned to the enslavement of African populations. They were captured, converted into goods, and trafficked across the Atlantic by European ships and slave entrepreneurs (and later also from entrepreneurs from the colonies and former colonies), to work as the property of their masters—most often to death—on *plantations* and other economic activities in the American colonial territories. If the transatlantic trade fed the lucrative colonial enterprise with the necessary labour power, the trade as a globalized enterprise (connecting three continents) was also, as we saw in Marx's discussion, one of the main forms of primitive accumulation.[144] It was based on this logic of capitalist accumulation that over 12.5 million human beings were ripped from their original lands and trafficked as commodities to the Americas, almost 6 million of them by ships flying Portuguese or Brazilian flags.[145]

In the English colonies of North America, it was only amidst conflicts between workers subjected to forced labour—imprisoned Native Americans, Europeans subjected to contracts as indentured labourers, or Africans captured and forced into slavery—and the plantation lords that demarcation lines based on racial criteria were created by law, seeking to demarcate the "whites" from the others. In this sense, the Bacon rebellion in 1676, in which a multi-ethnic alliance of "unfree" workers was outlined, served as a milestone from which, on the legal and ideological planes, the racial argument distinguishing the "white race" from black and indigenous peoples began to spread. As Asad Haider explains, the "insurrectionary alliance of European and African laborers was a fundamental existential threat to the colonial ruling class". It is in the face of this threat that such a "watershed moment in the long and complex process of the invention of the white race as a form of social control. The ruling class shifted its labor force decisively toward African slaves, and thus avoided dealing with the demand of indentured servants for eventual freedom and landownership".[146]

When the struggles against slavery—which have always existed, especially among enslaved workers—acquired the contours of a transatlantic abolitionist movement, as a counterpoint, ideological justifications increasingly coated with openly racist-scientific and Eurocentric tones gained prominence, to try to naturalize modern slavery as a result of the adaptability and/or limitation of the black "race" to manual labour. The application of this classification criteria directly extended from natural history to human beings, established as a "scientific" discourse in the eighteenth century; it was extended to Asians—yellow "race"—as the European (neo)colonialism of the nineteenth century advanced into eastern territories and racialist ideology also gained the input of a Eurocentric civilizational discourse. In this way, it presented the action of the "white man" in extensive regions of the Asian and African continents as beneficial to local peoples, for bringing modernity and Western-capitalist civilization to backward regions and societies due to the natural/racial inferiority of their populations. Later, scientistic racism would be amplified—and combined with "old" modalities of prejudice—to cover anti-Semitic and eugenic discourses, which composed the Nazi-Fascist ideologies of the twentieth century.[147]

The use of the expression race appears in previous moments to (dis)qualify Indigenous and African peoples in the colonial Americas, but the racialist justification expands it from the eighteenth century onwards and continues practically throughout the entire nineteenth century, amid the long struggle against slavery. Still, racism cannot be seen simply as a slavery ideological heritage. Twentieth-century science has completely overturned any claim to the scientificity of the racialist argument of the hierarchy between "races". However, racism continued and continues to guide oppressive forms of exercising power and interpenetrate itself in relations of production, creating hierarchies of functions, different levels of employment contracts, and significant differences in wage values, just as those that draw gender lines in the labour market.

Charles Post thinks about this issue based on the challenges posed to capital and labour by the systemic competitive logic of capital. It is this characteristic of contradictory capitalist social relations that "makes race—the ideological notion that humanity is divided into distinct groups with unchangeable characteristics—the logical way for capital and labor to spontaneously organize competition on the labor-market".[148] His argument about why racism, far from losing its historical meaning with the abolition of slavery, gained momentum across the working class in the United States, is centred on how "competition among workers produces systematic racial disparities among workers"[149] and is similar to that of the sociologist and historian Clóvis Moura, studying Brazil. According to Moura, "the dispute, the individual competition in the labour market, in terms of emergence of newly formed professional segments, in inferior extracts, sharpen the prejudice of colour or 'race'".[150]

This systemic sense of racism, amidst competition in the labour market, for capitalist exploitation was perceived by Marx who, in the debate of the First International, defended unrestricted support for the Irish national cause. Understanding that England had the most numerous working class and the most latent capitalist contradictions, thus being the central stage of the struggle for social revolution represented by the International, Marx also realized that there were objective and subjective obstacles to the revolution in England, associated with domination over Ireland. Racism and colonialism went together and needed to be fought together. From a strictly economic point of view, Marx understood that the strength of

English landowners lay, in large part, in control over Irish land, as well as in denouncing that the introduction of impoverished Irish workers into the English labour market served not only to lower the cost of the labour power as a whole, but it was also accompanied by an ideological effort to uphold prejudiced views. The main effect of which was to weaken the unity of the working-class social subject. The analogy he used, in an 1870 text, a few years after the end of the civil war, is with the racism manifested by white workers in the South of the United States:

> in fact in all the *major industrial centers of England* there is a profound antagonism between the Irish and the English proletarians. The ordinary English worker hates the Irish worker as a competitor who brings down his wages and standard of living. He also feels national and religious antipathies for him; it is rather the same attitude that the poor whites of the Southern states of North America had for the Negro slaves. This antagonism between the two groups of proletarians within England itself is artificially kept in being and fostered by the bourgeoisie, who know well that this split is the real secret of preserving their own power.[151]

Hence, Marx argued more and more emphatically throughout the 1860s that the emancipation of the English working class depended on the liberation of Ireland. He came to recognize that his position on the subject changed over the years, although he had always denounced prejudice and supported independence. His interpretation moved from a perspective that affirmed the ascendancy of the English proletariat on the struggle for self-determination, to another in which the struggle for independence in Ireland gained prominence, serving as the driving force of the socialist struggle in England. In an 1870 text, Marx stated: "After studying the Irish question for years I have come to the conclusion that the decisive blow against the ruling classes in England (and this is decisive for the workers' movement all over the world) cannot be struck *in England*, but *only in Ireland*".[152]

The valorization of struggles in the colonized peripheries as a trigger for the social revolution of the working class at the centre of industrial capitalism was not new to his reflections. Lucia Pradella draws attention to Marx's writings on China and India, in the 1850s, when he grows aware of the fact that anti-colonial struggles were aggravating factors to the capitalist crises that were beginning to manifest themselves on an international scale and, therefore, should be understood as an important part of anti-systemic struggles, as we would say today. Understanding imperialist expansion as a mechanism for coping with crises, Marx would have perceived in those writings both the possibility opened by colonial exploitation for a progressive increase in the wages of the working class in central countries and, contradictorily, the disruptive potential of the "agency of non-European people".[153] In a passage from one of his articles about China, rescued by Pradella, Marx says: "the next uprising of the people of Europe ... may depend more probably on what is now passing in the Celestial Empire – the very opposite of Europe – than on any other political cause that now exists".[154]

The greatest example of the importance of this more "global" view of the social struggles of his time is present in Marx's writings on the Civil War in the United States (1861–1865). Marx assessed, from the beginning of the conflict, that what was at stake was the issue of slavery, whose overcoming in the US South was part of the greater struggle of the European working class, defending, before its implementation, both the decree of total abolition of slavery by the central government and the arming of ex-slaves to face their former masters on the battlefield. For this reason, he welcomed the favourable attitudes towards Lincoln's central government by workers in the English textile industry (hit hard by the naval blockade imposed by the North, making southern cotton exports to supply British factories unfeasible) and included the theme in the Inaugural Address of the First International.[155] Thus, it is no wonder that in a passage from the preface to the first edition of *Capital* (1867), Marx attributes revolutionary dimensions to the Civil War: "As in the eighteenth century, the American War of Independence sounded the tocsin for the European middle class, so in the nineteenth century, the American Civil War sounded it for the European working class".[156]

Marx's writings, even if they were not often directed at racism, can help us locate the specificity of the identity criteria, based on the idea of race as a product of social conflicts and domination strategies that are historically and concretely located in social life. In this sense, proposals for the sociological (re)elaboration of the concept of race gain importance, such as the one presented by Antonio Sérgio Guimarães, when discussing the Brazilian reality, for whom the concept, which is only justified by the existence of racism, should, at the same time: "1- recognize the real and effective weight that the idea of race has in Brazilian society, in terms of legitimizing inequalities in treatment and opportunities; 2- reaffirm the fictitious character of such construction in physical or biological terms; and 3- identify the racial content of Brazilian social classes".[157] The racial issue, in this sociological sense, cannot be confused with other identity criteria, precisely because of the historical weight of the social relations that engendered and continue to sustain racism in capitalist societies.[158]

Such social relations—and here we can again resort to the concepts elaborated by Marx—engender specific forms of exploitation, oppression, and alienation, as highlighted by Abigail Bakan.[159] According to her, while exploitation refers to the social relations that guarantee the "economic extraction of surplus", alienation "refers to the general distancing of human beings from what makes them in fact human", and oppression "can be seen to operate in two distinct ways, as class oppression and as special oppression. Oppression is variable and contingent; it is, however, necessary to the reproduction of the social relations of capitalism".[160] In the synthesis she presents, aiming at putting Marx's concepts into dialogue with the criticisms of racism elaborated from the "politics of difference", Bakan says:

> Racism is a set of ideas and institutional practices that assign divisions of superiority/inferiority according to an ascribed and constructed set of biological and/or cultural characteristics that are falsely considered to be inherent and permanent within the human subsets. Racism is variable and adaptable but has proved to be remarkably valuable to capitalism and imperialist interests over centuries. Specific categories suggested here within this framework are racism as a codification of alienation, where alienation is articulated as hegemonic whiteness; racism as special oppression; and racial privilege as a historically concrete category that needs to be placed in specific lived contexts.[161]

Proposals such as Bakan's add effective arguments for establishing the necessary mediations, respecting the specificities of different forms of oppression and their articulated combinations in the social totality, to prominently include the struggles for the recognition of differences within the movement for human emancipation in general. A movement that has always been at the centre of Marx and Engels' project.

Hence, the importance of approaches such as the one proposed by the unitary feminist/Marxist theory, which perceives Marx's elaboration as a "critique of an articulated and contradictory totality of relations of exploitation, domination, and alienation", is to propose the need to integrate the analysis of productive and reproductive dimensions of labour under capital. In this way, it may be possible "to read relations of power based on gender or sexual orientation as concrete moments of the articulated, complex, and contradictory totality that is contemporary capitalism", also understanding that "gender oppression and racial oppression do not correspond to two autonomous systems which have their own particular causes: they have become an integral part of capitalist society through a long historical process that has dissolved preceding forms of social life".[162]

Reintroducing the issue of labour and, therefore, of class in the discussion of this contradictory capitalist totality, Susan Fergunson reminds us that "The forces of social oppression both shape and are shaped by the capitalist tendency to reduce life to labour power". Thus, "racism, sexism, and heterosexism (and the resistance they spawn) organize the institutions and practices of life-making in ways that are constantly articulated to—but not necessarily beholden to—capital's need for workers. But not just for any workers. For a socially differentiated (paid and unpaid) workforce".[163]

This process of social differentiation of the workforce, traversed by the way in which social oppressions operate, sustains and reinforces capitalist accumulation in two ways: (1) "it keeps the costs of social reproduction lower by ensuring some people take on that labour for free or at a low wage"; (2) "it ensures a steady supply of sufficiently marginalized and precarious workers prepared or forced to accept waged work that is unregulated, unhealthy, and poorly paid".[164]

Such a perspective is not completely new, as it can be, to some extent, found in formulations from the beginning of the twentieth century, in socialist thinkers more attentive to the importance of the race issue for understanding the profile of the working class, as well as for a socialist politic capable of unifying the groups integrated by capitalism in a fragmented and hierarchical way to its strategies of domination and exploitation. This was the case of Jose Carlos Mariategui, who sought to include "the problem of race" as a central theme in the Latin American communists' debate in the late 1920s. Having noticed both the functionality of racism in the way capitalist expansion incorporated labour relations based on the large estates' update of the exploitation of indigenous villages and the centrality of slavery and specific forms of exploitation of the black population after the abolition of slavery and recognizing that racism permeated the Latin American proletariat itself, the Peruvian revolutionary defended that:

> The reality of grounded and precise revolutionary politics in which the appreciation and utilization of the circumstances on which one must act in countries where the Indigenous or black population has an important size and role can and must convert the racial factor into a revolutionary factor. It is essential to provide the Indigenous or black proletariat movement, whether agricultural or industrial, a clear orientation as a class struggle.[165]

Going back a little further in time, let us recall again the Inaugural Address of the First International which already stated, a few lines before the famous cry "Proletarians of all countries, unite!", that an anti-slavery foreign policy against imperialist annexations was "part of the general struggle for the emancipation of the working classes" and this was attributed not to the "wisdom of the ruling classes, but [to] the heroic resistance to their criminal folly by the working classes of England", the European rejection to "an infamous crusade for the perpetuation and propagation of slavery on the other side of the Atlantic".[166]

On that other side of the Atlantic, as Angela Davis masterfully demonstrated, the American feminist movement was born from the womb of the abolitionist struggle and some of its most prominent characters demonstrated a deep consciousness "of the inseparability of the fight for Black Liberation and the fight for Women's Liberation", whereby they avoided falling into "the ideological snare of insisting that one struggle was absolutely more important than the other".[167]

Diverse, heterogeneous and historically constituted, the potentially transforming historical subject that Marx and Engels encountered in the nineteenth century continues to challenge the analytical capacity of those who intend to study it, as well as the political projects that intend to represent it.

Notes

1. E. P. Thompson, "Eighteenth-Century English Society: Class Struggle Without Class?", *Social History*, Vol. 3, No. 2, 1978, 148.
2. E. P. Thompson, *The Making of the English Working Class*, London, Penguin, 1991 (1963).
3. It is not my intention here to explore the biography of Marx and Engels extensively. For this the bibliography is abundant. I suggest, for example, reading Tristam Hunt, *The Frock-Coated*

Communist: The Revolutionary Life of Friedrich Engels, London, Penguin, 2009. Franz Mehring, *Karl Marx, The Story of His Life*, New York, Routledge, 2010 (1918). Mary Gabriel, *Love and Capital: Karl and Jenny Marx and the Birth of a Revolution*, New York, Little, Brown and Company, 2011. Michael Heinrich, *Karl Marx and the Birth of Modern Society: The Life of Marx and the Development of His Work*, New York, Monthly Review Press, 2019. Marcello Musto, *The Last Years of Karl Marx: An Intellectual Biography*, Stanford, Stanford University Press, 2020. As well as the biographies, in this chapter, section I benefited profoundly from the contribution of José Paulo Netto in his "Apresentação: Marx em Paris", In Karl Marx (ed.), *Cadernos de Paris & Manuscritos econômico-filosóficos de 1844*, São Paulo, Expressão Popular, 2015. And from the work of Michael Lowy, *The Theory of Revolution in the Young Marx*, Chicago, Haymarket, 2005 (1970).

4. On Chartism, see for instance, Asa Briggs, *Chartism*, London, Sutton, 1998; and Dorothy Thompson, *The Dignity of Chartism*, London, Verso, 2015.
5. Friedrich Engels, *The Condition of the Working-Class in England* (1845), In Karl Marx & Friedrich Engels (eds.), *Marx-Engels Collected Works*, vol. 4, London, Lawrence & Wishart, 1975, p. 517. Almost all quotations of Marx and Engels have been here referenced in the text by work title and publishing date and were consulted in this 50-volume edition of the *Collected Works*, henceforth identified as MECW, followed by volume and page.
6. Ibid., pp. 526–27.
7. *MECW*, vol. 1, pp. 240, 228.
8. *MECW*, vol. 3, p. 186.
9. *MECW*, vol. 3, p. 355.
10. *MECW*, vol. 3, p. 202.
11. J. P. Netto, "Apresentação", p. 28.
12. M. Löwy, *The Theory of Revolution in the Young Marx*, Chicago, Haymarket Books, 2005. pp. 63–96.
13. Ibid., p. 84.
14. Mikhail Bakhtin (Volochínov), *Marxism and the Philosophy of Language*, Harvard University Press, 1996, p. 21.
15. Ibid., p. 23.

16. Abbé Sieyès, *What Is the Third State?*, apud W. Sewell Jr., *Work & Revolution in France. The Language of Labor from the Old Regime to 1848*, New York, Cambridge University Press, 1980, p. 282.
17. Ibid., p. 283.
18. Asa Briggs, "The Language of Class in Early Nineteenth Century England", In A. Briggs & J. Saville (eds.), *Essays on Labour History*, London, Macmillan, 1960, p. 44.
19. Ibid., p. 44.
20. Daniel Bensaid, *Os irredutíveis: teoremas da resistência para o tempo atual*, São Paulo, Boitempo, 2008, p. 36.
21. *MECW*, vol. 35, p. 56.
22. Ibid., p. 57.
23. *MECW*, vol. 5, p. 77.
24. E. P. Thompson, "Eighteenth-Century English Society: Class Struggle Without Class?", *Social History*, Vol. 3, No. 2, May 1978, 133–65, p. 149.
25. Ibid., p. 149.
26. *MECW*, vol. 3, p. 241.
27. We discuss this distinction between extracting surplus value by extending the working day and by intensifying labour productivity through the introduction of new technologies further in the text.
28. *MECW*, vol. 34, p. 439.
29. Ibid., p. 443.
30. Ibid., p. 443.
31. Ibid., p. 448. Marx uses the same example of the schoolmaster to discuss productive labour in *Capital*, volume 1 (in the discussion on relative and absolute surplus value). "If we may take an example from outside the sphere of production of material objects, a schoolmaster is a productive labourer, when, in addition to belabouring the heads of his scholars, he works like a horse to enrich the school proprietor. That the latter has laid out his capital in a teaching factory, instead of in a sausage factory, does not alter the relation" (*MECW*, vol. 35, p. 510).
32. *MECW*, vol. 34, p. 446. It's important to explain that every time Marx presents some "law" in his analysis of capital, he is discussing a "tendency law", which suffers the effects of several "counter-tendencies".
33. Alex Callinicos, *Making History*, Chicago, Haymarket, 2009, p. 218.

34. *MECW*, vol. 35, p. 449.
35. Alex Callinicos, *Making History*, p. 218.
36. *MECW*, vol. 37, p. 871.
37. Alex Callinicos, *Deciphering Capital: Marx's Capital and Its Destiny*, London, Bookmarks, 2013, p. 191.
38. Daniel Bensaid, *Marx for Our Times: Adventures and Misadventures of a Critique*, London, New York, Verso, 2009.
39. Ibid., p. 100.
40. Ibid., p. 106.
41. Ernest Mandel, "Introduction", in Karl Marx, *Capital. A Critique of Political Economy*, volume one, London, Penguin, 1990, p. 33.
42. *MECW*, vol. 35, pp. 163–64.
43. Ibid., p. 53.
44. Ibid., p. 177.
45. Ibid., p. 184.
46. Ibid., p. 195.
47. Ibid., pp. 203–4.
48. Ibid., p. 227.
49. Ibid., pp. 241. The expression *ultima Thule* was used in medieval maps to designate the limits of the known world.
50. D. Bensaid, *Marx for Our Times*, p. 106.
51. *MECW*, vol. 36, p. 57.
52. Ibid., pp. 57–58.
53. Ibid., p. 62.
54. Ibid., p. 445.
55. Ibid., p. 446.
56. D. Bensaid, *Marx for Our Times*, pp. 107–8.
57. *MECW*, vol. 37, p. 210.
58. MECW, vol. 35, pp. 607–8.
59. Ibid., p. 609.
60. Ibid., pp. 613–14.
61. Ibid., p. 617.
62. Ibid., p. 617.
63. Ibid., p. 621.
64. Ibid., p. 617.
65. Ibid., pp. 625–26.
66. Ibid., p. 638.
67. Ibid., p. 707.

68. Ibid., p. 627.
69. Ibid., p. 634.
70. Ibid., p. 635.
71. Ibid., pp. 637–38.
72. Ibid., p. 637.
73. Ibid., p. 705.
74. Ibid., p. 706.
75. MECW, vol. 1, p. 228.
76. MECW, vol. 35, p. 748.
77. Ibid., p. 724.
78. Ibid., p. 747.
79. Ibid., p. 747.
80. Ibid., p. 748.
81. Ibid., pp. 749–50.
82. Ibid., pp. 750–51.
83. *MECW*, vol. 28, p. 37.
84. Alex Callinicos, *Deciphering Capital*, p. 196.
85. Ibid., p. 196.
86. *MECW*, vol. 11, p. 103.
87. R. Williams, *Keywords: A Vocabulary of Culture and Society*, Oxford, Oxford University Press, 1976, p. 200. Emphasis from the original.
88. *MECW*, vol. 5, p. 3.
89. *MECW*, vol. 35, p. 194.
90. *MECW*, vol. 29, p. 263.
91. Ibid., p. 263.
92. *MECW*, vol. 5, p. 36.
93. *MECW*, vol. 29, p. 263.
94. Jan Rehmann, *Theories of Ideology: The Powers of Alienation and Subjection*, Leiden, Brill, 2013, p. 118.
95. For two rich introductions to Gramsci's thought, see Carlos Nelson Coutinho, *Gramsci's Political Thought*, Leiden, Brill, 2012; and Alvaro Bianchi, *Gramsci's Laboratory*, Leiden, Brill, 2020.
96. Antonio Gramsci, *Cadernos do cárcere*, vol. 4, Rio de Janeiro, Civilização Brasileira, 2001, p. 51 (Notebook 16).
97. Ibid., pp. 51–52.

98. A. Gramsci, *The Antonio Gramsci Reader: Selected Writings, 1916–1935*, edited by David Forgacs, New York, New York University Press, 2000, pp. 331–32 (Notebook 11).
99. Ibid., p. 329.
100. Ibid., p. 332.
101. On the diversity of terms and their meanings in Marx's original texts in German, which are usually translated as "alienation", see J. Ranieri, *A câmara escura. Alienação e estranhamento em Marx*, São Paulo, Boitempo, 2001, p. 7.
102. R. Williams, *Keywords*, p. 35.
103. István Mészáros, *Marx's Theory of Alienation*, London, Merlin Press, 1970, p. 18.
104. Ibid., p. 14.
105. *MECW*, vol. 3, pp. 271–72.
106. *MECW*, vol. 35, pp. 82–83.
107. Ibid., p. 83.
108. Ibid., p. 83.
109. *MECW*, vol. 6, p. 210.
110. Ibid., p. 211.
111. Ibid., p. 211.
112. *MECW*, vol. 11, pp. 99–197.
113. Ibid., p. 187.
114. *MECW*, vol. 44, p. 258.
115. The category "hegemony" is one of the cornerstones of all Gramscian reflection in his Notebooks. Its complexity precludes any attempt to summarize it in a footnote. It is enough to remember that when he presented the analysis proposal he developed in his Notebooks, in a correspondence dated September 1931, Gramsci stated that his study "leads to certain determinations of the concept of State, which is usually understood as the political society (or dictatorship, or coercive apparatus, to shape the popular mass according to the type of production and the economy of a given moment), and not as a balance of political society with civil society (or hegemony of a social group over the entire national society, exercised through so-called private organizations, such as the Church, unions, schools, etc.)". Antonio Gramsci, *Cartas do cárcere*, vol. 2, Rio de Janeiro, Civilização Brasileira, 2005, p. 84.

116. Antonio Gramsci, *Selections from Prison Notebooks*, edited and translated by Quentin Hoare & Geoffrey Nowel Smith, London, Lawrence & Wishart, 1971, p. 181.
117. E. P. Thompson, *The Poverty of Theory*, pp. 221–22.
118. *MECW*, vol. 3, p. 186.
119. See, for example, Alex Callinicos, *Making History*, p. 214.
120. *MECW*, vol. 3, p. 187.
121. *MECW*, vol. 6, pp. 211–12.
122. *MECW*, vol. 20, p. 14.
123. *MECW*, vol. 35, p. 13.
124. Ibid., p. 16.
125. MECW, vol. 6, p. 482.
126. Ibid., p. 482.
127. *MECW*, vol. 35, p. 337.
128. Here, we chose to use "gender", as we understand it as the broadest concept to explain various social relations marked by oppression, which, however, maintain their specificities, such as those relating to LGBTQIA+ people. The text, however, focuses on the oppression of women. For a Marxist perspective on the relationship between capitalist exploitation and oppression against the LGBTQIA+ population, see, for example, Kevin Floyd, "Making History: Marxism, Queer Theory, and Contradiction in the Future of American Studies", *Cultural Critique*, No. 40, 1998; Alan Sears, "Situating Sexuality in Social Reproduction", *Historical Materialism*, Vol. 24, No. 2, 2016; and Peter Drucker, "The Fracturing of LGBT Identities Under Neoliberal Capitalism", *Historical Materialism*, Vol. 19, No. 4, 2011.
129. The image of "divorces" as well as possible "marriages" between Marxism and feminism is used, in reference to an earlier text by Heidi Hartmann, by Cínzia Arruzza, in her book *Dangerous Liaisons: The Marriages and Divorces of Marxism and Feminism*, London, Merlin Press, 2013.
130. *MECW*, vol. 6, p. 502.
131. *MECW*, vol. 26, p. 173 (first published in 1884). C. Arruzza does an interesting critical assessment of Engels' ideas in *Dangerous Liaisons*, pp. 82–86.
132. Wendy Goldman, *Women, the State and Revolution: Soviet Family Policy and Social Life, 1917–1936*, Cambridge, Cambridge University Press, 1993.

133. Lise Vogel, *Marxism and the Oppression of Women: Toward a Unitary Theory*, Chicago, Haymarket, 2013, p. 166.
134. Ibid., p. 177, See also the discussion, from this perspective, by David Macnally & Susan Ferguson, "Capital, Labour-Power, and Gender: Introduction to the Historical Materialism Edition of the Marxism and the Oppression of Women", in ibid., p. xxxii.
135. *MECW*, vol. 35, p. 181.
136. Tithi Bhattacharya, "Introduction", In T. Bhattacharya (ed.), *Social Reproduction Theory: Remapping Class, Recentering Oppression*, London, Pluto Press, 2017, pp. 2–3.
137. C. Arruza, "Remarks on Gender", *Viewpoint Magazine*, September 2, 2014, https://viewpointmag.com/2014/09/02/remarks-on-gender/, accessed on August 2021.
138. Ibid.
139. C. Arruzza, *Dangerous Liaisons*, p. 126.
140. The debate of black feminists was very important to bring up this issue. One of the possible interpretations from this debate is the one that emphasizes "intersectionality", a category presented by Kinberlé Crenshaw, among other thinkers, as a "metaphorical conceptualization" that seeks "to capture both the structural and dynamic consequences of the interaction between two or more forms of discrimination or systems of subordination. It specifically addresses the manner in which racism, patriarchy, economic disadvantages and other discriminatory systems contribute to create layers of inequality that structures the relative positions of women and men, races and other groups. Moreover, it addresses the way that specific acts and policies create burdens that flow along these intersecting axes contributing actively to create a dynamic of disempowerment". K. Crenshaw, Background Paper for the Expert Meeting on Gender Related Aspects of Race Discrimination, United Nations, 21–24 November 2000 Zagreb, Croatia. https://www.un.org/womenwatch/daw/csw/genrac/report.htm, accessed, August 2021. For a discussion that problematizes certain uses of the idea of "intersectionality", see David MacNally, "Intersections and Dialectics: Critical Reconstructions in Social Reproduction Theory", In T. Bhattacharya (ed.), *Social Reproduction Theory*, pp. 94–111.
141. Alex Callinicos, *Race and Class*, London, Bookmarks, 1993, pp. 23–30.

142. A very interesting discussion on the Middle Age and contemporary racism can be found in "Race, Racism and the Middle Ages", in *The Public Medievalist* blog, http://www.publicmedievalist.com/race-racism-middle-ages-toc/, accessed in March 2017.
143. *MECW*, vol. 35. In this regard, among the extensive bibliography, see the work of Peter Linebaugh e Marcus Rediker, *The Many-Headed Hydra: Sailors, Slaves, Commoners, and the Hidden History of the Revolutionary Atlantic*, Boston, Beacon, 2000.
144. See the aforementioned passage on profits from the trafficking of the Liverpool bourgeoisie in the chapter on primitive accumulation in K. Marx, *MECW*, vol. 35, p. 747. In the last chapter of volume 1, "The Modern Theory of Colonization", Marx explains the relationship between the colonial system and slavery from the perspective of capitalist accumulation.
145. The database of the project "Voyages: trans-Atlantic slave trade database" totals 12,521,337 people transported by force from different regions of the African continent to the Americas between 1501 and 1875, 5,848,266 to the Portuguese colony, later Brazil, or to other locations by Portuguese or Brazilian flag ships. http://www.slavevoyages.org/, accessed, March 2017.
146. Asad Haider, *Mistaken Identity: Race and Class in the Age of Trump*, London, Verso, 2018, p. 55. Haider resumes in this passage arguments by Neil Painter, *The History of White People*, New York, W. W. Norton, 2010.
147. For a comprehensive history of racism, Francisco Bethencourt, *Racisms: From the Crusades to the Twentieth Century*, Princeton, Princeton University Press, 2014.
148. Charles Post, "Marxism and the Race Problem", *Marxist Sociology Blog*, January 3, 2019. https://marxistsociology.org/2019/01/marxism-and-the-race-problem/?fbclid=IwAR1fTaFLwJTdX46R5rBuaP6zMysbIYX4FDBGNYSbfb7J_8ks_ezxvhoo-MM. Accessed on August 2021.
149. Ibid.
150. Clóvis Moura, *O negro: de bom escravo a mau cidadão?*, 2ª ed., São Paulo, Dandara, 2021, p. 77.
151. Apud. M. Musto (org.), *Workers Unite!*, pp. 249–50.
152. *MECW*, vol. 43, p. 473.

153. Lucia Pradella, "Crisis, Revolution and Hegemonic Transition: The American Civil War and Emancipation in Marx's Capital", *Science & Society*, Vol. 80, No. 4, 2016, 454–67, p. 457.
154. K. Marx, "Revolution in China and Europe" (May 20–21, 1853), apud L. Pradella, Crisis, Revolution, p. 457.
155. A very broad new edition of Marx and Engels' writings on the civil war, including an interesting preface by its organizer, was published in 2016. Karl Marx & Friedrich Engels, *The Civil War in the United States*, edited and with an Introduction by Andrew Zimmerman, New York, International Publishers, 2016.
156. *MECW*, vol. 35, p. 9.
157. Antonio Sérgio A. Guimarães, *Classes, Raças e Democracia*, São Paulo, Ed. 34, 2002, p. 56.
158. See in this regard the critique of attempts to replace the concept of race with that of ethnicity or ethnic identity in Kabengele Munanga, "Uma abordagem conceitual das noções de raça, racismo, identidade e etnia", In André Brandão (org.), *Cadernos PNESB*, vol. 5, Niterói, Ed. UFF, 2004, p. 29.
159. Abigail B. Bakan, "Marxism and Antiracism: Rethinking the Politics of Difference", *Rethinking Marxism: A Journal of Economics, Culture & Society*, Vol. 20, No. 2, 238–56.
160. Ibid., p. 252.
161. Ibid., p. 253.
162. C. Arruzza, *Remarks on Gender*, pp. 14–16.
163. Susan Fergunson, *Women and Work: Feminism, Labour and Social Reproduction*, London, Pluto Press, 2019, p. 116.
164. Ibid., p. 116.
165. Jose Carlos Mariategui, *The Problem of Race in Latin America* (1929), in Mariategui, *An Anthology*, p. 195, edited and translated by Harry E. Vanden and Marc Becker, New York, Monthly Review Press, 2011, p. 195.
166. K. Marx, "Inaugural Address" (1864), apud M. Musto (ed.), *Workers Unite! The International, 150 Years Later*. London: Bloomsbury Academic, 2014, p. 79.
167. Angela Davis, *Woman, Race & Class*, New York, Vintage Books, 1983, p. 59.

CHAPTER 3

Workers Today

Workers of the World!

The global population was estimated to be around 7.7 billion people in 2019, and we were less than half that 50 years ago.[1] In 1950, only 30% of the world's population lived in cities. In 2018, 55% of the world's inhabitants live in urban centres.[2] Such a change, extremely accelerated for the historical patterns of human life on earth, indicates an absurd intensification of the proletarianization process in recent years. After all, although conversion to wage earning is also growing in the countryside, the main reason for the migration from the countryside to the city is the complete expropriation of those who still found ways to survive mainly from their (and their family's) agricultural work, thanks to the ownership or possession of small plots of land.

Urbanization, as it is known, is older and more consolidated in countries that experienced the industrialization process earlier, in the Northern Hemisphere, considered more "developed", and it is more recent and aggressive in the countries of the Southern Hemisphere, where the industrialization is relatively late and domestic production of wealth is lower. Such differentiation is essential to explain certain demographic patterns that are reflected in the composition of the workforce.

In the world as a whole, the workforce (understood as the population over 15 years old who is employed, unemployed looking for a job,

M. B. Mattos, *The Working Class from Marx to Our Times*, Marx, Engels, and Marxisms,
https://doi.org/10.1007/978-3-030-97355-1_3

and looking for a job for the first time; excluding unpaid workers, family work, and students) was estimated by the International Labour Organization (ILO) to be 3.3 billion people in 2019. In 1990, they were 2.3 billion people. Taking this interval of about a quarter of a century, the percentage of the workforce in relation to the total population was 44.31% in 1990, in 2016, it reached 46.04%, and totalled 44.9% in 2019. There are significant regional imbalances, especially between the more developed national economies of the Northern Hemisphere and those of the Global South, where the least developed are to be found. Among those 47 nations that the UN considers less developed, for example, the participation of the workforce in the total population was 40.59% in 1990 and reached 42.27% in 2016. Even greater inequalities can be found if we add the generational and gender data. The percentage of women in the workforce was above 40%, throughout the period from 1990 (when they were 39.54% of the total) to 2019 (38.8%). In terms of distribution by sectors of the economy, in 2000, 39.6% of this workforce was employed in agriculture, while 19.5% in industry and 40.9% in services. In 2019, they were: 26.8% in agriculture, 22.7% in industry, and 50.5% in services.[3]

The increase in the number of jobs, however, is insufficient to absorb all workers who annually enter the labour market in search of their first job—40 million per year, according to the ILO, in a report dated back to 2015.[4] Women (occupying around 40% of the workforce, as we have seen) accounted for around 73% of the employment deficit.[5] In 2019, global unemployment reached 5.4%, involving 188 million people. The underutilization of the workforce (the sum of unemployed, time-related underemployed, and the potential workforce) involved 473 million people. Also revealing is the fact that around 50% of employment in the world is waged, but in regions such as Sub-Saharan Africa and South Asia, this percentage drops to 20%. In addition, it was estimated that 61% had informal jobs. Among these "precarious" workers, women are also a significant majority.[6]

Based on data of this type, the ILO has reinforced the statement that the great mark of the current world labour market is precariousness: "in short, the standard employment model is less and less representative of today's world of work since fewer than one in four workers is employed in conditions corresponding to that model". On the other hand, with regard to the "productivity" of work, the same document notes "the growing divergence between labour incomes and productivity, with the latter growing faster than wages in much of the word".[7]

Combined global data, however, can hide the profound diversity of uneven capitalist development, in which very different combinations of labour relations and working-class composition can take place.

Even in countries with advanced industrial development where the employment of the workforce in the industrial sector is still significant, precariousness has tended to grow in recent years. Germany, for example, is the industrial nation with the strongest economy in Europe, accounting for 30.5% of the added value produced by the European Union. It has not de-industrialized in recent decades and maintains relatively high employment rates in industry. According to ILO data, the relative decline in employees in German industry exists, but the proportion of manufacturing employment is still higher than in most European regions and in older industrial developing countries in general. Thus, in 2000, 2.6% of the jobs were in agriculture, 33.5% in industry, and 63.8% in services. In 2016, 1.4% were in agriculture, 27.7% in industry, and 70.9% in services.[8]

Furthermore, Germany did better than its neighbours during the situation caused by the capitalist crisis started in 2007/2008. Unemployment in December 2017 was 3.6%, significantly below the European average (at the same time, Spain's unemployment was 16.6%, 10.9% in Italy, 8.9% in France). That is why the economists-propagandists of capital speak of a "German miracle".

German sociologist, Klaus Dörre, however, explains that the issue is more complex. To answer the question "what lies behind the 'German job miracle'?", Dörre presents arguments to support his answer: "a return to 'undignified', because socially demeaning, work". Or, in other words, "the 'German employment miracle' conceals the transition to a society of full but precarious employment (…), by expanding insecure working, employment and living conditions".[9] Let's follow his presentation on the precariousness of work in the most advanced European industrial economy. Precariousness, in societies of advanced capitalism, is defined by him as follows:

> workers, on account of their work and its contractual constraints, fall well below the level of welfare protection and integration set as standard by society. Employment relationships and/or work activities may also, in such cases, be subjectively associated with loss of self-esteem, lack of participation and recognition and an inability to make secure plans.[10]

The data supporting Dörre's analysis are eloquent. Even before the 2008 international crisis, "non-standard employment"—temporary and fixed-term contracts, part-time work, mini-jobs (less than 12 hours a week) grew rapidly in the German labour market, at around 46.2% in 10 years (1998–2008). In 2008, 7.7 million workers occupied these "atypical" jobs, while 22.9 million were in "standard jobs" (contracts with no fixed term, of 20 hours or more per week), and 2.1 million were self-employed. Between 2000 and 2010, the proportion of "non-standard" jobs rose from 19.8 to 25.4%. For young people, women, immigrants, and those in low-skilled jobs, the proportion was much higher.

Focusing on wages, "23% of employees in Germany work in the low-wage sector, meaning that they earn less than two-thirds of the median wage".[11] Almost all "non-standard" jobs and 10.6% of full-time jobs receive low wages. In many cases, the state subsidizes the private sector to pay low wages, supplementing the income of workers via social security, through partial unemployment insurance for around 1.3 million employed people.

The result of this process is the growth of social inequality. In 1987, according to Dörre, managers of the largest German companies earned 14 times more than the average employee. In the early 2000s, they were already earning 24 times more, and in the early 2010s they started earning 54 times more. Inequality has grown to the point that the richest 10% own more than 50% of the income in German society, while the poorest 50% only 1%.[12]

It is a little more difficult to measure the precariousness of work in the dominant capitalist economy, that of the United States, especially since labour regulation there never reached the western European levels of the times of the so-called Welfare State. Even so, some data indicate that precariousness has advanced there too. Unlike the German case, industrial employment fell from 27% of employees in 1980 to 11% in 2010.[13]

The advance of social inequality and poverty is the most terrifying fact about the "heart" of capitalism. Out of an estimated population of 325.7 million people in 2017, more than 146 million lived in poverty, according to 2016 figures, among which more than 100 million received some form of state aid. In the midst of this population classified as poor, there are a large number of employees, but with wages that are very close to the minimum wage. John Russo estimated, in 2016, that 26.6 million people—30% of workers with contracts (non-self-employed) who are 18 or older—are in this situation, many of whom are dependent on public assistance.[14]

Although precariousness is a global issue and is present even in the central capitalist economies, as we have just shown, it affects, in a different way, the countries that industrialized later and that have a higher degree of dependence to those central economies. A strong example is India.

India is a country that in the last two decades has been watching the growing predominance of urban activities over rural ones and, therefore, has been in an accelerated course of that process of expropriations typical of proletarianization described by Marx in *Capital*, when referring to primitive accumulation. According to ILO data, in 2000, 59.9% of Indian jobs were still agricultural, 16.0% were in industry, and 24.1% in services. In 2016, the agricultural occupation was reduced to 45.1%, while industry and services occupied, respectively, 24.3% and 30.6%.[15]

The precariousness of labour is mainly reflected in "informality". According to recent data, 92.3% of the employed workforce in that country is classified as "informal workers". S. K. Sasikumar explains the strength of informality, not only as a result of the predominance of employment in non-formalized companies, but also because even in the formal/organized sector of the Indian economy there is a predominance of informal labour relations:

> The persistent duality between organised and unorganised sectors (based on the definition of enterprise size, the organised sector being defined as consisting of firms and establishments which have more than 10 workers) and between formal and informal work (based on regularity of employment and access to social security) has been a matter of concern, particularly since the 1990s. In India the overwhelming proportion of workers are employed in the unorganised sector, with nearly 83% in 2011-12, albeit with a declining trend during the last decade. While the total employment in the organised sector grew from 38.89 million in 1990-2000 to 81.6 million in 2011-12, the informal jobs within the organised sector increased from 15.95 million to 47.20 million during the same period. This indicated than an overwhelming majority (nearly three-fourth) of the new jobs generated in the organised sector in the last decade are informal in nature; at present informal jobs constitute 58% of the organised sector employment. This trend is reflected clearly in organised manufacturing where there has been a sharp increase in temporary and contractual jobs, which increased from 7.6% in the 1970s to 13.2% in 1995-6 to 33.9% in 2010-11.[16]

An excellent demonstration of this tendency towards labour informality in formalized/organized industrial companies, including large Indian industries, identified by Sasikumar, can be found in Andrew Sanchez's study of the most iconic among large Indian industrial corporations, the Tata group.[17] Tata Industries are now known worldwide, especially for their most recent acquisitions on a global level, such as the purchase of British automakers Land Rover and Jaguar, in 2008. Sanchez studies the labour relations in the recent period in the group's automotive companies based in Jamshedpur.

The ventures of the Tata family began with mining under a British concession in the 1880s. In the 1910s, the Tata Iron and Steel Company (TISCO) was formally created, and to implement it an entire industrial city was built from scratch, in a jungle area, in the Sakchi region, with industrial operations starting in the 1920s. The company became a symbol of industrial capitalist development with Indian national bases, being supported by the main nationalist leaders, such as Nehru and Gandhi, even before independence. Working for TISCO in Jamshedpur represented, for decades, the example of secure employment, with family recruitment and a paternalistic network involving business and housing in the typical *company town* model. With the opening of the Indian economy in 1991 and the neoliberal reforms of the 1990s, the company had its near monopoly in the steel and metal-mechanical/automotive sector threatened. The way out was a radical productive restructuring, with the complete precariousness of the workforce. In his work, Sanchez demonstrates how Tata companies were successful in reconfiguring themselves, through the complete breakdown of the collective organization of workers, especially through the precariousness of the workforce, but also through relations of dubious legality with agents of power and unclear links with local organized crime to silence (including through assassinations) resistant union leaders. Regarding the precariousness of labour relations, the data presented by the Sanchez study are impressive:

> In the late 1990s, the proportion of non-permanent workers in Tata Motors was less than a quarter. By 2006, this number had risen dramatically; the plant division in which I conducted fieldwork classified 76 per cent of their 1,471 employees in various grades of casual and trainee employment. Although the logic of casualisation is to replace unionised employees with cheaper casual workers, Tata recruitment structures remain

> directed towards traditional company families. Recruited through the still-functioning 'wards' scheme, a casual employee is invariability the son or sibling of a permanent worker employed in the very same division of the plant, suggesting a persistence of the Tata family despite changing patterns of employment.[18]

However, as the same study demonstrates, the wages of an "apprentice" or "intern", categories in which precarious workers are hired temporarily, were around 19% and 30% of the amount received by workers with a stable contract, with the addition that the precarious workers were still excluded from union representation.

Very low wages and the absence of union representation (or representation by unions fully controlled by the state and companies) are clear indicators of precariousness. In recent decades, the most populous country in the world (at least in official statistics, which give it a larger population than India), China, was seen as the greatest example of large-scale industrialization based on the exploitation of a working-class subject to very low wages.

The incorporation of huge contingents of workers to industrial companies installed in China in recent decades is a fact. According to the ILO, in 2000, half of the occupations were still in agriculture (50.3%), while industry accounted for 18.8% and services for 30.9%. In 2016, the change was already brutal, with 27.8% of jobs in agricultural activities, 23.9% in industries, and 48.3% in services.[19] Chinese statistic data further accentuate industrial concentration. Out of an estimated total population of 1.35 billion people, the workforce employed in 2011 was 764.2 million (almost a quarter of the world's workforce), with 359.14 million in cities and 405 million in rural areas. Using different criteria than the ILO, these statistics show 34.8% of jobs in the primary sector (agriculture), 29.5% in the secondary (industry), and 35.7% in services. An important data for the discussion is the reference, in the same sources, to 252.78 million migrant workers, 158.63 million among them working outside their province.[20]

Paula Nabuco analyzed the specific relationship between this migration process whose absolute dimensions are unprecedented in human history and the specificity of labour relations in large Chinese industries.[21] Since the reforms and economic opening of the 1990s, China has experienced such massive migration, in a movement that is not only directed from the countryside (mainly from the central region) to the city, but is specially designed to provide peasant's sons and daughters as workforce for the large and new industries (many of predominant foreign investment) installed in the east and south regions of the country.

Since 1958, China has adopted a system of residence registration (*hukou*) that sought to establish the population in its provinces, also establishing controls over the workforce, according to its origin and urban or rural employment, in order to ensure that the development of the country's industrial sector did not occur at the expense of excessive migratory flows from the countryside to the city, as did the capitalist industrialization throughout the world.[22]

Starting in the 1990s, however, these controls have been loosened, but the *hukou* system has not been abolished, although some provinces have recently begun to allow registration changes. Thus, migrant workers cannot use public services (schools, hospitals, etc.) and access other rights outside their provinces of origin. Recruitment systems were established between demanding provinces and other provinces supplying this migrant workforce, resembling the *coolie* model in the nineteenth century. The result is that these migrants are forced to submit to exploitative regimes based on long hours and lower wages, most often in factory-room systems, where places of residence and work (and confinement) are obscured.

The weight of this process on the Chinese economy is undeniable. According to Nabuco, "migrant labour and the income that migrated peasants sent to their provinces of origin represented 16% of the growth in Chinese gross domestic product (GDP) between 1987 and 2005".[23] In the most dynamic centres of industrialization in that country, this relationship is even more expressive. Within them, the combination of gender and ethnic origin ranks the degree of exploitation of the workforce. Women are preferred in the electronics industry for their anatomy and ability to work with microcomponents, but also because they are considered more sensible. Although a majority in the production lines, they rarely occupy managerial positions. Provincial origins (with their respective linguistic, cultural distinctions, and historical prejudices) are also elements that define the organization of work teams and the managerial hierarchy in the production process. Thus, according to Nabuco:

> Guangdong province, the great laboratory of reforms, has approximately 110 million inhabitants, with at least 400,000 factories and three Special Economic Zones. Of the total local workforce, the majority is female and

> migrant. Currently these workers make up about 60% of the total migrant workers [outside their home provinces] in China.[24]

Thus, there are a set of factors responsible for the subordination and dependence of the workforce on capital at very high levels, rather than simply lower wage levels; that explains the success (from the point of view of capital) of the recent Chinese industrializing leap. In fact, it is worth noting that wage levels in Chinese industry are not that low anymore. According to a survey released in 2017, and widely commented on in the world press, the average wage of Chinese industrial workers tripled between 2005 and 2016, from US$ 1.20 to US$ 3.60 per hour. These values are higher than those of workers in almost all of Latin America (with the exception of Chile). In Brazil, for example, the hourly wage of factory workers declined from US$ 2.90 to US$ 2.70 between 2007 and 2017.[25]

These values must be carefully analyzed, as they are highly influenced by exchange rate variation, but it is undeniable that, despite the high degree of subordination of the workforce, Chinese industrial wages have been rising as a result of very numerous collective struggles of the working class in that country, with an emphasis on strikes and other collective protests in companies. Marcel van der Linden has compiled data that demonstrate the growth of social struggles in China since 2004. Not only was there a numerical expansion, but the focus of demands has also changed: from labour rights to higher wages and better working conditions. According to him:

> The Chinese Academy of Social Sciences reported that there were more than 60,000 so-called 'mass incidents' (popular protests by waged workers and others, such as peasants and the quasi-religious group Falun Gong) in 2006, and over 80,000 in 2007. Since then, official figures on 'mass incidents' have no longer been published but experts believe that in recent years the number has further increased.[26]

Despite all the precariousness, labour conflicts have also increased in India in recent years. Since 1991, when neoliberal reforms began, until 2017, India has experienced 17 general strikes. The largest of them, probably the largest in the history of humanity so far, considering the number of strikers, took place on 2 September 2016, when between 150 and 180 million people stopped work across the country. Although only 4% of the workforce is unionized today, part of the unions has made an effort to organize not only formal workers, but also to support the organization and struggles of the overwhelming majority of informal workers.[27]

To resume, if the labour market, in its global dimension, is currently marked by precariousness, there are social sectors that are more affected, such as women and young people, and late industrialized countries are an even more fertile ground for the precariousness of labour relations.

However, even in the earliest and most advanced industrial development countries, this asymmetry in labour relations can be verified, not only in terms of generations or gender, but also in terms of ethnicity. Migratory flows are tremendous today, as we saw in the case of internal migrations in China, but they occur in many other regions and directions. Concerning earlier industrialized countries, migration is now a vital element in securing new supplies of the key commodity: labour power.

According to the OECD, migrants were responsible for 47% of the growth of the workforce in the United States and for 70% in Europe, between the years 2002 and 2012. The same report highlights the advantages of migration to countries with a more advanced capitalist development, among which the filling of "niches" in the labour market and its contribution to their "flexibility".[28] By "niche" markets we should understand that they are jobs with lower qualification requirements and lower pay, and "flexibility", as we know, is the sweetened term for contractual relationships with less guarantees for employees.

In Europe, where the issue of migration generates heated debates, 2017 data indicated that there are 35.1 million immigrants from outside the European Union (20.7% of them without citizenship in their countries of residence) and 19.3 million born in other EU countries. Even so, despite all the boasting, according to official data, only 4.1% of the population residing in the 28 countries of the European Union is made up of immigrants from other regions of the world who do not have European citizenship. Unemployment is the most eloquent fact of the precariousness of migrants in the labour market. In 2015, for a 9.2% unemployment rate among the population aged 20 to 64 in the 28 countries, non-citizens of the EU experienced 18.9% unemployment in the same age group. Among non-citizens, higher rates of temporary and part-time jobs are also observed.[29]

The positive contribution of migrants to the national economies of destination is beyond dispute due to the cold economic data. In many European countries, with their ageing native population and very low birth rates, the expectation is that only immigration flows could guarantee a labour supply to preserve the "natural (im)balance" of the capitalist labour market. In Portugal, for example, estimates have been released that, without immigration, the country's population will decline from the current 10.4 million inhabitants to 7.8 million in 2060.[30] Despite all the political rhetoric of the political right, that migrants steal jobs and enjoy the benefits of a Welfare State paid by taxpayers in the richest countries, the reverse is true. Data from a study on the United Kingdom showed that:

> Immigrants from [EU] member states who entered the country between 2000 and 2011 contributed 34% more in taxes than they received benefits and support from the UK Government. On the other hand, immigrants from outside the European Community contributed 2% more in taxes than they received in support. Interestingly, the same cannot be said of those born in England: on average, taxes paid by the British were 11% lower than the benefits received.[31]

Immigration therefore acts, most of the times, as an expansion factor of relative surplus-population and, for this very reason, job insecurity is very high among the contingents of workers who migrate. Still, the competition for jobs between immigrants and locals is, in most cases, not direct, as immigrants tend to occupy the "niches" of lower pay, which attract few local male and female workers, or in very specific situations they are recruited into highly skilled jobs for which local companies face an absolute shortage of skilled labour.

There are, however, situations in which even precarious work is a soft term. This is the case of forced labour relations and all sorts of modern forms of slavery. Immigrants, not by chance, are among the groups most vulnerable to the various forms of forced labour, which are perceived as "slavery-like labour", or "modern slavery". The 2016 edition of the *Global Slavery Index*, published by the *Walk Free Foundation*, estimates that worldwide there are 45.8 million people under modern slavery.[32] ILO's concepts and data on the subject are more conservative, registering 21 million "forced labourers". Still, they are important for revealing that 90% of these workers are enslaved by private companies, generating around US$150 billion in annual (illegal) profits.[33]

Regarding another cruel aspect of the labour market, the ILO's data from 2015 indicate that 168 million children are subjected to child labour in the world, among which 120 million are aged between five and fourteen. Five million children are under modern slavery, according to this same source.[34] It is curious (and hateful) to associate the data and realize that the jobs occupied by children who should be in schools are equivalent to almost 85% of the number of unemployed people in the world.

This data about the world of labour today, although very superficial, help to understand how, according to reports by the British non-governmental organization Oxfam, the richest 1% of the world's population holds the same amount of wealth as the remaining 99%. The 2017 version of the report drew even more attention by showing that the world's eight biggest billionaires hold property worth US$426 billion, equivalent to half the world's population (approximately 3.7 billion people).[35]

Among late industrialized countries, Brazil is one of the champions of inequality. Let us then approach the current picture of the working class in Brazil more attentively, in order to understand this picture of inequality.

Workers of Brazil!

In 2021, Brazil had more than 213.5 million inhabitants. Data from the 2010 census indicate that 84% of the Brazilian population resided in cities, versus 16% in the countryside. This picture contrasts sharply with the picture of the country a few decades ago. In 1940, only 31.2% of the 41,236,315 residents in the country lived in cities. It was only in the 1960s that the urban population surpassed the rural one. In 1970, 55.9% of the 93,139,037 people surveyed lived in cities.[36]

IBGE's 2015 National Household Sample Survey (PNAD), indicated that 13.9% of the employed population was linked to agricultural activities, 21.5% to industrial activities and 64.5% to services.[37] This implies recognizing that the working class in Brazil is deeply concentrated in the urban environment, but that this concentration took place rather quickly in the last decades of the twentieth century. This has had direct implications for life in large cities, which grew a lot in a short period of time, experiencing all kinds of social contradictions resulting from this swelling, as well as for the experience and culture of the class, whose composition still holds strong marks of life in the countryside, both individually and through older generations of the family who are still alive. Regarding these and all other data gathered below, the regional differences are immense, and we would not be able to account for them in such a short space. We will focus here on the major portion of the urban workforce.

Labour legislation in Brazil, since the 1930s, establishes that registration with a "work card" as a basis for recognizing labour rights. Initially restricted to urban workers, they were extended to rural workers only in the 1960s and 1970s, when they were already becoming a minority. Even numerically significant urban categories, such as domestic workers, have only recently been affected by this legislation. Such rights (working hours limitation, weekly rest and paid vacations, higher pay for overtime, regulation of hazardous, unhealthy work, etc.), which characterize "formal work" in the country were, from a legal point of view, therefore, conquered very slowly and by minority sectors of the working class until recently. It should also be considered that many workers, especially among the least qualified and worst paid groups, have experiences of transit between formally registered and unregistered work.

Informality in the Brazilian labour market is considered structural. In 2019. it reached 41.6% of the country's workers, or 39.3 million people. In the 1990s, the data were even more negative. In 1999, for example, wage earners with a formal contract were only 44.7% of the total, versus 26.9% without a formal contract and 23.5% self-employed. Over a period of about ten years, there was an increase in the percentage of formalized workers in the private sector (from 39.7% of those employed in 2003 to 49.2% in 2012).[38] Another way of perceiving the absence of workers' rights is to observe that in 2015, 62% of the employed contributed to social security. Thus, disregarding the 3.7% of employers, it was found that more than 40% workers did not contribute and were therefore excluded from social security rights and could at best be covered in future with assistance benefits from the social security system.

Considering unemployment rates, surveys by the IBGE (Continuous PNAD) calculated the average number of the unemployed in 2016 at 11.5%, 12.7% in 2017, 12.3% in 2018, 11.9% in 2019, and 13.5% in 2020. The composite rate of underutilization of the workforce reached 28.7% at the end of 2020. Such rate, which is composed of underemployed due to insufficient hours worked; unemployed and those who are part of the potential workforce, facilitates the understanding of the degree of insecurity in relation to the labour market.

However, this insecurity is unevenly experienced within the class. The same IBGE survey also shows a difference in the unemployment rate of men and women at the end of 2020. The percentage was 11.9% among men and 16.4% among women. According to the racial classification of the Institute, among black people, the rate was 17.2%, while that of brown people was 15.8%, both above the national average (13.9%). The rate for whites (11.5%) was below average. Data from 2019 show that, among employed people, the percentage of blacks or browns in informal occupations was 47.4%, while among white workers it was 34.5%. These indicators reflect the greater participation of the black and brown population in jobs characteristic of informality, such as agricultural activities, which had 62.7% of black or brown workers, construction, with 65.2%, and domestic services (where the vast majority are women), with 66.6%. Gender and race therefore have a very significant weight in the experience of unemployment.

Unemployment rose in Brazil from the 1990s onwards and constitutes an important factor for us to understand how the advance of the precariousness of labour relations has found fertile ground since then. Adding the "informally occupied" to the unemployed, we have an idea of the degree of precariousness of labour relations and the fragmentation of the working class in its urban majority contingent. But formal workers can also experience precarious work conditions.

Outsourcing data would help us complete the picture of this precariousness process. We don't find it in the form of general statistics. It was estimated, in 2011, that about 12 million employees (in an Economically Active Population of 105 million people) were outsourced workers, that is, formally hired, but through service providers for the companies they actually work for, with lower wages and less access to rights.[39]

Extreme poverty in the country reached 6.5% of the population in 2019, according to the international line set by the World Bank at US$ 1.90 a day. Among people below the World Bank's poverty lines, 70% were black or brown, while the population that self-declared as such was 56.3% of the total population. Poverty affected black or brown women even more: they were 28.7% of the population, but 39.8% of the extremely poor and 38.1% of the poor.

Poverty reflects the extremely low remuneration of the labour power in Brazil. In 2019, the average household income per capita was R$1,406 for the total Brazilian population. The national minimum wage that year was R$ 998.[40] However, 11.8% of the Brazilian population lived with up to a quarter of a monthly *per capita* minimum wage (approximately R$250) and almost 30% on up to half the per capita minimum wage (R$499).

This is the starting point for Ruy Braga's analysis, for whom the new jobs created between 2003 and 2013 were basically low-wage jobs, because of the "2.1 million new jobs created per year, around 2 million remunerate the worker up to 1.5 minimum wages. Here's the secret of jumping jacks: growth supported by cheap labour".[41]

While in the world, 8 billionaires currently hold the same amount of wealth as half of the planet's population, in Brazil, a champion of inequality, the picture is even worse: there are six billionaires who hold wealth equivalent to half the population (more than 100 million people).[42]

Valério Arcary comments on data such as those from surveys by the Institute for Applied Economic Research (IPEA) which indicate that the richest 1% of the population had an income equivalent to the poorest 50%, combined with the finding that the difference in income between those who live on wages has fallen in recent years, although the gap between the share of GDP and national wealth appropriated by capital in relation to that appropriated by labour has increased (the share of labour in national income fell from 45.4% in 1990 to 41.7% in 2008). Therefore, he concludes that: "in the last twenty years, workers have taken a smaller share of the national wealth and capital has taken a larger share, but among wage earners the wage gap has decreased because, at the same time, the base of the manual wage has increased, and the base level of the highly educated wage has fallen".[43]

In an attempt to establish comparative parameters, according to an OECD study, Brazil, in 2013, continued to present the second worst income distribution when compared to its fellow 34 member countries (Brazil, although participating in the Organization's forums, is not a member country), being preceded only by Mexico.[44] The Gini Index of 0.543 in 2019 makes Brazil the ninth most unequal country in the world, according to the World Bank.

Moving from working conditions and remuneration to living conditions, there is no single indicator that can summarize all the aspects involved. We can start from the Human Development Index (HDI), which combines income, education, and longevity rates. Although its income indicator is GDP per capita (unable to capture inequality in distribution), this index has become a reference and allows for some comparisons. For example, in relation to other countries, Brazil's negative position is noticeable, with a lower HDI than its neighbours Argentina, Chile, and Venezuela. In South America, its index is only higher than that of Paraguay. With a 0.807 HDI, Brazil was, in 2006, in the 70th position in the world ranking organized by the UN, which contrasts with its economy, considered to be among the ten largest in the world. This indicator, taken only in its national dimension, is nevertheless extremely misleading. When we look at the metropolitan regions we realize why. In the Rio metropolitan area, for example, with its almost 12 million inhabitants, the HDI of the city of Rio de Janeiro was 0.842 in 2000, but that of the city of Japeri, in Baixada Fluminense, was 0.724. Inside big cities, the contrast becomes even more evident. In the city of Rio de Janeiro, the HDI for the upscale neighbourhood of Gávea was 0.970. In the Acari favela, this index dropped to 0.720.

Focusing on housing indicators, the Ministry of Cities pointed to a housing deficit of 7,935,000 houses, 6,543,000 of which in cities, according to estimated data for 2006. In other words, more than 30 million Brazilians lived more directly with the problem of lack of housing in the country. Hence, it is not difficult to explain that, in 2010, the IBGE Census registered 6,329 favelas in the country ("subnormal agglomerations", in the somewhat politically correct technical definition of the census, which is more restrictive than other surveys on the subject). In the country's total population, the total number of slum dwellers was equivalent to 6%. In Belém, slum dwellers accounted for 54% of the city's total. In São Paulo, they were 11% of the total. The 763 favelas in the city of Rio de Janeiro (48.4% more than in 2000) concentrate almost a quarter (22%) of the city's inhabitants—1.39 million of the 6.2 million—making up the largest favela population in the country. Other data on living conditions would be important, but the information gathered so far seems to be sufficient for a first approximation to the symptoms of the visible social inequality prevailing in this capitalist periphery.

Given this quick overview of data about the working class in Brazil and in the world, we can return to the categories of analysis discussed in the first part of this book, confronting them with concrete reality.

Returning to Marx

Taking into account the elements presented above to synthesize the theoretical approach on the working class inaugurated by Marx and Engels and confronting them with the contemporary picture, many discussions seem to make as much sense today as they did in the time they were writing them. For example, we can recall the theses of *Capital*, associated with the idea of "the general law of capitalist accumulation", which we discussed earlier. This is the case of that statement by Marx according to which "accumulation of capital is, therefore, [an] increase of the proletariat", which still continues today, globally, given that the growth of the workforce available for capitalist exploitation has accelerated in recent decades. The contingent of more than three billion employed people is complemented by more than 200 million unemployed, which also recalls another Marxian thesis related to the "general law of accumulation": one that states that "the whole form of the movement of modern industry depends, therefore, upon the constant transformation of a part of the labouring population into unemployed or half-employed hands".[45] Certainly, data on poverty, hunger, and *favelas* (slums), among many others on the conditions of existence of the proletariat in the world (and in Brazil) today must arise as much indignation as the records of his time aroused in Marx and can still be illuminated by the analyses and "illustrations" he presented in *Capital*, concerning the British and Irish working class in the 1840s to 1860s.

From the estimates available for the planet, it is possible to see that the relative weight of productive workers—those who produce surplus value, which, as we have seen, are not restricted to factory workers—in the global workforce behaves quite unequally. International statistics do not contemplate the broadness of the meaning of the category "productive labour" in Marx, allowing us only an approximation based on the data on employment in the manufacturing industry. In Marx, as we have seen, productive labour involved many other sectors of the class, which statistics compute as service workers and even agricultural workers. Then, in view of this limitation, there has been a decline in the percentage of employees in factories in most countries with older industrial development, where agricultural work has very little weight and the service sector has grown significantly in recent decades. But we also observe that, in the more densely populated regions of the South of the globe, there has been tremendous recent industrial expansion, which has supported absolute growth and a relative equilibrium in the number and percentage, respectively, of industrial workers on a global scale. It is worth remembering, however, that the relative decline of productive employment (producer of surplus value) is not foreign to the discussion developed by

Marx. As already mentioned, in *Capital*, Marx states that "the extraordinary productiveness of modern industry (…) allows of the unproductive employment of a larger and larger part of the working class."[46]

Still, the more than 200 million Chinese employed in factories are a good indicator that global capitalism can be more "financialized", but it cannot do without extracting more value in increasing amounts in the production process. In other words, the factory worker is far from disappearing, in this as in other parts of the world. And they are still in movement.

However, let us again remember Marx, it is not only in the factory where we must look for the working class and, therefore, the potential subject of the revolutionary transformation of society. The proletariat is much broader and involves productive and unproductive workers, employed and unemployed, formal and informal, more or less precarious (although proletarianization always involves precariousness to some degree), regular wage earners or not. Despite the undeniable retreat of working-class mobilizations and their political weight, especially in the countries of the global North, since the 1980s, a topic to which we will return later, there are many ongoing movements led by this collective subject, as demonstrated by factory strikes, or the Indian general strike of 2016, among many other examples. It seems to us, for all that, that it remains valid to claim—with all the mediations of the political-ideological countertrends that limit social conflict—the relevance of that conclusion presented by Marx in his study of "primitive accumulation" in *Capital*, that we see the growth of "the mass of misery, oppression, slavery, degradation, exploitation; but with this too grows the revolt of the working class".[47]

The use of Marx's observations also allows us to explain more satisfactorily the apparent unevenness pointed out by the ILO through the observation of "the growing divergence between labour incomes and productivity, with the latter growing faster than wages in much of the world".[48] More than a mismatch, this is the very systemic logic of capitalist accumulation that Marx explains in his work. After all, the perspective presented in *Capital* allows us to better discern the contradictory dynamics through which capitalist uncontrollable impulse for accumulation always depends on a process of incessant transformation of human groups into proletarianized masses, although it tends to generate an also growing relative surplus-population, as well as pauperism (absolute and/or relative) which aggravates the so-called social issue.

In short, from the point of view expressed here, the understanding of the current reality can only gain from the categories of analysis and the method employed by Marx to apprehend the formation and composition of the working class amid conflicting capitalist social relations. However, from a partial (and, we could provocatively say, Eurocentric) view of changes in the composition and living and working conditions of workers, many analyses reached hypotheses and conclusions centred on a supposed decline, or even an end, of the working class. To arrive at such an assessment, as we will see below, they often consider what have always been exceptions as the rule in defining the class: "standard employment relations" in force for a minority of countries and workers (mostly men), in the period of the so-called thirty "glorious years" of the post-war period.[49]

We then proceed to examine some of these theses, comparing them with the references synthesized so far from the work of Marx and Engels, as well as with some more contemporary formulations in the field of historical materialism.

Notes

1. World population data and future growth prospects can be found in the UN report, *United Nations, Department of Economic and Social Affairs, Population Division (2019). World Population Prospects 2019: Highlights.* (ST/ESA/SER.A/423).
2. United Nations, Department of Economic and Social Affairs, Population Division (2019). *World Urbanization Prospects 2018: Highlights* (ST/ESA/SER.A/421).
3. According to World Bank data from various topics related to employment and gender, available in their digital database http://data.worldbank.org, accessed in August 2021. See also International Labour Organization, *World Employment and Social Outlook: Trends 2020*, Geneva, ILO, 2020.
4. ILO, *World Employment, and Social Outlook 2015: The Changing Nature of Jobs*, Geneva, ILO, 2015, p. 13.
5. Ibid., p. 18.
6. The precariousness of work is reinforced by the current forms of neoliberal "deregulation" of labour relations, but it is possible to see that working women were the majority among all precarious workers even at the time when the most advanced capitalist

economies lived under the domination (among men, especially white) of regular employment with guarantees from the Welfare State, as in the so-called glorious years of the post-European war. In this regard, see Eloisa Betti, "Gender and Precarious Labor in a Historical Perspective", *International Labour and Working-Class History*, Vol. 89, 2016, 64–83.

7. ILO, *World Employment, and Social Outlook 2015*, p. 13.
8. According to http://www.ilo.org/global/statistics-and-databases/lang--en/index.htm, accessed in June 2017.
9. Klaus Dörre, *The German Job Miracle: A Model to Europe?*, Brussels, Rosa Luxemburg Stiftung, 2014, p. 19 and 33.
10. Ibid., p. 17.
11. Ibid., p. 21.
12. Ibid., p. 34.
13. Kim Moody, The State of American Labor, *Jacobin*, June 2016, in https://www.jacobinmag.com/2016/06/precariat-labor-us-workers-uber-walmart-gig-economy/, accessed in January 2018. According to ILO data, the configuration of the American labour market is slightly distinct: in 2000, ILO estimates that 2.5% of the jobs were agricultural, 22.5% industrial, and 75% in services. In 2016, the estimates were 1.5% in agriculture, 17.2% in industry, and 81.3% in services. According to http://www.ilo.org/global/statistics-and-databases/lang--en/index.htm, accessed in June 2017.
14. John Russo, Poverty and Precarious work, *Laboronline*, 7/09/2016, at https://www.lawcha.org/2016/09/07/poverty-precarious-work/, accessed in January 2018.
15. According to http://www.ilo.org/global/statistics-and-databases/lang--en/index.htm, accessed in June 2017.
16. S. K. Sasikumar, "India's Labour and Employment Scenario: An Overview", *India Handbook of Labour*, Noida, V. V. Giri National Labour Institute, 2015, p. 20.
17. Andrew Sanchez, *Criminal Capital: Violence, Corruption and Class in Industrial India*, New Delhi, Routledge, 2016.
18. Ibid., p. 19.
19. According to http://www.ilo.org/global/statistics-and-databases/lang--en/index.htm, accessed in June 2017.
20. Labour statistics in China are available at https://www.statista.com/topics/1317/employment-in-china/, accessed in June

2017. I used the systematization presented by Gabriel Casoni, "Uma nota sobre a classe trabalhadora brasileira", available at http://maismovimento.org/2017/03/13/uma-nota-sobre-a-classe-trabalhadora-brasileira/#sdfootnote44anc, accessed in June 2017.

21. Paula Nabuco, "Hukou e migração na China: alguns apontamentos sobre divisão do trabalho", *Revista de Economia Contemporânea*, Vol. 16, No. 2, 237–258.
22. Ibid., p. 240.
23. Ibid., p. 242.
24. Ibid., p. 244.
25. João Pedro Caleiro, "Trabalhador industrial brasileiro ganha menos do que um chinês", in *Exame*, 02/03/2017, conforme http://exame.abril.com.br/economia/trabalhador-industrial-brasileiro-ganha-menos-que-um-chines/, accessed in July 2017.
26. Marcel van der Linden, "Global Labour: A Not-so-grand Finale and Perhaps a New Beginning", *Global Labour Journal*, Vol. 7, No. 2, 2016, p. 207. Sobre as greves na China, ver também Paula Nabuco, "As 'recentes' greves na China", *Revista Outubro*, Vol. 20, 2012.
27. Vijay Prashad, "India Is Making Labour History with the World's Largest General Strike", 07/09/2016, according to https://www.alternet.org/2016/09/india-worlds-largest-strike/, accesses in July 2017.
28. OCDE, *Migration Policy Debates*, May 2014, pp. 1–2.
29. The data in this paragraph come from the report *Eurostat, Migrant Integration*, 2017, pp. 14–29. Available at https://ec.europa.eu/eurostat/documents/3217494/8787947/KS-05-17-100-EN-N.pdf/f6c45af2-6c4f-4ca0-b547-d25e6ef9c359, accessed in August, 2021.
30. According to https://fronteirasxxi.pt/migracoes/, accessed in July 2017.
31. Data from a study conducted by Christian Dustmann and Tommaso Frattini, quoted by Joana Ferreira da Costa, "Imigrantes: como os estudos desmentem mitos de ameaça ao emprego e à economia", available at https://fronteirasxxi.pt/estudos-imigracao/, accessed in July 2017.

32. Walk Free Found, *Global Slavery Index*, 2016, http://downloads.globalslaveryindex.org/GSI-2016-Full-Report-1500913375.pdf, accessed in July 2017.
33. According to http://www.ilo.org/brasilia/temas/trabalho-escravo/lang--pt/index.htm, accessed in July 2017. For more: https://www.ilo.org/global/topics/forced-labour/lang--en/index.htm, accessed in August 2021.
34. OIT, *World Report on Child Labour 2015: Paving the Way to Decent Work for Young People*, Genebra, OIT, 2015. Available at http://www.ilo.org/ipec/Informationresources/WCMS_358969/lang--en/index.htm. Accessed in March 2017.
35. Oxfam's report, "An economy for the 99%", can be found at https://www.oxfam.org/en/research/economy-99, accessed in February 2017.
36. Any not explicitly referenced quantitative data come from the Brazilian Institute of Geography and Statistics (IBGE) and can be accessed at www.ibge.gov.br.
37. As a basis for comparison with the world data cited, the ILO estimates that for 2019 the distribution of the workforce in Brazil as 9.08% in agriculture, 19.99% in industry and 70.94% in services. According to http://www.ilo.org/global/statistics-and-databases/lang--en/index.htm, accessed in August 2021.
38. The growth in formalization has reversed in recent years. In 2017, the IBGE registered 34.31 million people working self-employed or without a formal contract, against 33.321 million employed in formal positions.
39. See, for example, the estimates presented by a Labour Court, at http://www.trt23.jus.br/tnt/2012_08_10/fique_sabendo.html, accessed in February 2014.
40. Exchange rate fluctuations can distort comparisons, but in January 2019, this value corresponded to around U$ 260.00.
41. Ruy Braga, "A maldição do trabalho barato", 13/08/2012, in http://blogdaboitempo.com.br/2012/08/13/a-maldicao-do-trabalho-barato/, accessed in July 2013.
42. According to Oxfam's survey for Brazil, at https://www.oxfam.org.br, accessed in August 2021.
43. Valério Arcary, *Um reformismo quase sem reformas: uma crítica marxista do governo Lula em defesa da revolução brasileira*, São Paulo, Sundermann, 2011, p. 49.

44. Marcelo Corrêa, "Brasil tem segunda pior distribuição de renda em ranking da OCDE", 19/03/2013, at http://oglobo.globo.com/economia/brasil-tem-segunda-pior-distribuicao-de-renda-em-ranking-da-ocde-7887116, accessed in September 2017.
45. *MECW*, vol. 35, p. 627.
46. Ibid., p. 449.
47. Ibid., p. 832.
48. ILO, *World Employment, and Social Outlook 2015*, p. 13.
49. Marcel van der Linden, in an analysis that places the current picture in a long-term historical perspective and in a non-Eurocentric perspective, calls attention to the fact that that model of "standard employment" under capitalist conditions was a "historical anomaly". Marcel van der Linden, "San Precario: A New Inspiration for Labor Historians", *Labor: Studies in Working-Class History of the Americas*, Vol. 11, No. 1, 2014, p. 19.

CHAPTER 4

The Debate on the Working Class Today

Class Exhaustion?

In the first part of this book, the objective was to synthesize the concept of working class that emerges from the work of Marx and Engels, in the second part a summary characterization of the current profile of the class, on a global and local scale, was confronted with that conception originating from historical materialism to assess its analytical validity in contemporaneity. On our part, the answer to the question posed here is affirmative, that is, the hypothesis supported in this book is that the analytical perspective based on historical materialism in its emphasis on the working class as a category of analysis and as a political subject remains valid. In this third part of the exhibition, the objective is similar, but the debate takes place on another level, centred on the critique of approaches built in recent decades which deny the working class a role as a historical subject of a transformation project, in certain cases even denying its objective relevance to capitalist accumulation today.

The most recent changes in the profile of the workforce, which we have sought to summarize in the preceding pages, reflect some contemporary capitalist processes. Since the capitalist crisis that began in the 1970s, the exits sought by capital have led to significant changes in the distribution of capitalist investments and the workforce around the world, as

M. B. Mattos, *The Working Class from Marx to Our Times*, Marx, Engels, and Marxisms,
https://doi.org/10.1007/978-3-030-97355-1_4

well as in the organic composition of capital and the form of organization and management of labour relations in companies, accompanied by an internationally concerted political action to withdraw labour and social rights, including a good part of those that characterized the so-called Welfare State, whose validity, we have already stated, was limited to certain national, especially European, formations. These and other characteristics of change in the dynamics of capitalist accumulation were defined from expressions, used with more or less weight as categories of analysis, such as: globalization, productive restructuring, and neoliberal policies.

These processes had a very negative impact on the organizations and struggles of the working class, with a visible decrease in the percentage of unionized workers,[1] in addition to a significant decline in the volume of strikes and other struggles (since the defeat of the miners' strike in 1984), especially in older industrial developing countries.[2] Of course, subjective reasons also explain this retreat. Among others, social democracy and Stalinism of the official Communist Parties failed to present themselves as references to the left since the fall of the Eastern European regimes and onwards, at the turn of the 1990s. There are, however, previous roots to explain the bankruptcy of the social-democratic pact, which generated in Western European countries—with significant differences between them—the Welfare State model in the three decades following the end of World War II. In view of the crisis of the 1970s, in various national situations, private sector labour unions, especially in the branches most directly affected by plant closures, sought agreements through social consultation in three-part mechanisms (business representatives, workers unions, and the State), that set wage and/or early retirement guarantees based on public social security funds. Such agreements, although confirming social security guarantees for a more mature generation of part of the formally employed working class of native-born origin, opened up scope for the intensification of precariousness among the less formalized groups in other sectors of the economy and this hit the new generations, those that entered the labour market from the 1990s onwards and immigrants, the hardest.[3]

Faced with such transformations in the organization of production, changes (unequally perceived according to the region of the world) in the composition of the class and the retreat of institutions and traditional class politics and union action, many analysts began to speak of an exhaustion of the possibilities of analysis of contemporary social reality (and the proposition of political alternatives) based on class criteria.

For some, the changes indicated the "end of the centrality of labour", in its use as a category of analysis or in the life experience of most of the population. To explain this phenomenon, a cumulative argument was used: among the contingent of people able to work, in each country of advanced industrialization, those who work were a minority (pensioners, students, housewives, among other groups, added up to the majority); among these, many have irregular jobs, or live off small businesses and self-employment, in addition to being unemployed for a long time; and among those who work regularly, the workday needed to maintain the volume of production of goods was ever more shorter, creating an expectation for a reduction in the workload and expansion of free time for vacations, leisure, and family life, which would consume the majority of the time and concerns of these workers. Claus Offe was one of the authors who, even in the 1980s, theorized about the end of the "labour society", stating that:

> contemporary forms of social activity normally designated as 'work' do not have a common rationality or shared empirical characteristics, and (...) in this sense work is not only objectively amorphous but is also becoming subjectively peripheral.[4]

Interestingly, Offe reached these conclusions in an advanced industrial economy such as Germany's, where employment levels and the occupational distribution of the working class across different sectors of the economy had changed little in that first decade of restructuring. In other words, his empirical bases for projecting the "end of labour" were, at the very least, very fluid projections.

Others reached very similar conclusions, adding more emphasis to the subjective element, to affirm an exhaustion of the proposal of social transformation centred on workers as the main actors. On a different path than Offe's, a few years earlier, in France, André Gorz understood that the new productive technologies would open up the possibility of a reduction in working time and enable the construction of a sociability full of meanings outside the work environment. The protagonists of a change of this type, however, would not be the workers, but, according to Gorz, they should be "the non-class of non-workers". According to him, the historical subject identified by Marxism and, consequently, Marxism itself, lacked transformative potential:

> There is a crisis in Marxist thinking because a crisis has developed within the labour movement. Over the past 20 years, the link between the development of the productive forces and the growth of class antagonism has been broken. (...) In fact, capitalist development has produced a working class which, on the whole, in unable to take command of the means of production and whose immediate interests are not consonant with a socialist rationality. This is the present state of affairs. Capitalism has called into being a working class (or, more loosely, a mass of wage earners) whose interests, capacities and skills are functional to the existing productive forces, which themselves are functional solely to the rationality of capital.[5]

The idea that the working class was not an antagonist of capital, but was—from the beginning, or due to the historical unfolding of capitalist development—inexorably committed to the reproduction of capitalism, gained more supporters in the following years. At the end of the 1990s, the perspective that productive restructuring, with the recent accentuated technological development, would lead to the inexorable overcoming of living labour by dead labour, in addition to this emphasis on the assertion that the working class is (was and always will be) "functional" to capitalism, with no revolutionary potential, was taken up again by the Krisis group's *Manifesto against Labour*, whose main herald was for some time Robert Kurz. Assuming a point of view of radical criticism of capitalist society, this proposal presented a programme of denial of labour and the political way to overcome it—understanding politics as an action aimed at the State. The starting point of the *Manifesto* was also, as in Offe or Gorz's statements in the previous decade, an affirmation of the imminent death of the labour society, based on the observation of ongoing technological changes. The entire ideological force of the valorisation of labour, which crossed actors such as the bourgeoisie in its neoliberal phase and the traditional unionist in its cry for more jobs, corresponded precisely to the phase in which the labour crisis would find itself in a terminal stage:

> A corpse rules society – the corpse of labour (...). In the wake of the microelectronic revolution, wealth production increasingly became independent from the actual expenditure of human labour power to an extent quite recently only imaginable in science fiction. No one can seriously maintain any longer that this process can be halted or reversed. Selling the commodity labour power in the 21st century is as promising as the sale of stagecoaches has proved to be in the 20th century.[6]

The termination of work resulted from a dictatorship of labour as an abstraction. The ongoing technological transformations decreed the end of any utopian possibility based on labour (and, therefore, on workers, who were also condemned to perish). The categorical distinctions between productive labour (which generates surplus value) and unproductive labour (which does not generate surplus value), as well as between concrete labour (creator of use values, humanity's sociometabolism with nature, etc.) and abstract labour (producer of exchange values, subsumed under capital, estranged/alienated, etc.), present in Marx's work, are neglected by an analysis of this type. Afterall:

> for the first time, the speed of process innovation is greater than the speed of product innovation. More labour is rationalised away than can be reabsorbed by expansion of markets. As a logical consequence of rationalisation, electronic robotics replaces human energy or new communication technology makes labour superfluous, respectively. Entire sectors and departments of construction, production, marketing, warehousing, distribution, and management vanish into thin air. For the first time, the labour idol unintentionally confines itself to permanent hunger rations, thereby bringing about its very own death.[7]

From this perspective, two fundamental problems are combined: on the one hand, a confusion between the tendency of capital to incorporate more and more dead labour (machines, technologies, etc.) into the production process with the supposed possibility of complete abolition of living labour as a result of the dynamics of capital expansion. On the other hand, a profound technological determinism that attributes the "microelectronic revolution", "robotics", and "communication technologies" to a role as subjects of the process of historical changes, in capitalist society or beyond. It is also worth noting that such an analysis suffers from an evident Eurocentric bias, generalizing to the whole world a relative decrease in the weight of the industrial sector in the composition of European economies.

In a less agitative and more analytical text, though marked by the same caustic style as the *Manifesto* he helped write, Robert Kurz is, in part, more careful. The existence of a distinction in Marx's analysis between the concrete and abstract dimensions of labour is not denied. However, the very definition of abstract labour is criticized, as this abstraction is, finally, the general characteristic of labour. In Kurz's reading, "Marx duplicates

(...) the abstract concept of labour itself, by delimiting the specifically historical commodity-producing 'labour' of 'ontological labour'". Therefore, for Kurz, "the famous concept of ***abstract labour*** that comes out of it is actually a strange expression, a rhetorical duplication, as if we were talking about an 'abstract green', since the definition of something like 'green' is already in itself an abstraction".[8]

Criticizing then what he considers to be dubiousness, a contradiction of Marx (not perceived as a dialectical explanation of a reality contradictory in itself), Kurz seeks to distinguish the "exoteric" of the "esoteric" side of Marxian elaborations. Starting from an equivalence between capitalist development in peripheral societies and the Soviet process, both understood by the category of "modernization", Kurz defines the "exoteric" face of Marx as:

> a theory of modernization and immanent to the fetish, it refers to the internal form of the movement and history of the imposing of capital as a juridification and reification of all relations, whose horizon of development was still positively fulfilled. And this is, in fact, the current and world-renowned Marx: the 'worker's point of view' and class struggle are the central concepts of this line that led to historical Marxism.[9]

On the other hand, the "esoteric" perspective, also present in Marx's work, according to Kurz's reading, "in a strict 'radical' sense (that is, that descends to the roots) refers to the real mystification of the form as such of the commodity and of money, 'in' which modernity, along with its immanent conflicts, exposes, imposes and develops itself".[10]

By homogenizing twentieth-century Marxism as "historical Marxism", and especially by associating Marx himself with a "theory of modernization", Kurz ends up treating him as a naive cultivator of capitalist modernization. There is no doubt that a significant part of the social theory that claimed Marx in the twentieth century confused the advance of the productive forces (understood in a reductionist way as technological progress) with the path to socialism. However, to refute such association between Marx and the theories of modernization in the twentieth century, which seek to convey the image of the founder of the International as an idolater of "progress" of the capitalist productive forces, it is enough to remember the reference he makes to productive labour in several passages from his writings on the critique of political economy, as when he states, in Chapter XVI of *Capital*, that "to be a productive labourer is, therefore, not a piece of luck, but a misfortune".[11]

Even in his writings on India from the 1850s, always associated to a perspective of uncritical positive valuation of capitalist expansion, it is worth remembering that Marx pointed out the destruction that the English caused in the "Hindostan" as greater than that operated by centuries and centuries of wars and previous occupations, as the public works necessary for the irrigation of plantations were cut and artisanal production was destroyed. In other words, the imperial advance of "modern" English capitalism over "backward" India, represented an enormous destructive impact, not only socially, but also from a strictly economic and technological point of view. In his words:

> There cannot, however, remain any doubt but that the misery inflicted by the British on Hindostan is of an essentially different and infinitely more intensive kind than all Hindostan had to suffer before. (...) All the civil wars, invasions, revolutions, conquests, famines, strangely complex, rapid, and destructive as the successive action in Hindostan may appear, did not go deeper than its surface. England has broken down the entire framework of Indian society, without any symptoms of reconstitution yet appearing.[12]

If it is possible to agree with Kevin Anderson that there are "problematically Eurocentric notions" in those articles—I think "ethnocentrism" would be more adequate, as Marx makes derogatory remarks about European countries as well—it is also possible to recognize with Anderson that the "suggestion of capitalist progressivism", in Marx's text is very small.[13] In the conclusion of that first article, and in the article he published the following month, Marx stated that the destructive character of the British occupation had a "positive" counterpoint, for creating the material conditions for India to undergo social struggles with modern characteristics and contribute, thus, for the anti-capitalist struggles on a planetary scale. There is no simplistic belief in the absolute positivity of material progress in this evaluation of capitalist expansion via colonization, as it is the case in a theory of "modernization". Even in that polemical text, what predominates is an affirmation of the need for the existence of capitalist material basis (and, therefore, of its contradictions) to overcome capitalism itself, as can be seen from the following passage:

> The bourgeois period of history has to create the material basis of the new world – on the one hand universal intercourse founded upon the mutual dependency of mankind, and the means of that intercourse; on the other hand the development of the productive powers of man and the transformation of material production into a scientific domination of natural agencies. Bourgeois industry and commerce create these material conditions of a new world in the same way as geological revolutions have created the surface of the earth. When a great social revolution shall have mastered the results of the bourgeois epoch, the market of the world and the modern powers of production, and subjected them to the common control of the most advanced peoples, then only will human progress cease to resemble that hideous, pagan idol, who would not drink the nectar but from the skulls of the slain.[14]

Returning to Kurz, by asserting the analytical validity of Marx's "esoteric" interpretation of capitalism, but rejecting his "exoteric" perspective, especially in the political dimension of his project, the German theorist characterizes both Marxism in general and specifically the theoretical basis of the working class movement (and therefore the workers' class consciousness) as "immanent critiques" of capitalist modernization. His project, therefore, discards any active role of the proletariat in overcoming capitalism, because social classes, in this perspective,

> are no longer subjects of conflict existing in themselves, without presuppositions, but nothing more than different functional bearers of its [fetishism of commodities] common basic and historical form; and also the so-called working class 'is' in this sense an inescapably integral part and moment of the capitalist relationship, but not its predestined opponent.[15]

Faced with the absence of possible social subjects for transformation, since the fetishized relationship of capital subjects everyone and everything, Kurz is inexorably betting on the "collapse" of the system, which was already in accelerated tempo, as the only possibility for the end of capital and of the society based on its logic. Kurz seeks to distinguish his theory of the collapse of modernization from technologically based determinisms. However, he leaves the impression that, if the development of the productive potential of capital is the factor that will generate its extinction, without any space for a somehow conscious collective action by the working class in the process, we face a modality of determinism, although apparently complexified, presented as:

> the theory of an absolute limit of globalized capital, with the overcoming of the commodity-money value, with the overcoming of the relationship between the sexes constituted by the fetishism of the commodity and with the overcoming of "labour" in all its avatars. The result would be an overcoming of the separation of different spheres of modern society, in which the individual is only the intersection point of countless functional moments, being, precisely for that reason, abstract.[16]

In this case, what stands out is Kurz's inconsistency in criticizing in Marx something that in his own texts appears with much more emphasis, the defence of "modernization" (in the sense of expansion of the capitalist productive forces). After all, it is Kurz who sustains the possibility of transformation resulting from a mechanical deepening (by mechanism, understood here as a machine moved by non-human force) of the contradictions generated by the—technical—"progress" of capitalism.

In Marx, on the contrary, we saw that the development of productive forces is inseparable from human action and, therefore, from class struggle. Returning to the much-criticized texts about India, from the beginning of the 1850s, there is an explicit affirmation there that the transformations of the productive forces are not independent from and do not substitute the action of great human collectives:

> All the English bourgeoisie may be forced to do will neither emancipate nor materially mend the social condition of the mass of the people, depending not only on the development of the productive powers, but on their appropriation by the people. (...) The Indians will not reap the fruits of the new elements of society scattered among them by the British bourgeoisie, till in Great Britain itself the now ruling classes shall have been supplanted by the industrial proletariat, or till the Hindoos themselves shall have grown strong enough to throw off the English yoke altogether."[17]

A second example of analysis, with arguments akin to Kurz's ones is offered by the works of Moishe Postone. His discussion of the critique of political economy produced by Marx is more sophisticated and complex than the set of propositions in the *Manifesto against Labour*, in addition to not presenting himself as "post-Marxist", as claimed by Kurz.[18] Even so, he has a lot in common with Kurz's positions and his (ex)comrades, with whom he collaborated, especially regarding the assessment of the critique of fetishism as the centre of Marx's analysis in *Capital*, as well as the emphasis on the denial of labour—in Postone presented as valuing

Marx's "negative critique" of labour under capitalism—accompanied by the refusal to attribute a revolutionary historical subject potential to the working class.

In his most important work for this discussion,[19] Postone presents relevant contributions to the understanding of what he defines as the "quasi-objective" social forms of commodity and capital, from which he thinks about value and labour, which are inserted in, and constitute the studied capitalist social mediation. All this from an in-depth analysis of *Capital* (especially its first volume) and the *Grundrisse*. His discussion of the imprisonment of time by the logic of this capitalist social mediation, involved in his use of the category of "abstract labour time", undoubtedly constitutes a relevant and original contribution to the debate.

On the other hand, the author's concern with countering what he labels "traditional Marxism" is visible. "Traditional Marxism" is sometimes very fluidly associated with a conception centred on the criticism of capitalism "from the standpoint of 'labour'", sometimes with an analysis of capitalism focused on the question of ownership of the means of production, or even to the historical experience of the USSR and Eastern Europe in the twentieth century. Such questions complement Postone's critique of any conception of socialism as a simple state appropriation of the means of production combined with state economic planning.[20] In this field of discussion, unlike the authors of the *Manifesto against Labour*, Postone does not circumvent the existence of a double meaning for labour (abstract/concrete; labour/work) in Marx's work, nor does he reject it, as does Kurz. On the contrary, he discusses it and argues that a socialist society can only be constituted from "a new structuring of *work*, but for a fundamental restructuring and resignification of social life in general".[21] He rejects, however, any ontological approach to labour, stating that:

> Marx's theory does not assert that labor is the transhistorical structuring principle of social life; it does not grasp the constitution of social life in terms of a subject-object dialectic that is mediated by (concrete) labor. Indeed, it provides no transhistorical theory of labor, class, history, or the nature of social life itself.[22]

Postone does not deny the existence of social classes and of class struggle between workers and bourgeois, which would distance himself completely from Marx, but presents a very peculiar reading of these categories and their historical meaning in capitalist societies. His reflection is apparently quite careful, in understanding the working class as a social relationship, historically formed, rejecting unilateral understandings of class as a simple result of relations of production. However, even with the exception of limited intentions and preliminary analysis, he emphasizes the economic dimension of the conflict between capitalists and workers to affirm that class struggle—reduced in the book to the pressure of the working class for higher wages, shorter working hours and better working and living conditions—turns out to be, in the final analysis, functional for the logic of capital. By putting pressure, organized and collectively, for the reduction of the working day, workers end up driving the movement of capital towards the expansion of relative surplus value, thus acting as "moments of the development of the totality".[23]

Thus, according to Postone's reading, the exploitative relationship between bourgeois and proletarians and the conflicts arising from it are not the centre of Marx's critical analysis of capitalist society, but classes emerge in *Capital* from the question of their relationship with "the specificity of the form of social mediation".[24] In summary, according to the author in question:

> "Class conflict between the workers and capitalists as it is developed in Volume 1 of *Capital*, then, is a moment of the ongoing, totalizing dynamic of capitalist society. It is structured by, and constitutes, the social totality. The classes involved are not entities but structurings of social practice and consciousness which, in relation to the production of surplus value, are organized antagonistically; they are constituted by dialectical structures of capitalist society and impel its development, the unfolding of its basic contradiction.[25]

Such an argument is the basis for Postone to deny the working class the role of a historical subject potentially capable of carrying out a revolutionary transformation towards socialism.[26] Postone is always defensive in asserting the limitations of his analysis with regard to the subjective dimensions of class (its cultural and political horizon, its collective action, class consciousness, in short), and he repeatedly claims to distance himself from any determinist perspective. However, the conclusion of his discussion on class struggles in capitalist society reduces the dimension of subjectivity—in Marx defined from the dialectical interaction between being and consciousness of being, from the category of praxis, in short—to a direct derivation of the shackles of the contradictory structural totality of capitalism, conceived in almost exclusively economic terms. To use the aforementioned Gramscian terminology in the analysis of correlations of strength, Postone's conclusion is that struggles (and therefore the consciousness of the working class) are generally stuck at the "economic-corporate" level, or when they exceed it to address the State, they always do so within the narrow limits of systemic logic. The critique of capitalism arising from these struggles, for Postone (in terms almost identical to those of Kurz), "remains immanent to its object".[27] This can be read as a rather abusive generalization of the reformist political horizon and a subsumed action to the system, which completely ignores the different moments and examples of open confrontation between the movements of the working class and capitalism, or even the possible accumulations from the point of view of class consciousness, resulting from defensive struggles.

Moving without further mediation between a necessary critique of the allegedly socialist experiences of the twentieth century and a rather questionable definitive assessment of the immanent character of the class consciousness of workers in capitalism, Postone, always claiming to faithfully interpret Marx's "intentions", thus states:

> the logical thrust of Marx's presentation does not support the idea that the struggle between capitalists and workers is one between the dominant class of capitalist society and the class that embodies socialism – and that such struggle therefore points beyond capitalism. The class struggle, viewed from the workers' perspective, involves constituting, maintaining, and improving their position and situation as members of a working class. Their struggles have been a powerful force in the democratization and humanization of capitalism, and have also played an important role in the transition to organized capitalism. However, (…), Marx's analysis of the trajectory of the capitalist process of production does not point toward the possible future affirmation of the proletariat and the labor it performs. On the contrary, it points towards the possible abolition of that labor. Marx's presentation, in other words, implicitly contravenes the notion that the relation between the capitalist class and the working class is parallel to that between capitalism and socialism, that the possible transition to socialism is effected by the victory of the proletariat in class struggle (in the sense of its self-affirmation as a working class), and that socialism involves the realization of the proletariat."[28]

In this specific aspect, Kurz's position seems to be more honest in relation to Marx's texts, since even though we disagree with the dissociation he establishes between his "esoteric/exoteric" sides, Kurz recognizes in Marx the strong presence of the idea of the proletariat as the subject of transformation, as well as the clear Marxian conception of the possibility of developing the consciousness of this class in a dimension that surpasses the "economic-corporate" and reformist limits, even in the face of the fetish of commodity.

We have seen here how, in several texts, Marx explains a definition of class in which his consciousness and collective action (his subjectivity, understood as the praxis of the social subject) surpasses, or may come to surpass, the limits imposed by the logic of capital. However, far from perceiving workers' struggles for wages or the reduction of working hours as elements that ultimately stimulate the development of capital, Marx attributes to them a much broader potential, precisely because his concept of social class has a political dimension, whose relation to the structural totality of the capitalist mode of production is much more complex. As we saw in the "Letter to Bolte", from 1871, mentioned above, in which the link between economic and political struggles, whether automatic or not, is potentially valued.

A few years earlier, in an internal debate at the First International (*Value, Price and Profit*, 1865), Marx had already harshly criticized the perspectives that neglected the economic struggle for wage increases and reduced working hours. His analysis of the capitalist economy recognized that "the general tendency of capitalistic production is not to raise, but to sink the average standard of wages, or to push the *value of labour* more or less to its *minimum limit*". For this reason, he emphasized the importance of workers' strikes for wage readjustments and reduction of working hours, as the need to dispute the price of their labour power with capitalists "is inherent in their condition of having to sell themselves as commodities". Renouncing this everyday conflict against capital would leave the workers as if to "disqualify themselves for the initiating of any larger movement".[29]

Therefore, even recognizing that the laws of tendency of the capitalist economy lead to a situation in which the pauperization (absolute and/or relative) of the working class is imposed, Marx understood the collective struggles against this process as an important "countertrend", but not because they allowed the working class simply to maintain, and improve their position within the capitalist order, as Postone wants. On the contrary, the crux of the matter for Marx was that such struggles against capitalists enabled the working class to undertake other larger movements. These are movements in which the systemic abolition of wage labour exploitation is the main objective. Thus, in that same text, Marx emphasizes:

> At the same time, and quite apart from the general servitude involved in the wages system, the working class ought not to exaggerate to themselves the ultimate working of these everyday struggles. They ought not to forget that they are fighting with effects, but not with the causes of those effects; (…) They ought to understand that, with all the miseries it imposes upon them, the present system simultaneously engenders the *material conditions* and the *social forms* necessary for an economical reconstruction of society. Instead of the *conservative* motto, '*A fair day's wage for a fair day's work*!' they ought to inscribe on their banner the revolutionary watchword, '*Abolition of the wages system*!'[30]

Returning to Postone, his denial of the role of the proletariat as a historical subject does not lead him to the same certainties as Kurz regarding the end of capitalism through its own "collapse". His analysis oscillates, sometimes presenting positions that emphasize the contradictions intrinsic to capitalist development in its maximum potential as the key commanding the transformation ("a growing gap between the possibilities generated by the development of capital and its current form"[31]), sometimes giving prospective to the transforming potential of other subjects (women, racial activists, ecologists) and their struggles.

In this sense, Postone seems, at the same time, to reject the role of the proletariat as a potential subject and to present a restricted definition of this proletariat, without considering the fact that one of the ways to understand the proletariat from Marx is precisely to see how in his texts the working class does not fit into narrow definitions. In any case, the balance of Postone's analysis is precarious, pressed by the difficult task assigned between denying the role of the proletariat as a historical subject, but agreeing with Marx that "it would be possible for the associated individuals to make their own history"[32]; besides criticizing the determinisms, he maintains, however, that the overcoming of capitalism will result directly from its maximum development. In the end, Postone concludes with a double exit, which affirms the "people" and the world of merchandise they created, as subjects of historical transformation:

> Marx's analysis can be understood as a very powerful and sophisticated attempt to show that, with the development of the commodity as a total social form, people already 'make' the world around them. (...) Marx analyses capital as the alienated form of historically constituted, species-general knowledge and skills and, hence, grasps its increasingly destructive movement toward boundlessness as a movement of objectified human capacities that have become independent of human control. (...) Marx's conception of the overcoming of capitalism can be understood in terms of people gaining control over such quasi-objective developments, over processes of ongoing and accelerating social transformation, which they themselves have constituted. Within such a framework, then, the issue is not so much whether people should try to shape their world – they already are doing so. Rather, the issue is the way in which they shape their world and, hence, the nature of this world and its trajectory.[33]

As far as I can understand Postone's proposal, it is a question of stating that the world fetishized by the commodity was previously constructed by the "people" and that is the means by which, as their fetishized relationships develop to the limit in capitalism, the doors of social transformation open up. The "people" in this case seem to make their own history not only in conditions they did not choose, but also without any space for the development of a transformative consciousness. Determinism, expelled through the front door of the author's statements, seems to return, albeit well-disguised, through the background of a theory of history that reserves little or no space for action by large human collectives (the "agency" of social classes), reducing them to people "subsumed as cogs of a rationalized mega-apparatus".[34]

In both Kurz's and Postone's perspectives, there are several important elements of analysis for the critique of the logic of capital and the limits of theories that, seeking reference in Marx, were restricted to advocating the overcoming of private property, or worse, the attenuation of capitalist exploitation as the centre of the socialist project. However, by presenting such a critique as opposed to a "workers' movement Marxism", or "traditional Marxism", they tended to overvalue the originality of their approaches and to caricature these opponents.

This supposed originality in face of "traditional" or "historical" Marxism needs to be relativized. Several examples can be taken from the tradition of critique of the maintenance of the logic of capital exploring alienated labour, in countries that went through socialist revolutions (or that came to be incorporated "from above" into the post-war Soviet orbit).[35] What to say then about Postone's categorical assertion that socialism does not represent the assertion of the proletariat as a class, as opposed to the point of view which he considers to be at the heart of "traditional Marxism"? Wouldn't this be an original point of analysis for him, or for the reading he claims to deduce from Marx?

In this case, it is enough to recall a classic example of "traditional Marxism" to relativize the originality of Postone's vision and, at the same time, call into question this conception of "traditional Marxism" itself. In the debate at the beginning of the 1920s on the proposal of a "proletarian culture", Leon Trotsky rejected such a proposal for categorically stating that the struggle of the proletariat was fully realized with its extinction as a class in communist society, having overcome the transitory stage of the dictatorship of the proletariat:

> The cultural reconstruction which will begin when the need of the iron clutch of a dictatorship unparalleled in history will have disappeared, will not have a class character. This seems to lead to the conclusion that there is no proletarian culture and that there never will be any and in fact there is no reason to regret this. The proletariat acquires power for the purpose of doing away forever with class culture and to make way for human Culture.[36]

The transitory "temporary – for a brief period only –"[37] character of the dictatorship of the proletariat is explained precisely around the central task of creating the foundations of a classless society. Thus, in Trotsky's analysis, during this transitory stage:

> The proletariat, however, will reach its highest tension and the fullest manifestation of its class character during this revolutionary period and it will be within such narrow limits that the possibility of planful, cultural reconstruction will be confined. On the other hand, as the new regime will be more and more protected from political and military surprises (…), the proletariat will be more and more dissolved into a Socialist community and will free itself from its class characteristics and thus cease to be a proletariat.[38]

István Mészáros, in a much more contemporary critique of current capitalism, but also of the societal construction that followed the 1917 Revolution in Russia, follows the same tone when recognizing the contradictory character—"class as such is both the necessary and the inherently problematical agent of emancipation"[39]—of the proletariat's role as a potential subject of a historical transformation. A transformation that, in the final analysis, means its extinction/abolition, since, "even the 'class for-itself' is in Marx's view consigned to pre-history. He always insists on the necessity to transcend all classes as the fundamental condition of making 'real history'."[40] But, of course, there is a fundamental difference there with the theses of Kurz and Postone: both Trotsky and Mészáros recognize this contradiction within an analysis of the also contradictory logic of capital and connect it to a revolutionary project in which the proletariat—the working class—has a potential: that of tipping the cross-roads of "socialism or barbarism" towards socialism. In other words, they maintain that the result of the struggle between bourgeois and proletarians can lead to a resolution in the first direction of the historical tension highlighted in the *Communist Manifesto*, in which, as we have seen, the different configurations of the class struggle over time ended "either in a revolutionary re-constitution of society at large, or in the common ruin of the contending classes".[41] And this defence of the political dimension of the collective action of the class does not need to be done through an exaggeratedly voluntarist bias, since it starts from the materialist methodological principle expressed in the statement that "mankind thus inevitably sets itself only such tasks as it is able to solve".[42]

Authors such as Trotsky and Mészáros, sticking to the ones I have just mentioned, both taking different positions and appearing at different moments of the twentieth century, do not seem to correspond to generalizations about a "historical Marxism", or "traditional Marxism", as proposed by Kurz and Postone. It is not difficult, therefore, to seek support in the diverse critical tradition of historical materialism, in order to reject deterministic conceptions—even if it is sophisticated and (at least apparently) critical of technological determinism—such as those that claim that the logic of capital can be overcome directly from the "collapse" of capitalism, or from the realization of the contradictory potential of the advance of "dead labour". While recognizing the contradictory character of the performance of a subordinate class such as the proletariat and the strong determinations of the logic of capital, on whose rupture depends on the project of social transformation "whose objective is to go beyond capital in order to create the social/economic structures of the 'new historic form'", analysis such as those of Mészáros advocate that the task of reorganizing the economic foundations of social metabolism is "primarily political/social and not economic".[43] Hence, according to Mészáros, class is, "paradoxically, both the necessary vehicle and active agent of the historical task of socialist emancipation and, at the same time, also a fundamental obstacle to its accomplishment".[44]

The critique of the "end of labour" theses or of the obsolescence of the affirmation of the proletariat as a revolutionary subject, which I have only rescued here from a few elements, is supported by a full debate in the field of social theory. A debate reviewed and presented in its best dimension by the work of sociologist Ricardo Antunes, who in several texts has insisted on a defence of the centrality of labour, taken not as a defence of the permanence of alienated labour in a society beyond capital, but as a finding that as long as the socio-metabolism of capital prevails—the extraction of surplus value in the process of capitalist production—the exploitation of labour, involved by the fetishism of the commodity, continues and will continue to be essential for the system.[45]

Antunes' analytical perspective is based on a recognition of the dual character of labour, in Marxian analysis and in capitalist social reality. Thus, "if we can consider work as a founding moment of human sociability, as the starting point of its humanization process, it is also true that in capitalist society, work becomes waged, taking the form of alienated, fetishized and abstract labour".[46]

The recognition of an ontological dimension of labour, therefore, in no way means a limit to the critique of fetishized abstract labour, or a defence of post-capitalist society as a simple overcoming of private ownership of the means of production, something that would be equivalent to the full realization of the working class. On the contrary, Antunes has a clear strategic definition of the need to have:

> a new system of social metabolism, a new mode of production and life based on free, autonomous and self-determined activity, based on the time available to produce socially necessary use values, against heterodetermined production (based on excess time for the exclusive production of exchange values for the market and for the reproduction of capital).[47]

To achieve this strategic objective, however, Antunes defends the fundamental role of the working class as a historical subject. His effort to criticize those who affirmed the end of class (or of the concept's pertinence), involved defending the analytical validity of Marx's concept of the working class today, which led him to an expanded notion of this class, including "the totality of those who sell their labour power, with the productive workers as the central nucleus", but also encompassing the unproductive workers, in order to incorporate, in addition to the rural proletariat, "the *precarious proletariat; the modern sub-proletariat; part-time* work; the new proletariat of fast-food restaurants; (…) the tertiarised and precarious workers of *lyophilised* enterprises (…); *wage-earning* workers of the so-called 'informal economy' who are very often indirectly subordinated to capital; as well as unemployed workers, expelled from the productive process and from the labour-market as a result of capital restructuring and expanding the industrial reserve-army, during the phase of expansion of *structural unemployment*".[48]

Such a broadened notion of the working class is not only relevant to the understanding of social relations in the present—influenced by the fragmentation and heterogenization of the class, as well as the expansion of the number of workers subsumed to the socio-metabolism of capital—but also fully compatible with Marx's reflections, presented in the first part of this book. To a large extent, those critics of Marx—either of his "exoteric side" or of "traditional Marxism"—regarding the idea of the proletariat as a potential subject of transformation, corroborate a very restricted understanding of the proletariat, seen almost exclusively as an industrial working class.

It is interesting to note that, not only on this point, a critic with a theoretical background somewhat different from Ricardo Antunes, such as Daniel Bensaid, can present analyses similar and complementary to his own.[49] Here, I return to a critique by Bensaid of the propositions of Gorz, another author criticized by Antunes in several of his writings (and claimed by Postone), which can be easily extended to the reasoning of the texts by the Krisis group and, to some extent, also to the more sophisticated analysis of Postone. In it, Bensaid highlights the limits of determinism in understanding the ongoing process:

> Abstract labour does not disappear: in its thirst for profit, capital always needs living labour, even though it must mobilize an increasing amount of dead labour to transform it into value. After Kasparov's chess match against a computer, the machine was said to have beaten the man. But *Deep Blue* was never anything more than a sizable mass of accumulated and socialized dead labour.[50]

Bensaid does not simply deny the crisis of labour, but qualifies it as a crisis of waged labour, of abstract labour as a general measure of social wealth. A crisis that, following his analysis, Marx predicted, when in the *Grundrisse* he affirmed the contradictory process in which capital took science and social communication to their maximum potential, but continued to seek to imprison them according to their value. In Marx's words, also cited by Postone and Kurz, who nevertheless draw other analytical consequences from them:

> The *theft of alien labour time, which is the basis of present wealth*, appears to be a miserable foundation compared to this newly developed one, the foundation created by large-scale industry itself. As soon as labour in its immediate form has ceased to be the great source of wealth, labour time ceases and must cease to be its measure, and therefore exchange value [must cease to be the measure] of use value. (...) On the one hand, therefore, it calls into life all the powers of science and Nature, and of social combination and social intercourse, in order to make the creation of wealth (relatively) independent of the labour time employed for that purpose. On the other hand, it wishes the enormous social forces thus created to be measured by labour time and to confine them within the limits necessary to maintain as value the value already created.[51]

In his discussion of this fragment, Bensaid draws attention to the fact that although in the current stage of capitalist development, as Marx predicted, the measurement of wealth through labour time has become a "miserable basis"—because mediate forms of labour have increasing weight in relation to immediate forms—capitalism is far from having abolished living labour and that "now miserable basis" continues to be the basis for measuring social wealth. Hence, for Bensaid, a change in the "organic composition of labour" can be perceived, but not its near end within capitalism. Regarding those who draw conclusions from this passage about the possibility of overcoming capital "almost automatically" by the complete realization of the Marxian prognosis, it is worth remembering that Marx describes in *Capital*, as we have seen, this situation as instituting "the material conditions" to create the destruction of capital. These are the material conditions that enable, but do not end, the transformation process. Even here, it is necessary to inquire about the social subject who will activate such an explosion of capital.

On the other hand, in his critique, Bensaid emphasizes the one-sidedness of the prophets of the end of labour (so critical, in turn, of the one-sidedness of the image of labour as liberator). For him, these analyses lack an understanding of the dual perspective of labour, as unveiled by Marx. The terminology he employs is slightly different, as Bensaid prefers to speak of the anthropological (rather than ontological) dimension of labour, but it seems to me that we have come here to the same point highlighted by Antunes:

> The dogma of the liberating labour and the prophecy of the end of labour have their one-sidedness in common. The first only considers the anthropological dimension of labour, abstracting its historically determined character. The second only considers its concretely alienated and alienating character, abstracting its creative potentialities. In fact, in the 'imbrication of action and labour', the anthropological and historical dimensions are closely combined. Even though alienation dominates waged labour, there is, at the same time, a 'forcibly ambivalent' socialization process. (...) It is not a question of denying this contradiction, but of installing oneself in it to work on it. Behind the imposed labour, there persists, albeit in a weak, deaf way, this 'need of the possible', which differentiates human activity from simply vegetative plenitude. It is the sign, even, of its finitude and its ability to 'go further', for better or worse.[52]

New Subjects? (II)

In recent years, given the limits—experienced by the struggles of actual workers—of the theses on the end of the working class in the style of those advocated two or three decades ago by Gorz, Offe, Postone and Kurz, it is surprising that they continue to be used on a relatively large scale in analyses of contemporary capitalism. They are, however, less visible references than there were 10 or 15 years ago. Nevertheless, some more recent theses approach those discussions in a different manner. This is the case of an analytical perspective that does not deny the existence of a subject of transformation but accepts as a presupposition the generalization of "de-industrialization" in the advanced capitalist countries of the Northern Hemisphere, to resume the argument of the decline of the proletariat. By that, a new subject emerged from this decline of the working class: the "precariat".

Even considering that there are different frameworks for the use of the term, there are authors more directly associated with its use, among which Guy Standing stands out, whose most important book in this direction is *The Precariat: The New Dangerous Class*, first edited in 2011.[53] In his analysis, Standing characterizes the precariat as a set of insecurities—in relation to the labour market, employment, career, working conditions, income, professional improvement, and collective representation—that constitute it as a "class- in-the-making", still lacking a collective conscience that would allow it to act as a "class-for-itself".[54]

The precariat is also defined by a contrasting perspective, that is, by differentiating from what Standing considers to be the proletariat/working class and from other categories of social stratification employed by the author, such as "salariat" (in the same sense employed by Gorz)—understood as the most stable sector and protected by social benefits among waged workers (presented by him as privileges). In his words:

> The precariat has *class* characteristics. It consists of people who have minimal trust relationships with capital or the state, making it quite unlike the salariat. And it has none of the social contract relationships of the proletariat, whereby labour securities were provided in exchange for subordination and contingent loyalty, the unwritten deal underpinning welfare states. Without a bargain of trust or security in exchange for subordination, the precariat is distinctive in class terms. It also has a peculiar status position, in not mapping neatly onto high status professional or middle-status craft occupations. One way of putting it is that the precariat has 'truncated status'. And, as we shall see, its structure of 'social income' does not map neatly onto old notions of class or occupation.[55]

Besides the possible criticisms of the way he combines different matrices of understanding the concept of social class to present his "new class", the biggest problem with this way of understanding the current picture seems to me to lie in the bases of comparison that allow Standing to say that the precariat is a "distinct class" from the proletariat. In other words, in his analysis, the definition of the proletariat—or working class—is directly associated with "standard employment"—a stable contract, a situation close to full employment and guarantees of social rights.

It turns out that, although Standing seems to recognize in some passages that this model only existed in post-war Europe, his analysis generally tends to ignore that the relation of "standard employment" under capitalist conditions was a "historical anomaly", to recall the already commented discussion by Marcel van der Linden.[56] An "anomaly" restricted in time to a period of less than three decades, following the end of World War II, confined in space to a group of countries that experienced advanced capitalist development in the North of the Globe and, even in these areas, restricted to male workers.[57]

It is also important to realize that this "historical anomaly" was only possible, in capitalist societies, due to social struggles with a very high impact from the working class. The Russian revolution, the defeat of fascism, the successful struggles for national liberation, are some of them. On the other hand, Marx's rich demonstration of the fact that forms of relative surplus-population are not outside the working class, but rather a constitutive part of its own "existence" as a class, does not seem to us to have been overcome by the recent hunt for "new subjects".

We have seen that, in the nineteenth century, lived and studied by Marx, the employment that we now call precarious represented the pattern. The exceptional situation of some advanced capitalist development countries in the post-war period resulted from historically specific conditions of the class struggle in the period following the 1917 socialist revolution in Russia. The high-impact struggles of the working class at that juncture operated as social-political "counteracting influences"—"multiple circumstances"—to the "general law of accumulation". Thus, the historical sense and the contradictory character of these, like the others, "laws" of capital are evident. Therefore, the prevalence of "stable employment" has never become widespread throughout the world. To some extent, in fact, it was only possible because of the "unequal exchanges" characteristic of the imperialist dynamic. Lucia Pradella, analyzing Marx's texts from the 1850s—in which he pays attention to the global dynamics of capitalist expansion and begins to give greater importance to struggles in colonial territories as potentially disruptive to accumulation in imperialist countries—explains:

> In the light of these studies, Marx questioned his previous belief in the "iron law of wages": as the wave of strikes in England in 1853 proved, technological innovation and imperialist expansion made it possible for the labor movement in imperialist countries to "demand their share" of the economic prosperity and achieve material improvements.[58]

From this point of view, precariousness as a rule can only be seen as a novelty if we abstract the long historical trajectory of the working class, since the time of Marx. The possibilities of diminishing its impact on the working class experience have always depended on specific historical conditions, under which the uneven and combined dynamics of capital expansion and class struggle have significant weight. In this line of reasoning, in a critical essay in relation to Standing's work and other analyses of the precariat as a "new class", Bryan Palmer presents a characterization of the proletariat that values expropriation/dispossession. Palmer presents expropriation—more than the condition in the labour market, formalization and the economic sector of employment, income, or even the wage relationship—as the constant element of a class that has always been characterized by heterogeneity and precariousness. According to him:

> Class has always embodied differentiation, insecurity and precariousness. Just as precariousness is historically inseparable from class formation, there are invariably differentiations that seemingly separate out those with access to steady employments and secure payments from those who must scramble for work and access to the wage. Expropriation, then, is a highly heterogeneous experience, since no individual can be dispossessed in precisely the same way as another, or live that process of material alienation exactly as another would. Yet dispossession, *in general*, nonetheless *defines proletarianization*. It is the metaphorical mark of Cain stamped on all workers, regardless of their level of employment, rate of pay, status, waged placement or degree of wagelessness.[59]

Palmer directly quotes analyses and passages from *Capital*, which were summarized in the first part of this book, to assert that "dispossession, then, is the basis of all proletarianization, which orders accumulation".[60] There are other analyses that, in a similar approach, reinforce Palmer's argument that expropriation—and the consequent dispossession—define proletarianization. Alex Callinicos rescues Robert Brenner's concept of "market dependence" to demonstrate how social property relations in capitalism have two central elements: on the one hand, the separation between economic agents and the means of providing for their livelihood (even those who may possess some kind of skill and tools/means of production, cannot possess all of their livelihoods); on the other hand, these agents have no means of extracting surplus labour from direct producers. Thus, it is ensured that workers "can only reproduce themselves by producing as efficiently as possible for the market. By making the first condition separation from the means of subsistence, rather than from the means of production, Brenner casts subsumption under capital more broadly than Marx's concepts of formal and real subsumption do, since (…) these both presuppose wage labour".[61]

It is worth mentioning, albeit briefly, that even giving such importance to dispossession as a central element to define the proletariat, Callinicos is quite critical of the analyses that attribute centrality of that concept in explaining contemporary capitalist accumulation. As in the case of some works by David Harvey, for whom the characteristics associated with "dispossession" and attributed by Marx to the process of primitive accumulation—"force, fraud, oppression"—have analytical precedence over the extraction of surplus value through waged labour, which is, "after all, a specific form of accumulation by dispossession, since it is nothing more or less than the alienation, appropriation and dispossession of the laborer's capacity to produce value in the labor process".[62] Callinicos uses passages from volume 1 of *Capital* to show there that Marx reinforces the fundamental difference between the historical stage of primitive accumulation and the accumulation of capital when the production process capitalist is fully developed, constantly generating a relative surplus-population, because in these conditions "Direct extra-economic force is still of course used, but only in exceptional cases".[63] This does not prevent us from recognizing that the use of "extra-economic" force to guarantee accumulation is far from being just an exceptionality, as we know. The point is that this is no longer a "previous" or "original" stage, but a subordination of traditional and "new" forms of expropriation to the process of expanded accumulation.

We have seen that expropriation is a key category for Marx's discussion in the chapter on primitive accumulation of *Capital*, and it maintains a close connection with the category of relative surplus-population, which is central to the debate in the previous chapters, on the "general law of accumulation". A recent analysis of contemporary capitalism that seeks to explain the precarious dynamics of labour relations on a global scale in the light of the elaborations of the "general law of accumulation" presented by Marx, combined with a reflection on imperialism, is that of John Foster and Robert McChesney. In their study on the capitalist crisis, more specifically in a chapter on "the global reserve army of labor and the new imperialism", they seek to analyze the current dynamics of the relationship between expansion of multinational capital and "the great global job shift", with the expansion of labour towards the market in the Global South, compared to the perception of its relative shrinkage in the North.[64]

According to these two authors, the expansion of the global workforce available to capital in recent decades is mainly the result of two processes:

> (1) the depeasantization of a large portion of the global periphery by means of agribusiness - removing peasants from the land, with the resulting expansion of the population of urban slums; and (2) the integration of the workforce of the former "actually existing socialist" countries into the world capitalist economy.[65]

Presenting data showing how the share of the Global South in the world's total industrial employment grew dramatically from 51% in 1980 to 73% in 2008, the authors seek to explain the correlation between the concentration of corporate control of the market and profits by big capital with the "abysmally low wages and the chronic insufficiency of productive employment" at the base of the system. Their central argument, which they develop through the conceptual arsenal made available by Marx—drawing attention to his indications that his analysis for Great Britain could be expanded to a world level, combined with the Marxian concern with unequal exchanges—is the following:

> the key to understanding these changes in the imperialist system (beyond the analysis of the multinational corporation itself, discussed in the two previous chapters) is to be found in the growth of the global reserve army (...). Not only has the growth of the global capitalist labor force (including the available reserve army) radically altered the position of third world labor, it also has had an effect on labor in the rich economies, where wage levels are stagnant or declining for this and other reasons. Everywhere multinational corporations have been able to apply a divide-and-rule policy, altering the relative positions of capital and labor worldwide.[66]

An analysis developed from the reality of the Global South, which seeks to explain the precariousness of labour relations using the category "precarious", however, articulated with Marx's definitions of the proletariat/working class, was presented by Ruy Braga. In his analysis, the precariat constitutes a portion within the working class and not a distinct and external group to it. Dealing with the mass movements that took to the streets of Brazil in June 2013, Braga identifies a leading role of the precarious: "young, educated, and underpaid workers, under precarious working and living conditions".[67] In his broadest work on the subject, he defines the precariat as: "the mass formed by unskilled and semi-skilled workers quickly entering and leaving the labour market, young people seeking their first job, workers who recently left informal jobs and underpaid workers".[68]

Braga thus explicitly considers the precariat as the "poorly paid and exploited urban proletariat and farm workers", which differs both from the more qualified and better paid "*professional sectors*" of the working class, and from the impoverished population and the lumpenproletariat.[69]

Considering that the proletariat/working class can be a category, according to the conception expressed by Marx, that is already sufficiently inclusive and given the polyphony involved in the term "precariat", we do not believe it is necessary to incorporate it into the analysis. But Ruy Braga is right in his assessment that large-scale social-political explosions (such as in Brazil in June 2013) may have as protagonists the most precarious sectors of the working class, precisely those furthest from traditional union organization, because they are less represented by it. For this reason, it is essential to understand both the forms of mobilization and struggle that represent these sectors, as well as those that refer to the more formally employed sectors, also bearing in mind their possible articulations. We are thus far from the idea that the proletariat, in the current phase of capitalism, has no potential as a transforming historical subject.

It's worth remembering that such situations, as Marx well demonstrates, are not fixed and immutable throughout the life of each worker, as the movement between employment and unemployment, formality and informality, etc. is common. In any case, resuming to Marx as a reference to the general law of accumulation, "every combination of employed and unemployed disturbs the 'harmonious' action of this law."[70]

I conclude this section by returning to a historical analysis, at the end of this book, which in a sense has come to be invoked here as a necessary antidote to certain absolutizations or naturalizations of particular situations. However, I intend to show, through the critical commentary of studies developed by historians, that they have many issues in common with the reflections on labour in present time developed by social scientists and other theorists discussed so far.

Notes

1. Marcel van der Linden presents international data that, although restricted to a few countries and years, show that the decrease in unionization levels is widespread. An estimate of union entities, presented by him, calculates at 7% of the total workforce the percentage of unionized workers in the world. According to the text already mentioned M. Linden, "Global Labour".

2. We can have an approach based on empirical research, with the volume of worker protest cycles, on a world scale, since the last decades of the nineteenth century, through the data presented by Beverly Silver, *Forces of Labour: Worker's Movements and Globalization Since 1870*, New York, Cambridge University Press, 2003.
3. On the changes in the ways of managing labour relations throughout the twentieth century, in a comparative perspective between different countries, see Bo Strath, *The Organization of Labor Markets: Modernity, Culture and Governance in Germany, Sweden, Britain and Japan*, London, Routledge, 1996.
4. Claus Offe, *Capitalismo Desorganizado*, São Paulo, Brasiliense, 1989, p. 194.
5. Andre Gorz, *Farewell to the Working Class: An Essay on Post-Industrial Socialism*, London, Pluto Press, 1982, pp. 14–15.
6. Krisis, *Manifesto Against Labour* (1999), at https://libcom.org/library/manifesto-against-labour-krisis-group, accessed in November 2019.
7. Ibid.
8. Robert Kurz, "O Pós-marxismo e o Fetiche do Trabalho: Sobre a Contradição Histórica na Teoria de Marx", 2003 Portuguese edition, accessed at http://obeco.planetaclix.pt/ (original published in *Krisis* magazine, no. 15, 1995), accessed in September 2017. The work in which he formulates the main theses in this article is R. Kurz, *O Colapso da Modernização: da Derrocada do Socialismo de Caserna à Crise da Economia Mundial*, São Paulo, Paz e Terra, 1999 (1st German ed. 1993).
9. Robert Kurz, "O pós-marxismo".
10. Ibid.
11. *MECW*, vol. 35, p. 510.
12. *MECW*, vol. 12, p. 126 (The British Rule in India, 1853). For an interesting analysis of the perspectives opened by Marx (and the limits of his analysis) in his writings on India, see Victor G. Kiernan, "Marx and India", In Prakash Karat (ed.), *Across Time and Continents. A Tribute to Victor G. Kiernan*, New Delhi, Left Word, 2003.
13. Kevin Anderson, *Marx at the Margins: On Nationalism, Ethnicity, and Non-Western Societies*, Chicago, Chicago University Press, 2010, pp. 19–20.

14. *MECW*, vol. 12, p. 222 (The future results of British Rule in India, 1853).
15. Robert Kurz, "O Pós-marxismo".
16. Ibid.
17. *MECW*, vol. 12, p. 221 (The future results of British Rule in India, 1853).
18. The "post-Marxism" proclaimed in the title of Kurz's article commented here is defined by the rejection not only of the "exoteric" side of Marx, but also of the thought of Engels and of the entire Marxism of the twentieth century. The only positive reference that he recognizes from the debate on the left is considered by him as distant from Marxism. Thus, according to him, "the only real original source within the 'New Left' (alongside Ernst Bloch, whose reception was however peripheral) was the Critical Theory of the Frankfurt School, which had been formulated long before and which in general remained on the fringes of Marxist affairs." Robert Kurz, "Post-Marxism".
19. Moishe Postone, *Time, Labor and Social Domination: A Reinterpretation of Marx's Critical Theory*, New York, Cambridge University Press, 1993.
20. Ibid., pp. 35 and 44. Regarding the characterization of the USSR, Postone associates it with the concept of "state capitalism", based on the analysis of the Frankfurtian F. Pollock (although he criticizes the use and consequences drawn from the category by Pollock for some situations of advanced capitalism). See pp. 498 and 501 of the book's conclusions, and especially the third chapter.
21. Idem, p. 364.
22. Idem, p. 388. While we may agree that in Marx there are no transhistorical categories, what Postone seems to deny here, implicitly, is what Kurz most explicitly rejects: an ontological understanding of the nature of social being (historical ontology). Postone's targets seem to be the Lukacsian matrix formulations about labour, although he only makes the critique of Lukács explicit in the marginal comment he makes on the question of class consciousness pages later. In note 120, on p. 356, apparently disregarding the distinction between labour/work, which he adopts in other passages, he asserts that "the centrality of proletarian labor to Marx's analysis of capitalism should not be taken as an affirmative evaluation on his part of its ontological primacy to social life".

23. Idem, p. 318.
24. Idem, p. 398.
25. Idem, p. 321.
26. It is interesting to note that the strongest moments of denial of the role of the working class as a historical subject are footnotes in which Postone agrees, with reservations, with authors such as G. A Cohen and J. Cohen, as in notes 27, p. 319 and note 121, p. 357.
27. Idem, p. 323.
28. Ibid., p. 324.
29. *MECW*, vol. 20, p. 148.
30. Ibid., pp. 148–149.
31. M. Postone, *Time, Labor, and Social Domination*, p. 369.
32. Ibid., p. 382.
33. Ibid., p. 384.
34. Ibid., p. 390.
35. From different theoretical traditions, the critique of the naturalization of the organization of work implemented by capitalism in the productive units managed by the Soviet state in the post-1917 period appears, for example, in Robert Linhart, *Lénine, les paysans, Taylor: Essai d'analyse matérialiste historique de la naissance du système productif soviétique*, Paris, Seuil, 1976; and in the works developed since the 1960s by István Mészáros, including his characterization of the Soviet economy as non-capitalist, yet dominated by the logic of capital, systematized in *Beyond Capital: Toward a Theory of Transition*, New York, Monthly Review Press, 1995.
36. Leon Trotsky, "Proletarian Culture and Proletarian Art". In: *Literature and Revolution*, 1924. Available at: https://www.marxists.org/archive/trotsky/1924/lit_revo/ch06.htm, accessed in November 2019.
37. Ibid.
38. Ibid.
39. I. Mészáros, *The Power of Ideology*, London, Zed Books, 2005, p. 258.
40. Ibid. p. 258.
41. *MECW*, vol. 6, p. 482.
42. *MECW*, vol. 29, p. 263.
43. I. Mészáros, *Beyond Capital*, p. 949.
44. I. Mészáros, *The Power of Ideology*, p. 259.
45. Ricardo Antunes, *The Meanings of Work*, Leiden, Brill, 2013.

46. Ricardo Antunes, "Trabalho uno ou omni: a dialética entre o trabalho concreto e o trabalho abstrato", *Argumentum*, Vol. 2, No. 2, jul./dez. 2010, p. 10.
47. Idem, p. 13.
48. R. Antunes, *The Meanings of Work*, p. 82.
49. I refer to the fact that Antunes draws inspiration for his analyses from Lukács' ontological critique, while Bensaid was trained in the Trotskyist tradition of the IV International. Yet, of course, the two move on the common ground of the best tradition of historical materialism.
50. Daniel Bensaid, "Trabalho e emancipação", In D. Bensaid & Michel Lowy, *Marxismo, modernidade e utopia*, São Paulo, Xamã, 2000, p. 90.
51. *MECW*, vol. 29, pp. 91–92.
52. D. Bensaid, "Trabalho e Emancipação", p. 100.
53. Guy Standing, *The Precariat: The New Dangerous Class*, New York, Bloomsbury Academic, 2011.
54. Ibid., p. 7 e 10.
55. Ibid., p. 8.
56. Marcel van der Linden, "San Precario", p. 19.
57. The precariousness of most of the female workforce, even in Europe in the "glorious years" of the post-war period, is mentioned by Van der Linden and is the object of the case study on Italian female workers developed in the aforementioned article by E. Betti, "Gender and Precarious Labor".
58. Lucia Pradella, "Crisis, Revolution and Hegemonic Transition: The American Civil War and Emancipation in Marx's Capital", *Science & Society*, Vol. 80, No. 4, 2016, 454–467, p. 457.
59. Bryan Palmer, "Reconsiderations of Class: Precariousness as Proletarianization", in Leo Panitch, Greg Albo & Vivek Chibber (eds.), *Socialist Register 2014: Registering Class*. London, Merlin Press, 2013, p. 49.
60. Ibid., p. 47.
61. Alex Callinicos, *Deciphering Capital*, p. 206.
62. David Harvey, *A Companion to Marx's Capital*, New York, London, Verso, 2010, p. 311.
63. Alex Callinicos, *Deciphering Capital*, p. 199. For another analysis (also critical of Harvey) of contemporary expropriations, which

emphasizes their violent continuity, but takes them as a presupposition for extracting surplus value, see Virgínia Fontes, *O Brasil e o capital-imperialismo: teoria e história*, Rio de Janeiro, EdUFRJ, 2010.

64. John Foster & Robert McChesney, *The Endless Crisis: How Monopoly-Finance Capital Produces Stagnation and Upheaval from the USA to China*, New York, Monthly Review Press, 2012.
65. Ibid., p. 127.
66. Ibid., p. 129.
67. Ruy Braga, "Brazil: For an Interpretation Worthy of June", according to blogjunho.com.br/brazil-for-an-interpretation-worthy-of-june/, Accessed in November 2019.
68. Ruy Braga, *The Politics of the Precariat: From Populism to Lulista Hegemony*, Leiden, Boston, Brill, 2017, p. 245.
69. Ibid., pp. 5–6.
70. *MECW*, vol. 35, p. 634.

CHAPTER 5

The Recent Historiographical Debates on the Working Class

It may seem like wordplay, but in this book, we insist that the defence of the topicality of the conception of the working class developed by Marx must not come only from the debate on the class today. Just as the recent situation has motivated social scientists and critical essayists to question the analytical validity of the category of working class/proletariat for understanding the current social dynamics, some historians have also done so, also calling into question the relevance of the category as a valid analytical tool for understanding historical processes, closer or more distant in time.

On the other hand, however, still analogous to the debate about the present time, other historians sought to understand the complexity and diversity of the working class in its historical dimensions, developing broader forms of understanding this analytical category. In this chapter, disagreeing with historians who deny the analytical validity of the concept, we will seek to dialogue with the different analytical perspectives that resort to an expanded definition of class, taking up the references to Marx that guided all the reflection so far.

M. B. Mattos, *The Working Class from Marx to Our Times*, Marx, Engels, and Marxisms,
https://doi.org/10.1007/978-3-030-97355-1_5

The Making of the Class in Debate

An example of the relativization of the analytical validity of the category of working class for the understanding of contemporary history, since the nineteenth century, can be found in a book by the British historian Patrick Joyce, published in 1994.[1] According to him, the intellectual production in social history of the nineteenth century, referring to England in particular, paid too much attention to class identity, to the detriment of other "social" or collective selves such as "the people" and "humanity", which also existed and were even more important in the construction of an identification of the politics, culture, and society in which they lived in democratically. Locating his reflection in the wake of the emergence of perspectives defined as "post-structuralist" and of "post-modernity", Joyce inserts himself affirmatively in the intellectual movement identified as "linguistic turn". For this reason, his definition of class does not come from the "real", but from "an imagined form". Thus, he argues that during the nineteenth century, in studies about it, "other forms of the self and of collective identity emerge, long obscured by the concentration on class. And class itself, like any other collective 'social' subject, is seen to be an imagined form, not something given in a 'real' world beyond this form".[2]

From his defence of the imaginary character of class, combined with his criticism of the supposed overemphasis of historiography on this identity among other more important ones, Joyce draws a conclusion about the end of class, in a particular sense. Explaining why the first idea for a title for his book was "the fall of class", he is definitive:

> There is a powerful sense in which class may be said to have 'fallen'. Instead of being a master category of historical explanation, it has become one term among many, sharing a rough equality with these others (which is what I meant by the 'fall' of class). The reasons for this are not hard to find. In Britain, economic decline and restructuring have led to the disintegration of the old manual sector of employment, and of what was, mistakenly, seen to be a 'traditional' working class. The rise of the right from the 1970s, and the decline of the left, together with that of the trade unions, pointed in a similar direction to that of economic change, towards a loosening of the hold class and work-based categories had, not only on the academic mind, but also on a wider public. Changes going on in Britain were mirrored elsewhere, but the greatest change of all was the disintegration of world communism, and with it the retreat of intellectual Marxism.[3]

That is, if at the time of the author, for various reasons, the class has "fallen" in its economic dimension and its political strength, this explains its fall also as a "superior category of historical explanation". Although the defence of a position like this lacks further logical support (theoretically, one could agree on the ineffectiveness of a category to explain the present, without questioning its relevance to understanding the past), it is manifested—usually in a more subtle way—in many other voices.

About a decade earlier, Gareth Stedman Jones had already criticized the assumptions of Marxist-inspired social historians (with whom he had identified in the 1970s), based on a defence of the centrality of language. Although referring to the "materiality" of language, Jones' analytic proposal anticipates Patrick Joyce's position in his assumed linguistic turn. After all, according to Stedman Jones, his study sought to explore "the systematic relationship between terms and propositions within the language rather than setting particular propositions into direct relation to a putative experiential reality of which they were assumed to be the expression".[4]

The result of this shift in perspective (from the emphasis on the "social" to the valuation of language) in his analysis of the English working class in the nineteenth century is summarized as follows by Jones: "class' is treated as a discursive rather than as an ontological reality, the central effort being to explain languages of class from the nature of politics rather than the character of politics from the nature of class".[5]

As the "denial" of class emerged among historians at the same time (1980s/1990s) as among social scientists and other thinkers discussed in the previous chapter, in order to understand the specifics of this historical conception of class as a discursive reality, or its rejection in the name of other "imaginary" identities, it is important to discuss the specific interlocutors of these historians. Both mention their background in British Social History from a Marxist framework directly, which would later be the central target of their criticism. Both, still, establish the opposition to this historiography presenting their alternative interpretations to the process of formation of the English working class, in the first half of the nineteenth century.

For this reason, to better situate the devaluation of class as a relevant historical category, suggested by Jones and directly defended by Joyce, it will be useful to resort to the original debate of social history with a Marxist framework in that historical moment. Thus, we will quickly follow the discussions of some of the best-known representatives of this historiography on the process of formation of the English working class in the period that began in the last decade of the eighteenth century and ended with the struggles of Chartism in the years 1830–1840. Therefore, the 1840s, by the way, where we started this book, presents Marx's "encounter" with the proletariat.

Interestingly, some of the first studies of this British social historiography identified with Marxism that bet on a totalizing perspective and invested heavily in research on the working class had the "language of class" as a starting point.

In a text published in 1960, already mentioned in Chapter 1, one of the pioneers of modern British Social History, Asa Briggs, showed how the plural "*working classes*" was widely used in England in the early nineteenth century to designate the group of poor workers in its various professional categories. Around the 1840s, however, the use of the expression in the singular began to expand, "*working class*", denoting in its use a feeling of internal solidarity to the social group and opposition to other groups, in a new apprehension of the natural social inequalities.[6] In this conception, however, the question is not simply discursive, as the relationship between words and movements constitutes the centre of Briggs' discussion.

> The change in nomenclature in the late eighteenth and early nineteenth centuries reflected a basic change not only in men's ways of viewing society but in society itself. It is with the relationship between words and movements - in an English context - that this essay is concerned.[7]

The most significant work, from the point of view of the social history of work, of that generation of studies was *The Making of the English Working Class*, by E. P. Thompson, published in 1963. In the first chapter of the book, Thompson deals with the *London Correspondence Society* (LCS), created in 1792 by shoemaker Thomas Hardy and eight companions with the aim of promoting parliamentary reform (expansion of the right to vote). Within six months, the Society announced it had 2,000 members. Despite relativizing the pioneering spirit of the London initiative, Thompson lists the elements that in his opinion defined the LCS as a new type of organization, for many the first "working-class political organisation":

> There is the working man as Secretary. There is the low weekly subscription. There is the intermingling of economic and political themes- 'the hardness of the times' and Parliamentary Reform. There is the function of the meeting, both as a social occasion and as a centre for political activity. There is the realistic attention to procedural formalities. Above all, there is the determination to propagate opinions and to organise the converted, embodied in the leading rule: 'That the number of our Members be unlimited'.[8]

The Correspondence Society, however, was not the only—or the main—reference for the organization of the new working class that was formed at the turn of the eighteenth to nineteenth century. In England, after the approval of the *Combination Acts* (1799–1800), which suppressed the right of association, other forms of worker organization, initially illegal, gradually emerged.[9] After the conquest of the right of association (with the repeal of the *Combination Acts* in 1824), unions, known there as *trade unions*, started to spread. The 1830s and 1840s marked the growth of mobilization, initially along union routes, culminating in the foundation, in 1834, of the *Grand National Consolidated Trade Unions*, cooperative-Owenist orientated, which had a short life. At the end of the decade, however, the labour movement regained its strength with the great "chartist" mobilizations (in defence of an electoral and parliamentary reform that guaranteed the extension of political rights to over-age male workers). The mobilizations at the height of Chartism resulted in some legal achievements, such as the limitation of working hours to 10 hours, but the reflux of Chartism at the end of the 1840s, under the effect of successive repressive waves, marked the beginning of a phase of containment of the English workers' struggles that lasted until the end of the century.

Following this process until the beginning of the Chartist phase, Thompson even points, in the last chapter of his book, to an already formed working class, around the mid-1830s. As when referring to the radical press of those years, stating that "an examination of this period would take us beyond the limits of this study, to a time when the working class was no longer in the making but (in its Chartist form) already made".[10] Or by stating that between the years 1831 and 1835 "the limits of this study have been reached, for there is a sense in which the working class is no longer in the making, but has been made".[11] In both cases, however, the statement is made with reservations—"in its Chartist form" and "there is a sense in which".

Thompson's definition of the working class was sufficiently broad to involve both the "objective" and the "subjective" dimensions of class, which we discussed in the first chapter. In one of the most quoted passages of twentieth-century historiography, Thompson proposes a procedural definition of class formation and, therefore, of class consciousness:

> class happens when some men, as a result of common experiences (inherited or shared), feel and articulate the identity of their interests as between themselves, and as against other men whose interests are different from (and usually opposed to) theirs. The class experience is largely determined by the productive relations into' which men are born--or enter involuntarily. Class-consciousness is the way in which these experiences are handled in cultural terms: embodied in traditions, value systems, ideas, and institutional forms. If the experience appears as determined, class-consciousness does not.[12]

Only through a thus delimited definition was it possible for Thompson to locate the making of the working class in a period considered unusual by the more traditional labour historiography, whose periodization often begins with Chartism, as the first moment of the process.

The periodization presented by Thompson, however, was not consensual even among his fellow generations in British social history. Eric Hobsbawm paid tribute to the originality of the analysis developed in *The Making* and shared several of his views on the English proletariat but criticized Thompson's proposed periodization for the process of constituting the English working class. Focusing on the turn of the nineteenth to the twentieth century, Hobsbawm ended up disagreeing with Thompson, as he identified in the Chartist and Pre-Chartist phase of English workers "the" formation of "the" class. For Hobsbawm, those were important "ancestors", but "the working class is not 'made' until long after Thompson's book ends".[13] In order to explain the reason for his periodization, Hobsbawm outlined four aspects: the growth and concentration of the working class; the change in their occupational composition; national economic integration, with concentration of capital and expansion of the economic role of the State; and, finally, the expansion of the right to vote and mass politics. From these parameters, he identified the British proletariat based on the following factors: "(...) by the physical environment in which they lived, by a style of life and leisure, by a certain class consciousness increasingly expressed in a secular tendency to join unions and to identify with a class party of Labour".[14]

It is possible to agree with Hobsbawm's valorization of unions and workers' parties as typical working-class organizations, but still disagree with the arguments of his divergence with Thompson over when the class was "made". After all, although Thompson actually pointed out a moment when the class would be "made", he did so with reservations and relativizations, because his perspective of "making" can support a procedural analysis in which the determination of a starting point, or a point of arrival, as Hobsbawm seems to want, would always be debatable. In this sense, if from the point of view of national dimensions and the weight in the economic dynamics of capitalist accumulation, it is indisputable that the class experienced a significant quantitative leap between the decades studied by Thompson and the period highlighted by Hobsbawm, this does not mean to say that the working class did not exist in England in those 1830s/1840s. After all, at the time Marx was writing about the relationship/distinction between this existence and class consciousness, in his 1847 critique of Proudhon, from the point of view of organizational experiences and collective action that characterized class consciousness (the class "for itself"). Discourses and practices with a class background also emerged in the midst of collective organizations with different dimensions and natures from the great unions at the turn of the twentieth century and before the emergence of workers' parties highlighted by Hobsbawm.

Thus, the attempt to assess class consciousness exclusively through participation in modern workers' parties and mass unions does not seem adequate to the historical process of class formation captured by Marx since the 1840s, which for the English case was rescued by Thompson in his classic study.

Ultimately, Hobsbawm's formulation could lead us to questions such as: if the working class of the Chartist period was just an "important ancestor", would the contact with this "ancestor" have been enough for Marx and Engels to carry forward their perspective that attributed to the proletariat the role of potential subject of social transformation, or did they just manifest an intuition based on a future projection of what the class could become? It would also be worth asking whether the formation of the *International Workingmen's Association* (1863), based in London and supported by sectors of the class movement in England, which, as we know, had an active participation by Marx, was just another episode of this "prehistory" of class consciousness, against the "true" British working class, which in Hobsbawm's periodization only began to manifest itself more than a decade later.

Mike Savage and Andrew Miles help us by discussing the formation of the working class in England not as a linear process, but as a movement subject to situations of such change that it could be considered a true "re-making" of the class. In an interesting synthesis of the process of class formation between 1840 and 1940, they criticize the authors associated with the "linguistic turn"—both for taking language out of reality and for trying to disqualify the centrality of class for the historical analysis—and incorporate reflections from Thompson and Hobsbawm to propose an analytical perspective of the past that can also reorient the present view of the working class:

> The working class is constantly being made and remade, and the political implications of class formation are often ambiguous and uncertain. This having been said, in the first three decades of the twentieth century the working class developed an unprecedented social and political presence in British society. Although politicians and commentators alike are wont to stress the declining salience of class in our own times, we should be cautious about projecting current scepticism back onto the historical record. Moreover, although the particular working class whose development we have examined in this book may today be undergoing a further process of re-making, this does not constitute an adequate basis for questioning the continued significance of class in general. For so long as we live in an unequal society, in which some people exploit others, class divisions are likely to have profound political ramifications.[15]

There are, however, more recent questions to Thompson's perspective (and English Social History in general) on the formation of the working class that must be considered if we are to think, from a historical point of view, of a definition of the working class broad enough to contemplate what Marx had seen as the proletariat and its potentiality.

Beyond Eurocentrism (Beyond Marx?)

Since the 2000s, a proposal to renew this field of study, self-defined as Global Labour History, willing to go beyond the limits of the Eurocentric perspective, raised new questions regarding the limits of a position like E. P. Thompson's on his path to understand the formation of the working class from the English historical process. The pointed-out problem, however, was not Thompson's definition of class from a chronological point of view—quite the contrary, as an even more elastic chronology was accepted—but rather its narrow confinement to the borders of the national state.

In a review article, in which he defines the publication of E. P. Thompson's best-known work as a milestone in a "new labour history", Marcel van der Linden states that the English historian "transformed labour history into working-class history".[16] The new labour history from the 1960s to the 1980s, according to Van der Linden, constituted a "genuine intellectual revolution", by introducing new themes into the research agenda in the area. After all, "not just labour processes and everyday culture, but gender, ethnicity, race and age also finally gained the attention they deserved, along with household structures, sexuality, and informal politics".[17]

However, says Linden, the new labour history has not escaped the traps of the "old" labour history in at least two fundamental aspects: methodological nationalism and Eurocentrism. The first "links society and the state together, and therefore considers the different nation states as a kind of 'Leibnizean Monads' for historical research". And "eurocentrism is the mental ordering of the world from the standpoint of the North-Atlantic region".[18] It is from this critique that Van der Linden advocates the need to overcome such limits, through a global labour history.

Taking *The Making of the English Working Class* as an example of those limits, Van der Linden refers to the book as follows:

> From the new global perspective, there is something peculiar about this book, something that probably no one noticed before, but which now, under different circumstances, commands our attention: Thompson reconstructs the English process of class formation (in the period 1792–1832) as a self-contained process. England is, according to his analysis, the logical unit of analysis – while external forces certainly influenced it, these are specifically portrayed as foreign influences. Thus, the French Revolution plays an important background role in Thompson's narrative, as a source

> of inspiration of working-class activities, but developments in the neighbouring countries always remain an 'externality'. Added to this is the fact that Thompson pays no attention in The Making to imperial connections. Colonialism, with its increasingly significant influence on the lives of the lower classes through the nineteenth century, is simply disregarded.[19]

One of the historiographic references that Van der Linden invokes to support his criticism is the work of Peter Linebaugh and Markus Rediker *The Many-headed Hydra*.[20] In this book, the authors compose an exemplary effort of historical analysis of the capitalism implantation process and the resistance struggles against it, starting from an analysis of the "Atlantic World"—which involved Europe, Africa and the Americas (North America and Caribbean of English language in the authors' analysis)—throughout the seventeenth and eighteenth centuries. The focus of their analysis is precisely on the heterogeneous and multi-ethnic mass of workers: enslaved Africans taken by force to the Americas; poor European immigrants, expropriated in their regions of origin (England, Ireland, etc.) and often sent forcibly to the New Continent; urban and rural poor in England during the process of primitive accumulation; along with the sailors, who could have any of the previous origins, and were like transatlantic links between the whole set. The hardships of work under various forms of coercion and the resistance struggles of that "Atlantic Proletariat" (their expression), rescued by the authors, end up composing a very rich example of the potential of a labour history that goes beyond national borders and Eurocentric traditional limits.

As the analysis of the book approaches the end of the eighteenth century, the authors value a potential unity between those who faced slavery, those who participated in the revolutionary struggles of that era of revolutions and the militants who became engaged in the construction of the first organizations, collective actions, and political projects of the working class. However, Linebaugh and Rediker conclude that the impact of the Haitian Revolution (1791–1804) generated panic among the ruling classes and intensified, in the English case, the repressive anti-Jacobin climate already initiated by the French Revolution (and expanded with the war). Hence, the paths of those struggles, up until the beginning of the 1790s, converging in their defence of the rights of the "human being", diverged a few years after, as the concepts of "race" and "class" were defined.

The tone of the authors' analysis seems charged with a double indictment. On the one hand, the renewed labour history of the 1960s—E. P. Thompson in particular—is held responsible for neglecting this potential unity (and the long history behind it) between the black and white faces of the "Atlantic proletariat". Where Thompson saw "an English agitation… for an English Democracy", Rediker and Linebaugh perceived an Atlantic circulation of ideas and emphasize that "what was most vigorous in the debate did not come from any single national experience, English or otherwise".[21]

On the other hand, the historical agents themselves are held responsible for the disjunctions. Such as Tomas Hardy, founder of the London Correspondence Society, defined by Thompson, as we saw, as "a new kind of organisation". Hardy, at the time of the foundation of the LCS, shared his house with Olaudah Equiano—who had been enslaved and was active in the early moments of English abolitionism, being the author of one of the most widely read works denouncing slavery at the time—who was also an articulator of the correspondence society. In its first meetings, the society even defined the objectives of the new organization as: fighting for equality between "the whole human race, black or white, high or low, rich or poor".[22] Soon after, with the repercussion of the revolution in São Domingos, however, Hardy and the LCS gave up the affirmation of ethnic/racial equality, fleeing from any association with a debate that was becoming more delicate and trying to ensure that the association's performance maintained the central focus on the issue of parliamentary reform. Thus, in August of that same year, instead of "the whole human race", the Society defined its scope of action, restricting it to "fellow members", "all Members were admitted high and low, rich and poor".[23] In the following years, in his writings, Hardy neglected Equiano's importance for the LCS and organizations like the correspondence society, according to the authors of *The Many-headed Hydra*, ended up making "their peace with the nation, as the working class became national".[24]

The argument has an impact, but to be somehow incorporated it deserves to be problematized. After all, as Linebaugh and Rediker acknowledge, it was not only Hardy who sought respectability for his movement—or at least hoped to escape the most violent repression—in those years. English abolitionism united figures such as Equiano and Cugoano (another former slave militant in the cause of abolition) with white militants from upper classes moved by humanitarian and, mainly, religious convictions. The path taken by the movement, prioritizing the abolition of slave trade as a first step towards a gradual end to slavery, was largely defined by the alliance built with figures of the English ruling class, such as William Wilberforce (Deputy for Yorkshire, converted to the Anglican church in 1785, who in 1787 joined Thomas Clarkson and the Quaker reformers led by Granville Sharp in the campaign for the abolition of the slave trade and was the main parliamentary spokesman for British abolitionism) and William Pitt the Younger (Prime Minister 1783 and in the 1800s, which carried on the violent repression of all radical movements in the 1790s). If Hardy abandoned the rhetoric of racial equality, that was not enough to escape the fury of Pitt's repression.[25] Equiano, on the other hand, withdrew from the more active militancy at the same time as Hardy's arrest and died shortly thereafter, in 1797.

Robin Blackburn, citing many of the same sources as Linebaugh and Rediker, sees much more collaboration and co-participation between the parliamentary and abolitionist reform movements, although he points out that "the radical democrats and 'rational Dissenters' tended to argue that the introduction of a new political system would be necessary before abolition could be effected and that slavery, not simply the slave trade, could then be overthrown".[26]

In the following decades, there was, to some extent, a bifurcation of the paths of mobilization in the struggles for the main legal reforms carried out in England: on the one hand, abolitionism (initially fighting for the end of the African slave trade, then for the end of slavery in the West Indies and beyond); on the other, parliamentary reform, understood as an extension of the right to vote. It is not so strange that it happened, after all, if English abolitionism, after successive defeats at the end of the nineteenth century, began its trajectory of legal conquests in 1807, with the passing of the end of trafficking in the following year, the moments of new parliamentary victories—such as the end of slavery in the West Indies in 1833 and the end of the apprenticeship system in 1838—coincide with the beginning of the phase of greater mobilization of the Chartist movement. And it is a fact that the working class movement faced that juncture with much more difficulty in achieving success in its demands for legal reforms. From the Peterloo massacre in 1819 to the repression of Chartist demonstrations from 1838 and onwards, passing through the containment of the disruptive potential of the radical unrest of 1831–1832, the English working class leaders faced many of the parliamentary supporters of the end of slavery in the colonies willing, at the same time, to implement all kinds of repressive measures to defend their class interests against the advances of the labour movement. The disagreements can be explained in part, therefore, less by the degree of sympathy with the cause of abolition itself and much more by the fact that some of its English parliamentary defenders—generally less engaged with the fate of enslaved populations than with liberal arguments on the economic advantages of ending slavery—remained, with analogous hypocrisy, blind to "child slavery" (as child labour in factories was commonly referred to) and other local barbarities.[27] Anyway, we saw how in the years of civil war, coinciding with the founding of the First International, as Marx insisted on recording and commemorating, the political position of the English working class was unequivocally in defence of abolition.

However, returning to the debate about the making of the working class, the central focus of the discussion so far, whether we agree to a lesser or further extent with Van der Linden's and Linebaugh-Redicker's criticisms of Thompson, must recognize that the geographical framework adopted in the work of the English historian really confined the process of "making itself" of the class to the English national space. The Atlantic perspective exemplified by *The many-headed hydra* and the proposal of a global history of labour synthesized by Van der Linden must be incorporated as important contributions, so that we can reach an understanding of the transnational processes that, by the very logic of capitalist accumulation, involved and involve the history of the working class. It should not be difficult to understand the importance of this perspective for historians located in Brazil, a territory (initially colonial and then national) that between the sixteenth and nineteenth centuries was the destination of the largest contingent of enslaved workers torn from Africa and traded as goods in the Americas, but that also experienced, between the second half of the nineteenth century and the 1920s, an intense migratory flow of European origin.

Amid this defence of a transnational, or global, perspective of labour history, a relevant debate about the concept of the working class used by labour historians also emerged. Van der Linden's proposition, in his effort to overcome Eurocentrism, led him to the realization that, in historical situations empirically studied in different parts of the globe (and particularly in the "Global South"), the borders between different forms of labour exploitation—enslaved or "free", by contracts, self-employed or waged, domestic or for the market, urban and rural—are presented in a more fluid and combined way. Therefore, he defends the need to redefine the working class. Exposing a conceptualization of class—"subaltern workers"—which takes the subordination of work (both slaves and wage earners) to the logic of capital as the central point, Van der Linden defines it as follows:

> Every carrier of labor power whose labor power is sold (or hired out) to another person under economic (or non-economic) compulsion belongs to the class of subaltern workers, regardless of whether the carrier of labor power is him- or herself selling or hiring it out and, regardless of whether the carrier him- or herself owns means of production.[28]

Van der Linden warns that his definition is provisional and that each element of it demands further reflection, but defines what for him is the centre of the common class base of all this variety of subaltern workers: "*coerced* commodification of their labor power".[29] In another text, the Dutch historian directly criticizes the limits imposed by Marx on the definition of the proletariat, for excluding slaves and the lumpenproletariat.[30] On the lumpen, Marcel's criticism of Marx is centred on the historical analysis undertaken by him on France since the Revolution of 1848. According to Van der Linden, the idea of lumpenproletariat presented in *The 18th Brumaire* involved: "i) displaced peasants; ii) displaced proletarians; and iii) self-employed; iv) dubious professions, including the mountebanks, tricksters, gamblers, brothel keepers and prostitutes".[31] We have already seen in this book how, years later, in his *Capital* chapter on the "general law of capitalist accumulation", Marx identified the unemployed and expropriated peasants, respectively, as the "floating" and "latent" contingents of relative surplus-population, therefore, as part of the proletariat. However, Van der Linden's criticism seems valid, at least for some moments in Marx's work, in the sense that the lumpenproletariat often "is not so much an analytical, as a moral category".[32]

Nevertheless, his emphasis on the specificities of labour relations in the Global South that involved not only the proletarians, but also relatively more coercive forms of exploitation, such as slavery, also subsumed under the logic of capital accumulation, seems to us more important. To say "more coercive" is to question the assumption of wage earning as simply "free" labour. We know that Marx defined the proletarian/waged worker as one who is free to sell his labour power in exchange for a wage, a condition that allows them to have the resources to go to the market to buy what he depends on to survive and continue working. This happens because the proletarian is also an expropriated individual, "liberated" by the advance of capital from any condition of autonomously providing for their subsistence, such as land and work tools. In this sense, the "freedom" to sell their labour power is, in fact, also a compulsion, since only in the market the "free" worker will be able to stay alive. Expropriation and exploitation are, therefore, inseparable elements in the proletarianization process, which led Ellen Wood to highlight the role of a "coercion by the state" that guarantees the "coercion of the market", referring to the legal arsenal used to legitimize the expropriation of workers.[33] Therefore, the analogy between wage labour and slavery, in Marx, refers to the political and economic constraints that are also inherent to wage earning. In his words, "the system of wage labour is a system of slavery, and indeed of a slavery which becomes more severe in proportion as the social productive forces of labour develop, whether the worker receives better or worse payment".[34]

Van der Linden's discussion, however, goes beyond analogy and emphasizes the unity between all forms of labour exploitation inserted in the value production circuit. In the following pages, we will focus more directly on this discussion, whose repercussions for labour history can be significant.

Subaltern Workers, Subaltern Classes, Working Class

During the debate opened by English social historians on the historical dimension of the category of working class, the proposition of the class of "subaltern workers" by Marcel van der Linden, as well as the definition of the "Atlantic proletariat" by Linebaugh and Redicker represent important contributions towards an expanded reading of the concept of class. Its strong point is precisely the recognition that, from a transnational point of view, the making of capitalism since the process of colonial expansion in the sixteenth century has subjugated different groups of male and female workers, through different forms of labour exploitation. In this specific sense, by pointing to the transnational interconnection of the processes of the Atlantic proletariat's class struggle since the beginning of colonial expansion, Linebaugh and Redicker provide, as we have seen, sufficient evidence for Van der Linden's claim on the limits of methodological nationalism for the labour history renewed by contributions such as E. P. Thompson's in the 1960s. Other authors also informed the Dutch historian's critique.

Jairus Banaji, for example, in a research effort on modes of production, addressing both pre-capitalist situations in the ancient and modern East, as well as European historical development up to contemporaneity, proposes an expansion of the most current understandings about the concept of relations of production, in order to perceive it as encompassing different facets of social relations and not only the forms of labour exploitation.[35] By this, he intends to demonstrate that if "accumulation of capital, that is, *capitalist* relations of production, can be based on forms of exploitation that are typically *precapitalist*, then clearly there is not one ostensibly unique configuration of capital but a series of *distinct configurations*, forms of the accumulation process, implying other combinations".[36]

In the periphery of capitalism, this issue was, in a way, already present in many historical studies, although the rigidity of a more deterministic framework led a good part of historians to seek to situate the reality of the South of the Globe in the same evolution stages—ancient slave, feudal, capitalist modes of production—which were supposed to be the explanatory key to European history. In different recent approaches, the understanding of the way in which forms of labour exploitation, marked at some level by compulsion, were functional to capitalist accumulation has led to very interesting results.

The Indian labour historiography has presented new contributions to this debate, by focusing on forms of unfree labour exploitation employed to ensure large-scale agricultural production on the plantation of colonial India, in the late nineteenth and early twentieth century, when slavery was already formally abolished in the "West Indies". This was the case for the *coolies* employed in the tea *plantations* of the province of Assam who, travelled long distances to take on work in gangs on the plantations; they were bound to long-term employment contracts (indentured), with very low wages, under the justification of covering the costs of large landowners with their transport and housing.[37] The criminalization of the "breach of contract" (attempted escapes and other forms of resistance to compulsory labour), including the transference by the colonial state of punitive power to the owners, was the main form of guaranteeing the workforce for the accumulation of English and Indian capital associated in that lucrative enterprise linked to intercontinental commerce.[38]

Regarding the South of the United States, Latin America, and the Caribbean of nineteenth-century slavery, an interesting parallel can be drawn from Dale Tomich's discussion of a "second slavery", a proposition that aims to account for the moment when slavery was integrated to the dynamics of an industrial capitalism already developing in Europe. That was a different moment from the first centuries of exploitation of slave labour in the Americas, in which slave relations were part of the process of primitive accumulation of capital (or "commercial capitalism" as other authors prefer to characterize the period from the fourteenth to the eighteenth centuries). In Tomich's words, in the nineteenth century, when the typically capitalist relations of production already dominate in England, "the systemic meaning of slavery was transformed". As Tomich explains,

> The products of slave labor entered directly into the consumption of the European wage working class on an increasing scale. They were important on two counts: as a means of maintaining the exchange relation between wage labor and capital and as a direct contribution to lowering the cost of reproducing the labor power of wage labor. As the capital/wage labor relation became widely established, a systemic imperative to increase surplus value by reducing the value of labor power emerged, which required slave producers to provide cheaper and cheaper goods for working class consumption.[39]

This refinement of the researchers' view has produced interesting analysis results also regarding Europe and even the first industrial capitalist economy. Alessandro Stanziani, for example, has been publishing studies in which he demonstrates how the dominant notion of "free" work in most of Europe—including England—until the mid-nineteenth century was "as service", regulated by civil and criminal law, limiting significantly the mobility and the possibility of "free choice" of those workers. According to Stanziani, the concepts of free and unfree that we share today about labour relations were only established as dominant in the twentieth century.[40]

These contributions have as their main merit to demonstrate that the immediate and direct association between capitalist accumulation and exclusivity, or even the predominance, of free wage labour, should not be a presupposition of historical analyses. Even acknowledging the relevance of all these contributions by contemporary historians, it is still necessary to ask: are these concerns with the degree of articulation between "free" and "unfree" forms of labour completely original elaborations of the new labour historiography?

It doesn't seem to be the case. Returning to the central reference for this book, in its own way, the question of the role of other exploited social groups, beyond the waged working class was already essential for Marx, especially in writings with more direct political content, in which he sought to define the scope of social struggles that could give rise to and sustain the socialist revolution. In his last studies, when he came across the real movements of class struggle in countries of the European "periphery" (Russia in particular), in the 1870s and 1880s, Marx affirmed the impossibility of taking the English case of working-class formation, addressed in *Capital*, as a model of universal validity. According to him, the "sketch of the genesis of capitalism in Western Europe", presented in the book, was not "a historico-philosophical theory of general development, imposed by fate on all peoples, whatever the historical circumstances in which they are placed",[41] as he stated in a letter to the editor of a Russian newspaper in 1877. Four years later he repeated, in his famous letter to Vera Zasulitch, for which he wrote several more detailed drafts, that "the 'historical inevitability' of this process [the genesis of capitalist production] is expressly limited to the *countries of Western Europe*".[42] Instigated to reply, in the same correspondence, and in his more general contacts with the Russian *Narodniks*, about the revolutionary potentiality of the peasants, Marx outlined arguments around the specificity of the Russian rural commune, which generated a situation very different from the one through which, in Western Europe, an earlier form of private ownership of land had been converted into capitalist private ownership. In the same letter to Vera Zasulich he states that, having eliminated the "deleterious influences which are assailing it", the commune could be "the falcrum of social regeneration in Russia".[43]

In the following year, the preface to the second edition of the *Communist Manifesto* in Russian, signed by Marx and Engels, we can read that the "historical inevitability" of the peasant's conversion into a proletarian through their separation from the means of production (land in particular) was only fully manifested in the West, as it was a matter of converting "one form of private property into another form of private property". There, they outlined a more affirmative answer to the question of the subject of transformation: "If the Russian Revolution becomes the signal for a proletarian revolution in the West, so that the two complement each other, the present Russian common ownership of land may serve as the starting point for communist development".[44] In these considerations, Marx and Engels were careful to avoid taking the possibility that a revolution initiated by the peasants in the periphery could suffice by itself, since only combined in an international dimension with the proletarian revolution it could triumph.

We have seen that Marx did not realize this potential of other social groups subjected to the domination of capital only in the final years of his life. In the 1850s, he already foresaw the possibility that class struggles in the Asian colonies (China and India in particular) would have a decisive impact on the process of the European proletarian revolution. In his writings from the 1860s on the revolutionary dimension of overcoming slavery in the Civil War in the United States, also commented on above, he advanced in his understanding of enslaved workers fighting for their freedom as subjects of their own history. In *Capital*, he categorically stated that "labour cannot emancipate itself in the white skin where in the black it is branded".[45]

The classics of revolutionary thought from the turn of the nineteenth to the twentieth century, therefore, had solid references (although not all the texts by Marx and Engels cited here were available at that time) and they also paid attention to the issue. Thus, they valued the international dimension of the socialist revolutionary process and pointed out that the unequal and combined character of capitalist development, in its phase of global imperialist expansion, generated a coexistence between old and new forms of relations of production, which acquired specificities in relation to the process of capitalist industrial development in the first nations that underwent it, such as England.[46]

In explaining, in 1930, why the socialist revolution took place first in Russia, where the proletariat was a minority (though concentrated in large, modern factories) in relation to the peasant mass of the rural population, León Trotsky synthesizes the main arguments of the theory of uneven and combined development. Working with the "backward countries"/"advanced countries" pair to account for the difference between the centre and the periphery of the capitalist system in its imperialist stage, and with the notion of "laws" to define Lenin's theoretical proposals and his, Trotsky thus presented the question:

> The laws of history have nothing in common with a pedantic schematism. Unevenness, the most general law of the historic process, reveals itself most sharply and complexly in the destiny of the backward countries. Under

> the whip of external necessity their backward culture is compelled to make leaps. From the universal law of unevenness thus derives another law which, for the lack of a better name, we may call the law of ***combined development*** – by which we mean a drawing together of the different stages of the journey, a combining of the separate steps, an amalgam of archaic with more contemporary forms.[47]

It was a similar interpretative perspective that allowed the Peruvian Marxist José Carlos Mariategui to perceive the Latin American specificity and propose a political defence of the revolutionary potential of the indigenous element in the socialist struggles of the Andean countries, even in the 1920s. For Mariategui, the indigenist claim remained isolated, or manipulated by different populisms, manifesting itself strictly to ethnic, cultural, or educational aspects. It demanded economic and political expression, through its link with the land issue. Understanding the potential that could arise from such a change in the orientation of the indigenous movement as being decisively linked to its "inbreeding" with international proletarian socialism, Mariategui explained that:

> Faith in the renaissance of the Indian is not pinned to the material process of 'Westernizing' the Quechua country. The soul of the Indian is not raised by the white man's civilization or alphabet but by the myth, the idea, of the Socialist revolution. The hope of the Indian is absolutely revolutionary. That same myth, that same idea, are the decisive agents in the awakening of other ancient peoples or races in ruin: the Hindus, the Chinese, et cetera. Universal history today tends as never before to chart its course with a common quadrant. Why should the Inca people, who constructed the most highly-developed and harmonious communistic system, be the only ones unmoved by this worldwide emotion? The consanguinity of the Indian movement with world revolutionary currents is too evident to need documentation. I have said already that I reached an understanding and appreciation of the Indian through socialism.[48]

Given that capital operates in different ways to expropriate and exploit, according to the previous realities it confronts, both Marx's perspective on Russian peasants, inspiring the analyses that highlighted the unequal and combined forms of capitalist development in the periphery, and the valorization of the Indigenous element (the communitarian peasant) in Latin American social struggles, present in Mariategui, are far from treating the historical specificities of "peripheral" situations in relation to

European/Western capitalism as revealing absolute particularities. They understand them in connection with a broader totality of the contradictory movement of history. Hence, Mariategui can, at the same time, reject the Eurocentrism of the "civilizing" project of capital and proclaim the universality of the socialist emancipatory project, understanding the necessary link between the specific demands of indigenous Peruvians (related to the issue of land and labour exploitation, under the aegis of capitalism in its imperialist phase) and the international struggle of the proletariat for socialist revolution.

Still regarding Latin America, it was with the so-called dependency theory, in its Marxist version, from the 1960s, that the study of the specific but subordinate path of capitalist development in this peripheral space began more incisively to free itself from the attempts to reproduce a European model of evolution of modes of production. One of the most expressive representatives of this perspective was Ruy Mauro Marini.[49] As far as our discussion in this book is concerned, one of the most important suggestions put forward by the Marxist theory of dependency as developed by Marini concerns the specificities of labour exploitation in the capitalist periphery. Pressed by its dependence on imperialism, a peripheral capitalism like the Brazilian one could only develop by extracting a sufficiently high amount of surplus value, to guarantee not only the reproduction of capital internally, but also the remuneration of central capitalism, in a kind of compensation for their relative disadvantages. This "value transfer" took place, according to Marini, through "unequal exchanges" that characterize foreign trade (and the remittances of profits from multinationals, payment of *royalties* for patents, external financing, etc.) between a dependent economy, with lower organic composition of capital, and imperialist central economies. To compensate for this external appropriation, it is therefore necessary to perpetuate forms of "compression of wages below their value", typical of dependent economies, in addition to "relative" forms (always limited by a lower productivity in comparison to central countries) and "absolute" expansion of the surplus value. The central condition for dependent capitalist development is therefore this "overexploitation" of labour force. This category was not designed to account for each specific situation of labour exploitation but aimed to explain the combination of various forms of exploitation in the set of Latin American capitalist social relations. According to Marini:

> the problem posed by unequal exchange for Latin America is not exactly that of opposing the transfer of value it implies, but compensating for the loss of surplus value, and that, incapable of preventing it at the level of market relations, the dependent economy's reaction is to compensate it in terms of internal production.[50]

Faced with such a problem generated by dependency, the solutions adopted by the peripheral economies of Latin America combined three forms of expansion of the extraction of surplus value commented by Marx: the increase in labour intensity, the extension of the working day and the reduction of consumption capacity of workers—by reducing the value of wages, "normally" equivalent to the average values necessary, in a given socio-historical circumstance, for the reproduction of labour power—to levels below the standard necessary for the adequate reproduction of this labour power.

Thus, in a movement of formation of capitalism in the dependent periphery that started from imperialist determinations to impose a standard to local production in the periphery, Marini locates both slavery and hybrid systems of labour exploitation (between wage-earning and serfdom, as in the example of the sharecropping with debt ties to farm shops [sistema de barracão] in the Brazilian countryside) in export agriculture, as "one of the ways through which Latin America reaches capitalism".[51]

The arguments compiled so far reinforce, on the one hand, the need for a very broad definition of the working class to account for the set of situations in which "*coerced* commodification of their labour power" predominates, as proposed by the notion of "subaltern workers" by Van der Linden. However, as we have seen, the definition of the working class proposed by Marx—and followed by the debate on the most critical strand of twentieth century Marxism, of which we are seeking just a few examples here—goes far beyond the more strictly economic dimension of labour power as a commodity subordinated to capital, since it also comprises a political dimension of the class as a social subject.

How to combine the recognition that the subsumption of capital involves unwaged labour relations, especially on the periphery of the world market, with the concern to identify the social subjects of historical transformation? We suggest here that, through the category "subaltern classes (or social groups)" it is possible to point out a path of analysis that respects the distinctions in the level of collective consciousness and, therefore, of its society projects, among different groups of workers subordinated to capital, because they are compulsorily submitted to a process of commodification of their labour power. To reach this, we can start from Van der Linden's own definition of subaltern workers, seeking to go beyond the abstract homogeneity of the exploitation of the labour power commodity by capital, to try to achieve the concreteness of the social action of collective subjects. The category "subaltern" appears in Van der Linden's proposal with reference to the term as used by the so-called Subaltern Studies, which emerged from the initiative of the Indian historian Ranajit Guha.

Concerned with overcoming the limits of both the colonialist vision and the Indian nationalist historiography, which paid special attention to the anti-colonial struggles of urban social groups, but completely neglected the peasant majority of the population and its fragmented but relevant manifestations of resistance, Guha defined the subaltern, in the writings that inaugurated a whole line of studies in the following decades, in opposition to the colonial and local elites. Thus, his broad definition treated "people" and "subaltern classes" as synonyms, quite inclusively:

> The social groups and elements included in this category represent the demographic difference between the total Indian population and all those whom we have described as the 'elite'. Some of these classes and groups such as the lesser rural gentry, impoverished landlords, rich peasants and upper-middle peasants who 'naturally' ranked among the 'people' and the 'subaltern', could under certain circumstances act for the 'elite', as explained above, and therefore be classified as such in some local or regional situations – an ambiguity which it is up to the historian to sort out on the basis of a close and judicious reading of his evidence.[52]

A few years later, Asok Sen, in the midst of the same movement, reinforced the use of the term subaltern classes to define "the entire people that is subordinate in terms of class, caste, age, gender, and office, or in any other way".[53] At the turn of the 1990s, however, the subaltern studies were strongly influenced by the already mentioned "linguistic turn" and distanced themselves, in most cases, from analytical concerns involving social classes and their conflicts.

However, in its first phase, Guha and the Indian historians linked to his project sought the "subaltern" category in Antonio Gramsci. Gramsci was also referred to by Van der Linden. Resuming Gramsci's original explanatory key can be a fruitful way to face, in the past as well as in the present, the emancipatory potential of all sets of workers subjected to exploitation by capital.

The concept of subaltern classes/groups in Gramsci allows for more than one approach. On the one hand, referring to the "subalterns" when approaching the complex capitalist societies of the twentieth century, he introduces a reflection on the moment when the "masses" abandon passivity and assume the role of "historical person, protagonist". It is an analysis of the process through which class consciousness "rises" from common sense, when the limits of a messianic worldview, fuelled by deterministic readings, is surpassed by the philosophy of praxis (historical materialism) in its most elaborate manifestation.[54] In this sense, the "subaltern classes" correspond to those that, in the revolutionary struggle, can constitute an anti-capitalist "united front", particularly the proletariat and the peasantry.

The concept of subaltern groups/classes is also useful for Gramsci to discuss the "spontaneous" and "organized" dimensions of the movements conducted by these classes. Spontaneity historically represented a constitutive role of the action of the subaltern classes:

> It may be said that spontaneity is therefore characteristic of the "history of the subaltern classes", and indeed of their most marginal and peripheral elements; these have not achieved any consciousness of the class "for itself", and consequently it never occurs to them that their history might have some possible importance, that there might be some value in leaving documentary evidence of it.[55]

Based on the example he lived from the revolutionary strikes in Turin at the turn of the 1910s to 1920s (the "red biennium"), Gramsci seeks to demonstrate how the organization that emerged from the more conscious sector of the subaltern classes must start precisely from the spontaneous element of their manifestations of revolt to drive them, with a programme of "intellectual and moral reform" (a revolutionary consciousness in this case). Avoiding to immediately repudiate "spontaneism", his aim is to go beyond it in order to triumph over the tendency towards the fragmentation of struggles. In other words, through this concept, Gramsci updates the discussion on the potential of the proletariat (in alliance with other sectors subordinated by uneven capitalist development, as the peasants) as a transforming historical subject. Recalling the "red biennium", Gramsci states that the element of spontaneity was not neglected by the political leadership, on the contrary:

> It was educated, directed, purged of extraneous contaminations; the aim was to bring it into line with modem theory – but in a living and historically effective manner. The leaders themselves spoke of the "spontaneity" of the movement, and rightly so. This assertion was a stimulus, a tonic, an element of unification in depth; above all it denied that the movement was arbitrary, a cooked-up venture, and stressed its historical necessity. It gave the masses a "theoretical" consciousness of being creators of historical and institutional values, of being founders of a State. This unity between "spontaneity" and "conscious leadership" or "discipline" is precisely the real political action of the subaltern classes, in so far as this is mass politics and not merely an adventure by groups claiming to represent the masses.[56]

It is precisely the discussion of the tendency to be spontaneous and fragmentary in the subaltern classes, combined with the debate on the forms of consciousness, that serves as a bridge to understand the broader dimension, in terms of its historicity, that Gramsci had attributed to the concept of subaltern classes, employing it, for example, to deal with Roman slaves and medieval peasants under lordship. In this historical dimension, what Gramsci proposed was a methodological path of analysis—sometimes in the form of a study plan—that sought to rescue the "fragmented and episodic" history of these groups, seeking to perceive in it a "tendency to (at least provisional stages of) unification", which is "continually interrupted by the activity of the ruling groups; it therefore can only be demonstrated when a historical cycle is completed and this cycle culminates in a success".[57]

Returning to the central problem of the discussion, I turned to Gramsci to highlight that both in the analysis of his present—closely related to the revolutionary social project he proposed—and especially in his methodological notes for the study of the past, his conception of subaltern classes can be quite pertinent for the historical studies developed today. In his analysis, as in those of Lenin, Trotsky and Mariátegui highlighted above, the concern with the subjective dimension, of class consciousness and, therefore, of the action of class as a historical subject, is clearly present, in a sense that resumes and develops the conception of Marx.

By replacing the aforementioned examples, through the category "subaltern classes", it may be possible to account for the class dimension of the process of formal subsumption of waged labour, but also unfree, or self-employed—to capital, in "peripheral" (or even "central") situations in which different forms of labour exploitation coexist. But, without losing sight of the complex ways of defining the collective subjectivity of social classes, that is, including the diversity of society projects that such different forms of exploitation can generate, bearing in mind their tendency to unify, which can only be completed in historical movements in which the aspects of organization and spontaneity successfully complement each other, with an emphasis, of course, on revolutionary experiences. In other words, in certain historical situations in which capital subordinates different social groups, through labour relationships that do not always involve wage earning, we could better understand the process if, instead of relating it to a single class of *subaltern workers*, as Van der Linden suggests, we paid attention to the specifics, but also to the possible tendencies towards unification in collective action that Gramsci refers to through the category of *subaltern classes*. Social groups that, despite having the subordination to capital in common, can be distinguished by different forms of social consciousness, whose tendency towards unification tends to manifest itself in certain specific moments of intensification of social struggles.

The specificities of the predominantly waged proletariat do not disappear from this explanation, nor does the potential of this working class as a subject of social transformation. On the other hand, the unequal and combined way in which capitalism, in its necessary global expansion, has subordinated the workforce around the world throughout its historical path is not reduced to free/wage labour. Thinking about the diversity, in time and space, of the subaltern classes, without losing sight of the specificities of the working class (also diverse and broad), can be useful for us not only to understand the past of the capitalist mode of production, but also its present, in times of expanded reproduction of expropriations and implementation of precariousness as a norm.

Notes

1. Patrick Joyce, *Democratic Subjects: Studies in the History of the Self and the Social in Nineteenth Century England*, Cambridge, Cambridge University Press, 1994.

2. Ibid., p. 1.
3. Ibid., p. 2.
4. Gareth Stedman Jones, *Languages of Class: Studies in English Working Class history, 1832–1982*, Cambridge, Cambridge University Press, 1983, p. 21.
5. Ibid., p. 8.
6. Asa Briggs, "The Language of Class in Early Nineteenth Century England", In A. Briggs & J. Saville (eds.), *Essays on Labour History*, London, Macmillan, 1960, pp. 43–44.
7. Ibid., p. 44.
8. E. P. Thompson, *The Making of the English Working Class*, New York, Vintage Books, 1966, pp. 20–21.
9. We would not have the conditions, nor the competence, for a more accurate reconstruction of the English process. Among "classical" and contemporary references, we suggest G. D. H. Cole & A. W. Filson, *British Working Class Movements; Select Documents, 1789–1875*. London, Macmillan, 1967. Mike Savage & Andrew Miles, *The Remaking of the English Working Class. 1840–1940*. London, Routledge, 1994. Eric Hobsbawm, *Worlds of Labour*. London, Weidenfeld and Nicolson, 1984.
10. E. P. Thompson, *The Making*, pp. 728–729.
11. Ibid., p. 807.
12. E. P. Thompson, idem, pp. 9–10.
13. Eric Hobsbawm, "The Making of the Working Class, 1870–1914", In *Worlds of Labour*, op. cit., p. 196.
14. Ibid., p. 194. It is interesting, however, that in another article published in the same collection—"Notes on Class Consciousness"—Hobsbawm states that the first manifestations of this consciousness took place in the 1830s and 1840s, referring to the change in vocabulary, which as we saw was discussed by Asa Briggs. Ibid., p. 36.
15. M. Savage & A. Miles, *The Remaking*, p. 90.
16. Marcel van der Linden, "Labour History: The Old, the New and the Global", *African Studies*, Vol. 66, No. 2, 2007, 169–180. p. 169.
17. Ibid., p. 169.
18. Ibid., p. 171.
19. Ibid., p. 170.

20. Peter Linebaugh & Marcus Rediker, *The Many-Headed Hydra: Sailors, Slaves, Commoners, and the Hidden History of the Revolutionary Atlantic*, Boston, Beacon Press, 2000.
21. Ibid., p. 285.
22. Thomas Hardy, April 1792. Apud., P. Linebaugh & M. Rediker, *The Many-Headed Hydra*, p. 339 e 354.
23. Ibid., p. 340.
24. Ibid., p. 352.
25. In 1794, two years after the founding of the London Correspondence Society, Hardy was arrested and charged with high treason. E. P. Thompson, *The Making*, Vol. 1, pp. 18–20.
26. Robin Blackburn, *The Overthrow of Colonial Slavery (1776–1848)*, Verso, 1988, p. 147.
27. Royden Harison, British Labor and American Slavery, *Science & Society*, Vol. 25, No. 4, December 1961, pp. 291–319. Philip S. Foner, *British Labor and the American Civil War*, New York, Holmes & Meier, 1981.
28. Marcel van der Linden, *Wokers of the World: Essays Towards a Global Labor History*, Leiden, Brill, 2008, p. 33.
29. Ibid., p. 34.
30. Marcel van der Linden, "Who Are the Workers of the World? Marx and Beyond", *Workers of the World*, Vol. 1, No. 2, January 2013.
31. Ibid., pp. 70–71.
32. Ibid., p. 72.
33. Ellen Wood, *The Origin of Capitalism*, London, Verso, 2002, p. 69.
34. *MECW*, vol. 24, p. 92.
35. Jairus Banaji, *Theory as History: Essays on Modes of Production and Exploitation*, Leiden, Brill, 2010.
36. Idem, p. 9.
37. The largest work on work in Assam's tea plantations is Rana Behal, *One Hundred Years of Servitude. Political Economy of Tea Plantations in Colonial Assam*, Delhi, Tulika Books, 2014.
38. Prabhu Mohapatra, "Regulated Informality: Legal Constructions of Labour Relations in Colonial India, 1814–1926", In Sabyasachi; Lucassen (org.), *Workers in the Informal Sector*: Studies Labour in History, 1800–2000, Nova Delhi, Macmillan, 2005.
39. Dale Tomich, *Through the Prism of Slavery: Labor, Capital, and World Economy*, Lanham, Rowman & Littlefield, p. 70.

40. Alessandro Stanziani, "Introduction: Labour Institutions in a Global Perspective, from the Seventeenth to the Twentieth Century", *International Review of Social History*, Vol. 54, Part 3, December 2009.
41. *MECW*, vol. 24, p. 200.
42. *MECW*, vol. 24, p. 370.
43. Ibid., p. 371.
44. *MECW*, vol. 24, p. 426.
45. *MECW*, vol. 35, p. 305.
46. See the idea of "unequal growth" in Lenin, for instance in *Imperialism: The Higher Stage of Capitalism*, Resistance Books, 1999, p. 139.
47. Leon Trotsky, *History of the Russian Revolution*, Marxists Internet Archive, 2000, p. 3. For a recent discussion on the theory of unequal and combined development that includes considerations about its developments by authors like Novak and Mandel, see Marcel van der Linden, "The 'Law' of Uneven and Combined Development: Some Underdeveloped Thoughts", *Historical Materialism*, Vol. 15, 2007, pp. 145–165.
48. Jose Carlos Mariátegui, "Prologue to Tempestad en los Andes by Valcarcel", In J. C. Mariátegui, *Seven Interpretative Essays on Peruvian Reality*. Available at: https://www.marxists.org/archive/mariateg/works/7-interpretive-essays/essay02.htm, accessed in November 2019.
49. Ruy Mauro Marini, "Dialética da Dependência" (1973), In Roberta Traspadini e João Pedro Stédile (orgs.), *Ruy Mauro Marini: vida e obra*, São Paulo, Expressão Popular, 2005. It worth briefly noting, that Marini's Marxist dependence theory is distinct from those studies that have also been identified as dependence theory, developed for example by Fernando H. Cardoso & Enzo Faletto, *Dependência e Desenvolvimento na América Latina: Ensaio de Interpretação Sociológica*, 4ª ed., Rio de Janeiro, Zahar Editores, 1977 (originally written in 1966). An excellent synthesis of the main assumptions of Marini's proposal and of the Marxist theory of dependency can be found in Marcelo D. Carcanholo, *Dependencia, Super-explotación del Trabajo y Crisis: una Interpretación desde Marx*, Madrid, Maia Ediciones, 2017.
50. Idem, p. 154.
51. Idem, p. 160.

52. Ranahit Guha, "On Some Aspects of the Historiography of Colonial India", In *Selected Subaltern Studies*, New York, Oxford Press, 1988, pp. 37–44. The mentioned essay was originally published in 1982.
53. Asok Sen, "Subaltern Studies: Class, Capital and Community", In Ranajit Guha (ed.), *Subaltern Studies V. Writings on South Asian History and Society*, Delhi, Oxford University Press, 1987.
54. A. Gramsci, *Selections from the Prison Notebooks*, pp. 334–337.
55. Ibid., p.196.
56. Ibid., p. 198.
57. Ibid., pp. 54–55.

CHAPTER 6

Final Considerations

The thesis defended in this book is simple: the working class, also called the proletariat, as it appears in the work of Karl Marx, was and still is valid as an analytical category for the understanding of social life under capitalism. The way to defend such thesis was, as it should be, starting from the reflections of Marx himself, whose synthesis constituted the first part of this work.

What is simple, however, can still be complex. The working class is not a category of analysis invented in an office of philosophical studies. Since the first decades of the nineteenth century, it went through a process of formation, as a concrete historical reality, a social relationship that existed when Marx (and Engels) became familiar and identified with it. And, like all concrete reality, the working class is also a synthesis of multiple determinations.

The starting point for understanding it is the material determinations that dispose men and women in different positions in relations of production, opposing the owners of the means of production to the wide range of dispossessed, expropriated of any means of their own to reproduce their life, in a world governed by the logic of commodities. They are left with their labour power, also commodified, to be exchanged, usually for some form of wage, to seek the reproduction of life, mainly through the purchase of other goods. The working class, however, is not only defined

M. B. Mattos, *The Working Class from Marx to Our Times*, Marx, Engels, and Marxisms,
https://doi.org/10.1007/978-3-030-97355-1_6

by its position in relation to the means of production, but it defines itself, insofar as it develops a class consciousness and presents a potential to act as a subject of social transformation. That is why Marx identified with it, because he found proletarian organizations and political projects to overcome capitalism in his wanderings from his homeland, (the not yet fully unified) Germany, to his exiles in France, Belgium, and England in the 1840s.

Bearing in mind these different dimensions of the working class category, as they appeared in Marx's texts, or by some of his best interpreters, which were resumed here in a very synthetic way, the book also presented the discussion about its validity, in three steps. Given the current picture of labour relations in the world (in the "centre" as in the "periphery"), does the category of proletariat/working class, as systematized by Marx, still have analytical validity? Or were those who affirmed that this category had no explanatory potential to account for the current transformations in this contemporary "world of labour", or even those who define the proletariat as a collective actor inherently conforming to the logic of capital, correct? And in the historical analyses of the formation and historical development of capitalism, in the North as well as in the Global South, does the working class category maintain its analytical potential? Anyone who has read this book to the end knows that the answers given here to the first and last question were affirmative, as well as the negative answers given to the second set of questions.

As it is a synthesis work based on previously developed reflections, and not specific empirical research, these questions and answers structured the writing plan in the second half of the book. Its main conclusion is that the alternatives presented by those interpretations that questioned the analytical validity of the working class category, its potential as a social subject, or even its concrete existence, so far have proved to be of little use in understanding the complex and contradictory reality in which we live, and that there is nothing to indicate that they may have contributed to transforming it.

Perhaps, such criticisms projected onto Marx and his discussion of the proletariat the simplifications and determinisms produced throughout the twentieth century (often appealing to his name), ignoring, or purposefully disregarding, what was effectively written by the German revolutionary. The ironic thing is that, under the justification of overcoming deterministic and simplifying readings, they produced other determinisms and simplifications that contrast sharply with the complexity of the analytical and political treatment that the working class had in Marx's work.

Marx did not produce a theory of social stratification, which is why he does not provide us with econometric parameters for the delimitation of classes, because at least he did not reduce, as we have seen, class to an economic phenomenon. He did not nurture a fetishist faith in a labour or working class society, as he bet on the historical-transforming potential of this class precisely because he understood that its struggle for emancipation could only be successful if it resulted in its self-abolition, in the midst of the emancipation of all humankind from the logic of abstract, exploited, alienated labour. He did not present homogenizing or static definitions, as he referred to a dynamic historical process, which engendered a set of social relations.

This is not to say that Marx's reflection on the working class exhausts our analytical and/or political problems. On the contrary, Marx did not explore all the analytic insights that his analyses of capital and capitalist society engendered, nor could we expect him to. Furthermore, if class can only be understood as a historical process and social relationship, the nearly two centuries that separate us from its first encounters with the working class place us with the obligation to permanently confront such reflections with the reality of contemporary capitalism.

Marx does not fare badly in this confrontation. As long as we recognize that the proletariat he sought to understand (and in whose struggles and organizations he sought to act) was perceived by him, in many moments of his work, as heterogeneous and crossed by several contradictions. During the long process of researching and writing *Capital*, Marx had the opportunity to study and discuss the internal divisions among workers. Some were directly derived from the complexity of the large industry, whose birth he was witnessing. In the modern factory, he saw the emergence not only of differences in payment levels, but also in the roles of waged workers especially charged with overseeing the production process, acting as representations of capital on the factory floor. Other divisions had their origin in ideological forms (never devoid of material ground) of prejudice and oppression—national, ethnic, racial—the result of which turned out to be the intensification of competition and disputes within the class, which at the political level resulted in the weakening of its potential to confront the interests of capital.

In the case of other aspects of the heterogeneity of the proletariat and other internal cleavages, which are ideologically anchored in (and reproduce, but transforming) pre-existing forms of oppression to capitalism, such as gender oppression (and the permanence of the patriarchal family), its specific analysis may have captured only a few characteristics. The totalizing analyses that Marx produced about capital and the dynamics of capitalist accumulation, however, make room for an understanding of the theme that is absent in other interpretative perspectives. Thus, Marx and Engels denounced it in several works the oppression of women within the patriarchal family and in *Capital* the first pointed to the drama of female industrial work. What could be seem as the main contribution to the understanding of the unity between this form of oppression and capitalist accumulation, however, was not developed by him, but by Marxist feminists who wrote more than a century later and pointed to the centrality of reproductive labour, as an essential element to the maintenance, reproduction (biological and social), and regulation of the price of labour power.

This is one of the best examples of how a reflection that recognizes the insufficiencies of certain specific discussions in Marx's work often finds richer answers in his own writings—at least from the point of view of the totalizing method of understanding the contradictions of social life under capital—than in perspectives that isolate a specific aspect of the class from its role in the set of social relations. Recognizing the heterogeneity, diversity, and historical dynamics of the working class collective subject, without losing sight of its existence as a relational unit, is a challenge, for which I believe we are better accompanied with Marx.

The first edition of this book was completed 200 years after Marx's birth. We live in an era in which humanity finds itself increasingly dominated by the destructive logic of commodities; in which social inequalities have reached such a point that only a handful of capitalists, less than the number of fingers on two hands, appropriate the same amount of wealth produced by the men and women who work across the planet as half of the world's population (almost 4 billion human beings). We live in a time in which the new forms of digital communication, in which great hopes are placed on the democratization of information, have often served to expand the ideological and fetishizing limits that oppose a full and critical understanding of the world in which we live. These are times when the democratizing masks of the bourgeois state seem less and less relevant in face of the growth of the open forms of coercion that characterize contemporary class domination. It should not be difficult to recognize that, in our context, an understanding of social dynamics that explains the forms of exploitation, alienation, and oppression that characterize social relations—conflicting relations between social classes—under the rule of capital, as Marx left us, is increasingly current. It is as current as the political project of overcoming class society, presented and represented by the social subject working class, which Marx so deeply understood and defended.

Bibliography

Anderson, Kevin, *Marx at the Margins: On Nationalism, Ethnicity, and Non-western Societies*. Chicago: Chicago University Press, 2010.

Antunes, Ricardo, "Trabalho uno ou omni: a dialética entre o trabalho concreto e o trabalho abstrato", *Argumentum*, vol. 2, no. 2, jul./dez. 2010.

———, *The Meanings of Work*. Leiden: Brill, 2013.

Arcary, Valério, *Um reformismo quase sem reformas: uma crítica marxista do governo Lula em defesa da revolução brasileira*. São Paulo: Sundermann, 2011.

Arruzza, Cínzia, *Dangerous Liaisons: The Marriages and Divorces of Marxism and Feminism*. London: Merlin Press, 2013.

———, "Remarks on Gender", *Viewpoint Magazine*, September 2, 2014, https://viewpointmag.com/2014/09/02/remarks-on-gender/.

Bakan, Abigail, "Marxism and Antiracism: Rethinking the Politics of Difference", *Rethinking Marxism: A Journal of Economics, Culture & Society*, vol. 20, no. 2, March 2008.

Bakhtin, Mikhail (Volochínov), *Marxism and the Philosophy of Language*. Harvard: Harvard University Press, 1996.

Banaji, Jairus, *Theory as History: Essays on Modes of Production and Exploitation*. Leiden: Brill, 2010.

Behal, Rana, *One Hundred Years of Servitude. Political Economy of Tea Plantations in Colonial Assam*. Delhi: Tulika Books, 2014.

Bensaid, Daniel "Trabalho e emancipação", in Bensaid, D. & Lowy, Michel, *Marxismo, modernidade e utopia*. São Paulo: Xamã, 2000.

———, *Os irredutíveis: teoremas da resistência para o tempo atual*. São Paulo: Boitempo, 2008.

M. B. Mattos, *The Working Class from Marx to Our Times*, Marx, Engels, and Marxisms, https://doi.org/10.1007/978-3-030-97355-1

———, *Marx for Our Times: Adventures and Misadventures of a Critique*. London: Verso, 2009.

Bethencourt, Francisco, *Racisms: From the Crusades to the Twentieth Century*. Princeton: Princeton University Press, 2014.

Betti, Eloisa, "Gender and Precarious Labor in a Historical Perspective", *International Labour and Working-Class History*, n° 89, 2016.

Bhattacharya, Tithi (ed.), *Social Reproduction Theory: Remapping Class, Recentering Oppression*. London: Pluto Press, 2017.

Bianchi, Alvaro, *Gramsci's Laboratory*. Leiden: Brill, 2020.

Blackburn, Robin, *The Overthrow of Colonial Slavery (1776–1848)*. London: Verso, 1988.

Braga, Ruy, "A maldição do trabalho barato", August 13, 2012, http://blogdaboitempo.com.br/2012/08/13/a-maldicao-do-trabalho-barato/.

———, "Brazil: for an interpretation worthy of June" (2015), blogjunho.com.br/brazil-for-an-interpretation-worthy-of-june/.

———, *The Politics of the Precariat: From Populism to Lulista Hegemony*. Leiden: Brill, 2017.

Briggs, Asa, "The Language of Class in Early Nineteenth Century England", in Briggs, A. & Saville, J. (eds.), *Essays on Labour History*. London: Macmillan, 1960.

———, *Chartism*. London: Sutton, 1998.

Caleiro, João Pedro, "Trabalhador industrial brasileiro ganha menos do que um chinês", *Exame*, March 2, 2017, http://exame.abril.com.br/economia/trabalhador-industrial-brasileiro-ganha-menos-que-um-chines/.

Callinicos, Alex, *Race and Class*. London: Bookmarks, 1993.

———, *Making History*. Chicago, Haymarket, 2009.

———, *Deciphering Capital: Marx's Capital and Its Destiny*. London: Bookmarks, 2013.

Carcanholo, Marcelo D., *Dependencia, super-explotación del trabajo y crisis: una interpretación desde Marx*. Madrid: Maia Ediciones, 2017.

Cardoso, Fernando Henrique & Faletto, Enzo, *Dependência e desenvolvimento na América Latina: Ensaio de interpretação sociológica*. 4ª ed., Rio de Janeiro: Zahar Editores, 1977.

Casoni, Gabriel, "Uma nota sobre a classe trabalhadora brasileira", 2017, http://maismovimento.org/2017/03/13/uma-nota-sobre-a-classe-trabalhadora-brasileira/#sdfootnote44anc.

Cole, G. D. H. & Filson, A. W., *Britsh Working Class Movements; Select Documents, 1789–1875*. London: Macmillan, 1967.

Corrêa, Marcelo, "Brasil tem segunda pior distribuição de renda em ranking da OCDE", March 19, 2013, http://oglobo.globo.com/economia/brasil-tem-segunda-pior-distribuicao-de-renda-em-ranking-da-ocde-7887116.

Costa, Joana Ferreira da, "Imigrantes: como os estudos desmentem mitos de ameaça ao emprego e à economia", https://fronteirasxxi.pt/estudos-imigracao/.

Coutinho, Carlos Nelson, *Gramsci's Political Thought*. Leiden: Brill, 2012.

Crenshaw, K., "Background Paper for the Expert Meeting on Gender Related Aspects of Race Discrimination", United Nations, November 21–24, 2000, https://www.un.org/womenwatch/daw/csw/genrac/report.htm.

Davis, Angela, *Woman, Race & Class*. New York: Vintage Books, 1983.

Dörre, Klaus, *The German Job Miracle: A Model to Europe?* Brussels: Rosa Luxemburg Stiftung, 2014.

Drucker, Peter, "The Fracturing of LGBT Identities Under Neoliberal Capitalism", *Historical Materialism*, vol. 19, no. 4, 2011.

Engels, Friedrich, *The Condition of the Working-Class in England* (1845), in Marx, Karl & Engels, Friedrich, *Marx-Engels Collected Works* (MECW), vol. 4. London: Lawrence & Wishart, 1975.

———. *The Origin of the Family, Private Property and the State* (1884), *MECW*, vol. 26. London: Lawrence & Wishart, 1990.

Eurostat, *Migrant Integration*, 2017, http://ec.europa.eu/eurostat/documents/3217494/8081569/KS-01-17-539-EN-N.pdf/3eba7121-91fd-4512-aeb5-b820a55517e2.

Fergunson, Susan, *Women and Work: Feminism, Labour and Social Reproduction*. London: Pluto Press, 2019.

Floyd, Kevin, "Making History: Marxism, Queer Theory, and Contradiction in the Future of American Studies", *Cultural Critique*, no. 40, 1998.

Foner, Philip S., *British Labor and the American Civil War*. New York: Holmes & Meier, 1981.

Fontes, Virgínia, *O Brasil e o capital-imperialismo: teoria e história*. Rio de Janeiro: EdUFRJ, 2010.

Foster, John & McChesney, Robert, *The Endless Crisis: How Monopoly-Finance Capital Produces Stagnation and Upheaval from the USA to China*. New York: Monthly Review Press, 2012.

Gabriel, Mary, *Love and Capital: Karl and Jenny Marx and the Birth of a Revolution*. New York: Little, Brown and Company, 2011.

Goldman, Wendy, *Women, the State and Revolution: Soviet Family Policy and Social Life, 1917–1936*. Cambridge: Cambridge University Press, 1993.

Gorz, Andre, *Farewell to the Working Class: An Essay on Post-Industrial Socialism*. London: Pluto Press, 1982.

Gramsci, A., *The Antonio Gramsci Reader: Selected Writings, 1916–1935*, edited by David Forgacs. New York: New York University Press, 2000.

———, *Cadernos do cárcere*, vol. 4. Rio de Janeiro: Civilização Brasileira, 2001.

———, *Cartas do cárcere*, vol. 2. Rio de Janeiro: Civilização Brasileira, 2005.

———, *Selections from Prison Notebooks*, edited and translated by Quentin Hoare & Geoffrey Nowel Smith. London: Lawrence & Wishart, 1971.

Guha, Ranahit, "On Some Aspects of the Historiography of Colonial India", in Guha, Ranahit (ed.), *Selected Subaltern Studies*, New York, Oxford Press, 1988.

Guimarães, Antonio Sérgio, *Classes, raças e democracia*. São Paulo: Ed. 34, 2002.

Haider, Asad, *Mistaken Identity: Race and Class in the Age of Trump*. London: Verso, 2018.

Harison, Royden, "British Labor and American Slavery", *Science & Society*, vol. 25, no. 4, December 1961.

Harvey, David, *A Companion to Marx's Capital*. London: Verso, 2010.

Heinrich, Michael, *Karl Marx and the Birth of Modern Society: The Life of Marx and the Development of His Work*. New York: Monthly Review Press, 2019.

Hobsbawm, Eric, *Worlds of Labour*. London: Weidenfeld and Nicolson, 1984.

Hunt, Tristam, *The Frock-Coated Communist: The Revolutionary Life of Friedrich Engels*. London: Penguin, 2009.

ILO, *ILO Monitor: COVID-19 and the World of Work*, April 29, 2021. https://www.ilo.org/wcmsp5/groups/public/---dgreports/---dcomm/documents/briefingnote/wcms_743146.pdf.

ILO, *World Employment and Social Outlook: Trends 2020*. Geneva: ILO, 2020.

ILO, *World Employment and Social Outlook*. Geneva: ILO, 2021.

ILO, *World Employment, and Social Outlook 2015: The Changing Nature of Jobs*. Geneva: ILO, 2015.

ILO, *World Report on Child Labour 2015: Paving the Way to Decent Work for Young People*. Geneva: ILO, 2015.

Jones, Gareth Stedman, *Languages of Class: Studies in English Working Class History, 1832–1982*. Cambridge: Cambridge University Press, 1983.

Joyce, Patrick, *Democratic Subjects: Studies in the History of the Self and the Social in Nineteenth Century England*. Cambridge: Cambridge University Press, 1994.

Kiernan, Victor G., "Marx and India", in Karat, Prakash (ed.), *Across Time and Continents. A Tribute to Victor G. Kiernan*. New Delhi: Left Word, 2003.

Krisis, *Manifesto Against Labour*, 1999, https://libcom.org/library/manifesto-against-labour-krisis-group.

Kurz, Robert, "O pós-marxismo e o fetiche do trabalho: Sobre a contradição histórica na teoria de Marx", 1995, http://obeco.planetaclix.pt/.

———, *O colapso da modernização: da derrocada do socialismo de caserna à crise da economia mundial*. São Paulo: Paz e Terra, 1999.

Lenin, V. I., *Imperialism: The Higher Stage of Capitalism*. London: Resistance Books, 1999.

Linebaugh, Peter e Rediker, Marcus, *The Many-Headed Hydra: Sailors, Slaves, Commoners, and the Hidden History of the Revolutionary Atlantic*. Boston: Beacon, 2000.

Linhart, Robert, *Lénine, les paysans, Taylor: Essai d'analyse matérialiste historique de la naissance du système productif soviétique*. Paris: Seuil, 1976.

Lowy, Michael, *The Theory of Revolution in the Young Marx* (1970). Chicago: Haymarket, 2005.

MacNally, David, "Intersections and dialetics: critical reconstructions in social reproduction theory", in Bhattacharya, Tithi (ed.), *Social Reproduction Theory: Remapping Class, Recentering Oppression*. London: Pluto, 2017.

Macnally, David & Ferguson, Susan, "Capital, Labour-Power, and Gender: Introduction to the Historical Materialism Edition of the Marxism and the Oppression of Women", in Vogel, Lise, *Marxism and the Oppression of Women: Toward a Unitary Theory*. Chicago: Haymarket, 2013.

Mandel, Ernest, "Introduction", in Marx, Karl, *Capital. A Critique of Political Economy*, vol. 1. London: Penguin, 1990.

Mariátegui, Jose Carlos, "Prologue to Tempestad en los Andes by Valcarcel". In Mariátegui, J. C., *Seven Interpretative Essays on Peruvian Reality* (1928), https://www.marxists.org/archive/mariateg/works/7-interpretive-essays/essay02.htm.

———, *The Problem of Race in Latin America* (1929), in Mariategui, J. C., *An Anthology*, edited and translated by Harry E. Vanden and Marc Becker New York: Monthly Review Press, 2011.

Marini, Ruy Mauro, "Dialética da dependência" (1973), in Traspadini, Roberta & Stédile, João Pedro (ed.), *Ruy Mauro Marini: vida e obra*. São Paulo: Expressão Popular, 2005.

Marx, Karl, "Proceedings of the Sixth Rhine Province Assembly" (1842), *MECW*, vol. 1. London: Lawrence & Wishart, 1975.

———, *Economic and Philosophic Manuscripts* (1844), *MECW*, vol. 3. London: Lawrence & Wishart, 1975.

———, *Contribution to the Critique of Hegel's Philosophy of Law. Introduction* (1844), *MECW*, vol. 3. London: Lawrence & Wishart, 1975.

Marx, K., "Critical Marginal Notes on 'The King of Prussia and Social Reform'. By a Prussian" (1844), *MECW*, vol. 3. London: Lawrence & Wishart, 1975.

———, *Letter to Feurbach* (August 11, 1844), *MECW*, vol. 3. London: Lawrence & Wishart, 1975.

———, *Theses on Feuerbach* (1845), *MECW*, vol. 5. London: Lawrence & Wishart, 1976.

———, *The Poverty of Philosophy* (1847), *MECW*, vol. 6. London: Lawrence & Wishart, 1976.

———, *The Eighteenth Brumaire of Louis Bonaparte* (1852), *MECW*, vol. 11. London: Lawrence & Wishart, 1979.

———, "The British Rule in India" (1853), *MECW*, vol. 12, London: Lawrence & Wishart, 1979.
———, "The Future Results of British Rule in India" (1853), *MECW*, vol. 12, London: Lawrence & Wishart, 1979.
———, *The Grundrisse* (1857), *MECW*, vols. 28–29. London: Lawrence & Wishart, 1986–1987.
———, *A Contribution to the Critique of Political Economy* (1859), *MECW*, vol. 29. London: Lawrence & Wishart, 1987.
———, *Economic Manuscripts* (1861–1863), *MECW*, vol. 34. London: Lawrence & Wishart, 1994.
———, *Provisional Rules of the International Working Men's Association* (1864), *MECW*, vol. 20, London: Lawrence & Wishart, 1985.
———, *Provisional Rules of the International Working Men's Association* (1864), *MECW*, vol. 20, London: Lawrence & Wishart, 1985.
———, *Capital: A Critique of Political economy*, vol. I (1867), *MECW*, vol. 35. London: Lawrence & Wishart, 1996.
———, "Letter to Sigfrid Meyer and August Vogt" (April 9, 1870), *MECW*, vol. 43. London: Lawrence & Wishart, 1988.
———, "Letter to Sigfrid Meyer and August Vogt" (April 9, 1870), *MECW*, vol. 43. London: Lawrence & Wishart, 1988.
———, *Critique of the Gotha Programme* (1875), *MECW*, vol. 24, London: Lawrence & Wishart, 1989.
———, "Letter to Otechestvenniye Zapiski" (1877), *MECW*, vol. 24, London: Lawrence & Wishart, 1989.
———. "Letter to Vera Zasulich" (1881), *MECW*, vol. 24, London: Lawrence & Wishart, 1989.
———, *Capital: A Critique of Political Economy*, Volume II (1885), *MECW*, vol. 36. London: Lawrence & Wishart, 1997.
———, *Capital: A Critique of Political Economy*, Volume III (1894), *MECW*, vol. 37. London: Lawrence & Wishart, 1998.
Marx, Karl. & Engels, Friedrich, *The Communist Manifesto* (1848), *MECW*, vol. 6, London: Lawrence & Wishart, 1976.
———, *The German Ideology* (1845), *MECW*, vol. 5. London: Lawrence & Wishart, 1976.
———, "Preface to the Second Russian Edition of the Manifesto of the Communist Party" (1882), *MECW*, vol. 24, London: Lawrence & Wishart, 1989.
———, *The Civil War in the United States*, edited and with an Introduction by Zimmerman, Andrew. New York: International Publishers, 2016.
Mattos, Marcelo Badaró, "Classes sociais e luta de classes: a atualidade de um debate conceitual", *Em Pauta*, vol. 20, 2007.

———, *Escravizados e livres: experiências comuns na formação da classe trabalhadora carioca*. Rio de Janeiro: Bom Texto, 2008.
———, *Reorganizando em meio ao refluxo: ensaios de intervenção sobre a classe trabalhadora no Brasil*. Rio de Janeiro: Vício de Leitura, 2009.
———, *E. P. Thompson e a tradição de crítica ativa do materialismo histórico*. Rio de Janeiro: Editora UFRJ, 2012.
———, "Marx, o marxismo e o sujeito histórico", *Marx e o Marxismo - Revista do Niep-Marx*, vol. 1, 2013.
———, "A classe trabalhadora: uma abordagem contemporânea à luz do materialismo histórico", *Outubro*, vol. 20, 2014.
———, "Abolicionismo e formação da classe trabalhadora: uma abordagem para além do nacional", in Gomes, Flávio & Domingues, Petrônio (orgs.), *Políticas da raça: experiências e legados da abolição e do pós-emancipação no Brasil*. São Paulo: Selo Negro, 2014.
———, "Trabalho, classe trabalhadora e o debate sobre o sujeito histórico, ontem e hoje", in Neves, Renake B. D. (org.), *Trabalho, estranhamento e emancipação*. Rio de Janeiro: Consequência, 2015.
———, "A Classe Trabalhadora no Brasil de Hoje", in Braga, Ialê Faleiros & outros (orgs), *O Trabalho no Mundo Contemporâneo: fundamentos e desafios para a saúde*. Rio de Janeiro: EdFiocruz, EPSJV, 2016.
———, *Sete Notas introdutórias como contribuição ao debate da esquerda socialista no Brasil*. Rio de Janeiro: Consequência, 2017.
———, "A lei geral da acumulação capitalista e as relações de trabalho na atualidade", in Paço, António Simões do & outros (coord.), *Trabalho, acumulação capitalista e regime político no Portugal contemporâneo*. Lisboa: Colibri, 2017.
———, "Movimentos sociais: aproximações teóricas e um exemplo histórico forte", in Pestana, Marco Marques; Oliveira, Tiago Bernardon de & Costa, Rafael Maul de C. (orgs.), *Subalternos em movimento: mobilização e enfrentamento à dominação no Brasil*. Rio de Janeiro: Consequência, 2017.
Mehring, Franz, *Karl Marx, the Story of His Life* (1918). New York: Routledge, 2010.
Mészáros, István, *Marx's Theory of Alienation*. London: Merlin Press, 1970.
———, *Beyond Capital: Toward a Theory of Transition*. New York: Monthly Review Press, 1995.
———, *The Power of Ideology*. London: Zed Books, 2005.
Mohapatra, Prabhu, "Regulated Informality: Legal Constructions of Labour Relations in Colonial India, 1814–1926", in Sabyasachi, S. & Lucassen, J. (ed.), *Workers in the Informal Sector: Studies in Labour History, 1800–2000*. New Delhi: Macmillan, 2005.
Moody, Kim, "The State of American Labor", *Jacobin*, June 20 2016, https://www.jacobinmag.com/2016/06/precariat-labor-us-workers-uber-walmart-gig-economy.

Moura, Clóvis, *O negro: de bom escravo a mau cidadão?* 2ª ed., São Paulo: Dandara, 2021.

Munanga, Kabengele, "Uma abordagem conceitual das noções de raça, racismo, identidade e etnia", in André Brandão (ed.), *Cadernos PNESB*, n. 5. Niterói: EdUFF, 2004.

Musto, Marcello (ed.), *Workers Unite! The International, 150 Years Later.* London: Bloomsbury Academic, 2014.

Musto, Marcello, *The Last Years of Karl Marx: An Intellectual Biography.* Stanford: Stanford University Press, 2020.

Nabuco, Paula, "As 'recentes' greves na China", *Revista Outubro*, nº 20, 2012.

———, "*Hukou* e migração na China: alguns apontamentos sobre divisão do trabalho", *Revista de Economia Contemporânea*, 16/2, 2012.

Netto, José Paulo, "Apresentação: Marx em Paris", in Karl Marx, *Cadernos de Paris & Manuscritos econômico-filosóficos de 1844.* São Paulo: Expressão Popular, 2015.

Nossa, Leandro & Monteiro, Tânia, "Nova classe média é uma das grandes conquistas do País, afirma Dilma", *O Estado de São Paulo*, April 26, 2011, http://politica.estadao.com.br/noticias/geral,nova-classe-media-e-uma-das-grandes-conquistas-do-pais-afirma-dilma,710974.

Offe, Clauss, *Capitalismo Desorganizado.* São Paulo: Brasiliense, 1989.

Oxfam, "An economy for the 99%", 2017, https://www.oxfam.org/en/research/economy-99.

———, *The Inequality Virus. Bringing Together a World torn Apart by Coronavirus Through a Fair, Just and Sustainable Economy.* Oxford: Oxfam, 2021.

Painter, Neil, *The History of White People.* New York: W. W. Norton, 2010.

Palmer, Bryan, "Reconsiderations of Class: Precariousness as Proletarianization", in Panitch, Leo; Albo, Greg & Chibber, Vivek (ed.), *Socialist Register 2014: Registering Class.* London: Merlin Press, 2013.

Pochmann, Marcio, *Nova classe média? – O trabalho na base da pirâmide social brasileira.* São Paulo: Boitempo, 2012.

Post, Charles, "Marxism and the Race Problem", *Marxist Sociology Blog*, January 3, 2019, https://marxistsociology.org/2019/01/marxism-and-the-race-problem/?fbclid=IwAR1fTaFLwJTdX46R5rBuaP6zMysbIYX4FDBGNYSbfb7J_8ks_ezxvhoo-MM.

Postone, Moishe, *Time, Labour and Social Domination: A Reinterpretation of Marx's Critical Theory.* New York: Cambridge University Press, 1993.

Pradella, Lucia, "Crisis, Revolution and Hegemonic Transition: The American Civil War and Emancipation in Marx's Capital", *Science & Society*, vol. 80, no. 4, 2016.

Prashad, Vijay, "India Is Making Labour History with the World's Largest General Strike", September 7, 2016, https://www.alternet.org/2016/09/india-worlds-largest-strike/.

Ranieri, J., *A câmara escura. Alienação e estranhamento em Marx*. São Paulo: Boitempo, 2001.

Rehmann, Jan, *Theories of Ideology: The Powers of Alienation and Subjection*. Leiden: Brill, 2013.

Ricci, Rudá, "O Maior Fenômeno Sociológico do Brasil: a nova classe média", http://www.escoladegoverno.org.br/artigos/209-nova-classe-media?tmpl=component&print=1&page=.

Russo, John, "Poverty and Precarious Work", *Laboronline*, September 6, 2016, https://www.lawcha.org/2016/09/07/poverty-precarious-work/.

Sanchez, Andrew, *Criminal Capital: Violence, Corruption and Class in Industrial India*. New Delhi: Routledge, 2016.

Sasikumar, S. K., "India's Labour and Employment Scenario: An Overview", *India Handbook of Labour*. Noida: V. V. Giri National Labour Institute, 2015.

Savage, Mike & Miles, Andrew. *The Remaking of the English Working Class. 1840–1940*. London: Routledge, 1994.

Sears, Alan, "Situating Sexuality in Social Reproduction", *Historical Materialism*, February 24, 2016.

Sen, Asok, "Subaltern Studies: Class, Capital and Community", Guha, Ranahit (ed.), *Subaltern Studies V. Writings on South Asian History and Society*. Delhi: Oxford University Press, 1987.

Sewell Jr., William, *Work & Revolution in France. The Language of Labor from the Old Regime to 1848*. New York: Cambridge University Press, 1980.

Silver, Beverly, *Forces of Labour: Worker's Movements and Globalization since 1870*. New York: Cambridge University Press, 2003.

Standing, Guy, *The Precariat: The New Dangerous Class*. New York: Bloomsbury Academic, 2011.

Stanziani, Alessandro, "Introduction: Labour Institutions in a Global Perspective, from the Seventeenth to the Twentieth Century", *International Review of Social History*, vol. 54, Part 3, December 2009.

Strath, Bo, *The Organisation of Labour Markets: Modernity, Culture and Governance in Germany, Sweden, Britain and Japan*. London: Routledge, 1996.

Sturtevant, Paul (ed.), "Race, Racism and the Middle Ages", *The Public Medievalist*, http://www.publicmedievalist.com/race-racism-middle-ages-toc/.

Thompson, Dorothy, *The Dignity of Chartism*. London: Verso, 2015.

Thompson, E. P., *The Making of the English Working Class* (1963). London: Penguin, 1991.

———, "Eighteenth-Century English Society: Class Struggle without Class?", *Social History*, vol. 3, no. 2, May 1978.

———, *The Poverty of Theory and Other Essays*. London: Merlin, 1978.

Tomich, Dale, *Through the Prism of Slavery: Labor, Capital, and World Economy*. Lanham: Rowman & Littlefield Publishers, 2003.

Trotsky, Leon, "Proletarian Culture and Proletarian Art" (1924), https://www.marxists.org/archive/trotsky/1924/lit_revo/ch06.htm.

———, *History of the Russian Revolution* (1930), Marxists Internet Archive, 2000.

United Nations, *World Population Prospects 2019: Highlights*, New York: UN, 2019.

Van der Linden, Marcel, "Labour History: The Old, the New and the Global", *African Studies*, vol. 66, no. 2, 2007.

———, "The 'Law' of Uneven and Combined Development: Some Underdeveloped Thoughts", *Historical Materialism*, 15, 2007.

———, *Wokers of the World: Essays Towards a Global Labor History*. Leiden: Brill, 2008.

———, "Who Are the Workers of the World? Marx and Beyond", *Workers of the World*, vol. 1, no. 2, January 2013.

———, "San Precario: A New Inspiration for Labor Historians", *Labor: Studies in Working-Class History of the Americas*, vol. 11, no. 1, 2014.

———, "Global Labour: A Not-so-Grand Finale and Perhaps a New Beginning", *Global Labour Journal*, vol. 7, no. 2, 2016.

Vogel, Lise, *Marxism and the Oppression of Women: Toward a Unitary Theory*, Chicago: Haymarket, 2013.

Voyages: Trans-Atlantic Slave Trade Database, http://www.slavevoyages.org/.

Weber, Max, *Economy and Society. An Outline of Interpretative Sociology*. Berkeley: University of California Press, 1978.

Williams, Raymond, *Keywords: A Vocabulary of Culture and Society*. Oxford: Oxford University Press, 1976.

Wood, Ellen, *The Origin of Capitalism*. London: Verso, 2002.

World Bank, *Poverty and Shared Prosperity 2020: Overview—Reversals of Fortune*. Washington DC: World Bank, 2020.

Wright Mills, C., *White Collar. The American Middle Classes*. London: Oxford University Press, 1956.

Index

M. B. Mattos, *The Working Class from Marx to Our Times*, Marx, Engels, and Marxisms,
https://doi.org/10.1007/978-3-030-97355-1

The manufacturer's authorised representative in the EU is Springer Nature Customer Service Centre GmbH, Europaplatz 3, 69115 Heidelberg, Germany. If you have any concerns regarding our products, please contact ProductSafety@springernature.com

Printed and bound by CPI Group (UK) Ltd, Croydon, CR0 4YY
30/09/2026
02225499-0001